The Future Inheritance of Land in the Pauline Epistles

The Future Inheritance of Land in the Pauline Epistles

By MIGUEL G. ECHEVARRIA JR.

Foreword by Brian Vickers

PICKWICK *Publications* · Eugene, Oregon

THE FUTURE INHERITANCE OF LAND IN THE PAULINE EPISTLES

Pickwick Publications
An Imprint of Wipf and Stock Publishers
199 W. 8th Ave., Suite 3
Eugene, OR 97401

www.wipfandstock.com

PAPERBACK ISBN: 978-1-5326-3282-2
HARDCOVER ISBN: 978-1-5326-3284-6
EBOOK ISBN: 978-1-5326-0182-8

Cataloging-in-Publication data:

Names: Echevarria, Miguel G., Jr., author. | Vickers, Brian J., foreword

Title: The future inheritance of land in the Pauline epistles / by Miguel G. Echevarria Jr.; foreword by Brian J. Vickers

Description: Eugene, OR : Pickwick Publications, 2019 | Includes bibliographical refer-ences.

Identifiers: ISBN 978-1-5326-3282-2 (paperback) | ISBN 978-1-5326-3284-6 (hard-cover) | ISBN 978-1-5326-3283-9 (ebook)

Subjects: LCSH: Bible. Epistles of Paul—Criticism, interpretation, etc. | Inheritance and succession—Biblical teaching.

Classification: LCC BS2655.I63 E27 2019 (print) | LCC BS2655.I63 (ebook)

01/23/19

To my wife Hollie
and my daughters Miriam, Esther, and Eunice
without whom life would not be near as rich

Contents

Foreword

BRIAN VICKERS
Professor of New Testament Interpretation
The Southern Baptist Theological Seminary

LAND IS CENTRAL TO the story of the Bible. If we take a "big-picture" approach to the theme, the story begins on the third day of the creation account—God creates the land, that is, the earth (Gen 1:9–13). This land will be the home of the human race, the pinnacle of God's creation work. The story of land and the story of humanity is forever brought together in Genesis 2. There the story takes a decidedly narrow focus on a particular piece of land, specifically the Garden of Eden. This garden is a special piece of land, for it is the place on earth where God communes with humanity. It is God's gift to Adam and Eve, the place where they enjoy a special relationship with him. Their job is to take care of the land and expand it. When Adam and Eve decide to redefine the rules of that relationship, their punishment is exile from the garden, away from the presence of God. Their new land is now the earth and, in this case, bigger is not better—humanity and the land are still bound together but now joined under a curse. From that point on the story of the Bible is all about restoring the lost relationship between God and humanity and the land. The story moves back and forth from broad perspective, the nations (Gen 11), to a specific promise of a new land—an inheritance—to Abraham and his children. Embedded in that promise (Gen 12), however, is a broader vision, the nations will take part in the fulfillment of the promise (Gen 15). The story of redemption is forever linked to the land promise.

Centuries later, Abraham's children, the nation of Israel, inherit the promised-land. Like Eden, it is a special place, a place where God's presence dwells with his chosen people. That land is promised to them forever. The land is theirs both now and in the future. The land-inheritance promise is

central to the national identity of Israel. The promise stands even in their unbelief and disobedience, which results ultimately in exile from the land. The
prophets point the people forward to a time when Yahweh will restore them,
and restoration for Israel means restoration of Israel in the land. When they
come back from exile, however, they are in the land but life there is not what
their prophets promised. There is no milk and honey, no holy city—there is
a city, though it is far from holy. Rather than an eschatological, golden era,
the land is dangerous, increasingly filled with enemies. Their literature from
that time, the Second Temple era, reflects the reality of living in the land
without the fulfillment of all the inheritance promises. They adopt the future perspective of the Old Testament prophets, looking for a Messiah who
will establish them according to Yahweh's promises. The New Testament
writers take up the inheritance promises in the context of their fulfillment
in the life and ministry of Jesus of Nazareth. The land-inheritance takes on
a decidedly global perspective as his followers go out into the world with a
message until the final consummation when the land will be the new earth.

Large-scale, birds-eye views of the biblical teaching on land-inheritance (or any theme or topic), however accurate or helpful they may be, can
only go so far. For one, we would be hard-pressed to find two Bible readers who would put the big-picture together in the same way. Secondly, and
more importantly, big picture approaches to the Bible are not identical to
the teaching of the Bible itself. They are reconstructions of themes and ideas
selected by the interpreter and presented in ways that by nature are necessarily different than their presentation in the Bible. Big-story presentations
often move along without taking much notice of historical, literary, and/
or genre questions and considerations. A large scale approach may, though
not necessarily, become all forest but no trees. Such views and perspectives
have a place as summaries of interpretations, as introductory Bible teaching,
and as proposals for theological readings of the Bible. If we only exist at the
big-picture level, we never enter into the world(s) of the Bible itself and can
be in danger of building on a foundation that is something less than biblical.

What I most appreciate about Miguel Echevarria's book is that he
guides the reader exegetically through biblical texts in their historical
and literary settings. His main subject is the writings of the Apostle Paul
and Echevarria grounds his work in Paul's own main source, namely, the
Old Testament. He establishes his hermeneutical and intertextual playing
field, then works his way, carefully and thoughtfully, through the relevant
narratives in the Hexateuch and historical books. It's accurate to say that
those narratives are the foundation upon which the writings and prophets
develop their own land-inheritance emphases. In his treatment of the Old
Testament, Echevarria guides his readers to listen in on the intertextual

discussion about land and inheritance as the various writers take up the theme in ever-increasing scope in the context of national disobedience, foreign threats, and finally exile. Though we often locate questions about the fulfillment of the inheritance promises in relation to the New Testament, questions about "literal" and/or "spiritual" inheritance (though that's not the way they would have put it), whether inheritance is present, future (or somehow both), and whether inheritance is inclusive or exclusive of the nations, are part and parcel of the Old Testament itself. Scholars and Bible readers often assume that in the Old Testament the "land" was simply Canaan, and the inheritance simply the physical possession of the land. Questions beyond the physical inheritance of land arose, it is often assumed, only later in the Second Temple literature and subsequently in the New Testament. Echevarria shows decisively that the issue of inheritance was a much broader question before the Second Temple era and the Apostle Paul.

Of course, readers, myself included, will be most interested in how Echevarria interprets Paul. What he shows is a development of the inheritance theme that is at once old, in that Paul picks up on the emphases established in the Old Testament and Second Temple literature, but also new as Paul brings these various strands of promise together to their fulfillment in the Spirit pointing forward to a future, physical inheritance in a renewed earth under the kingship of the risen Jesus.

Whether readers agree, disagree, or find themselves somewhere inbetween, this book must be included in any discussion of inheritance in Paul, and in the Bible generally. Echevarria provides a thoughtful account of how the biblical writers from the Old Testament narrative up through Paul in his epistles discuss and interpret the promises to Abraham and his children. It is precisely the kind of foundation upon which we may build, with confidence, a larger biblical-theological picture.

Preface

COMPLETING THIS BOOK REPRESENTS the fruit of several years of struggle with Paul's view of the promised inheritance (e.g., Rom 4:13; Gal 3:15–18). My interest in this theme began in doctoral seminars at The Southern Baptist Theological Seminary. Preparing for seminars on Paul's epistles, I read many of the commentaries on Romans and Galatians. One thing stuck out to me: There was no agreement regarding the meaning of the inheritance theme. Most scholars gave a passing nod at the Old Testament use of the word, saying that it is the land promised to Abraham. But, then, without much explanation, they would make a hermeneutical pivot, arguing that the inheritance is life in Christ; others that it is the Spirit, all the promises to Abraham, or any number of other possibilities. Such exegesis left me perplexed, especially at the way interpreters had "deterritorialized" the inheritance, without really explaining why. It was almost as if they were saying: "Why would Paul care about a physical land? That can't be what he intended. After all, we all know that Paul now thinks like a Christian, not as a Jew." It was hard for me to drink the Kool-Aid. I kept thinking: "If Paul was a Jew, whose worldview was grounded primarily in the Old Testament and Second Temple literature—not Greek philosophy—why would he depart from a Jewish reading of the inheritance?" Certainly, Christ makes it possible for believers to receive an inheritance. I am not disputing that. But, why would he depart from a faithful understanding of the inheritance, that which gave Jews hope that they would one day be free from their enemies and dwell in peace in a renewed cosmos? It made no sense to me. It still doesn't.

James Hester's *Paul Concept of Inheritance* was the only book that attempted an exhaustive examination of the inheritance in Paul's letters. For reasons I will discuss in the upcoming chapters, I was not satisfied with his partial spiritualizing and incomplete—thus certainly not exhaustive—treatment of the inheritance. In view of the fact that most scholars (in some sense) spiritualize the inheritance, and that the only volume on this theme in Paul is deficient in said facets, I decided to write my doctoral dissertation on this topic.

In the present volume, I revise and add needed support to my argument. Works from New Perspective scholars such as N. T. Wright and Richard Hays have been especially helpful in widening my horizon to see how Paul's theological framework is grounded in Jewish literature. I do not claim to have exhausted Paul's view of the inheritance. I do, however, believe that this book presents a more faithful perspective of what Paul understood the inheritance to be—more faithful than the majority of scholars who dismiss any sense of territory in Paul, or partially spiritualize this promise.

It is my prayer that this book will give the reader a clearer vision of Paul's future hope—the inheritance of a restored cosmos over which Jesus will reign. After all, Paul did not think he would spend eternity in heaven. He, like most every other Jew, longed for the Messiah to establish his kingdom upon a radically transformed earth.

Acknowledgments

This book is a revised version of my PhD dissertation submitted to The Southern Baptist Theological Seminary. It represents several years of research, writing, and revising. Of all the people who have assisted in the completion of this book, I owe a special debt of gratitude to the following.

I am most grateful for my wife, Hollie Echevarria. She has been an incredible support and encouragement to me as a graduate student and now a professor. Throughout the course of our marriage, we have lived in Dallas, Louisville, Mobile, and Wake Forest. Most of this time she has served at home with our three beautiful girls, Miriam, Esther, and Eunice. Such ceaseless sacrifice has allowed me to dedicate considerable time to the completion of this work.

I also owe a debt of gratitude to my doctoral supervisor, Brian Vickers. His close reading of each chapter of my dissertation and valuable critique and feedback have sharpened my writing. Just as important are the conversations we had about my research or anything else on my mind. He is the model of a patient, caring scholar. The academy would be enriched to have more professors like him.

I also want to thank my doctoral committee members, Jim Hamilton and Robert Plummer, and my external reader, Ben Merkle, for their helpful insight and feedback on my work. I now have the privilege of serving on faculty with Ben at Southeastern Baptist Theological Seminary. I am so grateful to observe his excellence in both teaching and scholarship. I am also thankful for Jerod Harper, who graciously read several chapters and individual sections of my dissertation. His comments have also sharpened my work.

Michael Wilder was a mentor of mine during my time at The Southern Baptist Theological Seminary, serving as his assistant in the Professional Doctoral Studies office. He entrusted me with valuable academic administration and teaching experience. I am a better director and professor as a result of sitting under his leadership.

The churches in which I have been involved during my time in graduate school and as a professor (Denton Bible Church, Grace Bible Church, Kenwood Baptist Church, River Hill Baptist Church, and Christ Covenant) have greatly shaped the way I read Paul's epistles. Thank you for your faithful preaching and ministry.

I am also grateful for my students and fellow faculty at University of Mobile and Southeastern Baptist Theological Seminary. At University of Mobile, I served as Assistant Professor of Christian Studies. Relationships with faculty members, such Bob Olson, Jay Robertson, and Steve Schuller, have increased my appreciation of Paul's letters for historical studies (Bob), interdisciplinary work (Steve), and pastoral ministry (Jay). In class my students' questions and insights have forced me to see more clearly Paul's vision of a renewed cosmos. I presently serve at Southeastern Baptist Theological Seminary as Assistant Professor of New Testament and Greek and Director of Hispanic Leadership Development. I am thankful for the generous resources and support Southeastern provides for faculty to grow in their teaching and research, which have aided in the completion of this book. I pray that God will grant me the privilege of serving at this fine institution for many years.

Finally, I want to thank God for giving me the grace to believe in the gospel of Jesus Christ. It is because of Him that I even have the capacity to complete this book. I owe my gifts, talents, and abilities to Him. May I use them for his glory until the day he resurrects his saints from the grave and we inherit the world.

Abbreviations

BHS   *Biblica Hebraica Stuttgertensia*

BDF   F. Blass, A. Debrunner, and Robert W. Funk, *A Greek Grammar of the New Testament and Other Early Christian Literature*

BDAG   Walter Bauer, William Fredrick Danker, William F. Arndt, and F. Wilber Gingrich, *A Greek-English Lexicon of the New Testament and Other Early Christian Literature*

HALOT   *Hebrew and Aramaic Lexicon of the Old Testament*

LSJ   Henry George Liddell, Robert Scott, and Henry Stuart Jones, *Greek-English Lexicon*

LXX   Septuagint

NA 28   *Novum Testamentum Graece*, 28th ed.

1

Introduction

THE THEME OF INHERITANCE has suffered from severe neglect in biblical scholarship. Interpreters prefer to speak of heaven rather than eternal life in the land promised to Abraham, i.e., the inheritance. One may speculate that this is due to platonic or gnostic influences throughout the history of the church, which deny the goodness of creation in favor of a bodiless existence in a realm devoid of matter. Consequently, the goal of a new creation for mankind has largely been forsaken, replaced by spiritualized themes such as "heaven" or "life in Christ."[1]

In recent years, Oren Martin and J. Richard Middleton have made significant contributions to the rise of interest in the land theme in biblical scholarship. In *Bound for the Promised Land*, Martin argues that the land promise throughout Israel's story is a type that anticipates an even greater land, a new creation on which God's people will dwell under the lordship of Christ.[2] In *A New Heavens and a New Earth*, Middleton acknowledges that in recent years some Christians have moved away from an eschatology

1. Wright, in speaking of salvation in Israel's story, makes an astute observation: "Let us, of course, be clear: *this is not to say that personal 'salvation' is not at issue* or deemed unimportant. This is a regular slur against fresh interpretations of Paul, but it misses the point entirely. Of course 'salvation' matters. What is being said, however, is (a) that salvation does not mean what western tradition has often taken it to mean (escaping to a disembodied 'heaven'), (b) that it is in any case not the main topic of most of the texts and (c) that it is not the main narrative they are trying to explicate. In the New Testament the rescue of human beings from sin and death, which remains vital throughout, serves a much larger purpose, namely that of God's restorative justice for the whole creation" (*Paul and the Faithfulness of God*, 1:164–65).

2. Martin, *Bound for the Promised Land*.

focused on heaven in favor one fixed on participation in God's reign in a new heavens and new earth.[3] These works have made a reasonable impact in turning the attention of Christians toward the true end of their sojourn: a kingdom in the new creation.

In this book, I hope to contribute to this modest rise in biblical scholarship. My work will focus on Paul's epistles, showing how the apostle's eschatology is sourced in his Jewish heritage, the OT and Second Temple writings, anticipating a distinctly earthly eternal existence for God's people.[4] Paul uses the inheritance theme to carry the freight of this expectation. It is not necessary for him to unpack this motif every time he uses it, for he assumes that this term will recall the longing expectation of every Israelite: the entrance into a new creation.

What follows is a brief introduction to this Pauline study. Here, I provide an introduction proper to the inheritance theme in the Pauline epistles, a history of research on the topic, and a statement of my thesis. Lastly, I provide a preview of the book.

INTRODUCTION TO THE INHERITANCE IN PAUL

Paul's view of inheritance is rooted in the land promised to Abraham and his descendants in Genesis (e.g., 12:7; 13:15; 15:18; 17:8; 24:7; 28:4). This is the land that the people of God are to receive as their permanent, physical dwelling. Throughout the OT, the inheritance remains a central hope for God's people (e.g., Deut 6:10–11; 8:7–10; Jer 24:4–5; 33:6–9; Ezek 36:22–28; Zech 9:16–17).

Paul discusses the expectation of such an inheritance in six of his epistles (Rom 4:13–17; 8:12–17; Gal 3:15—4:7, 21–31; 5:19–21; Eph 1:11–18; 5:3–7; Col 1:12; 3:24; 1 Cor 6:9–10; 15:50–6; Titus 3:7).[5] For example, in Galatians 3:18 Paul states that "if the inheritance is from the Law, it is no longer from the promise," and in Romans 4:13 he states that Abraham "is the heir of the world." Like the larger discussion of land in the Bible, the inheritance in Paul has received little attention. When scholars examine this

---

3. Middleton, *New Heavens*.

4. I agree with the twentieth-century shift in Pauline studies, from understanding the apostle in light of Greek thought (Baur, Bultmann) to situating him primarily within a Jewish context (Schweitzer, Sanders, Wright). I am not saying that Paul was not influenced by Greek philosophy or culture. What I am saying is that Paul thinks primarily through a Jewish lens, especially regarding themes grounded in the OT, such as the inheritance.

5. I will argue for the Pauline authorship of these letters in the appropriate chapters.

notion, they often do so in a portion of a book or monograph, a section of an OT or NT theology, or a journal article or essay.

Consequently, the following important questions seldom receive a satisfactory explanation. Are Paul's references to the inheritance fulfilled in the present for those who are in Christ or possess the Spirit? Is the inheritance a notion that will be fulfilled in both a future earthly and present spiritual manner? Is the inheritance a concept that will be fulfilled only in a future earthly sense (i.e., the future land promised to Abraham and his descendants), since this is the primary meaning of the inheritance in the OT (Gen 13:15; 17:8; 24:7)? Such questions are often not clarified, because rarely does someone provide an extensive discussion, especially an entire work, dedicated to the concept of inheritance in Paul's letters.

The sole exception to this trend is James Hester. In 1968 Hester published a 128-page monograph titled *Paul's Concept of Inheritance*, providing the most extensive study of the concept of inheritance in Paul's letters.[6] In the decades since it was first published, Hester's work is still considered to be "the most detailed study of inheritance in Paul."[7]

According to Hester, Paul's use of the inheritance concept is in line with its central understanding in the OT as the land of Canaan promised to Abraham and his seed (Gen 13:15; 17:8; 24:7). Thus, Paul does not spiritualize the inheritance but employs this notion in line with its original territorial sense. Yet, this is not solely the case in the OT, for the land continues to be the central interpretation of the inheritance during the Second Temple period (Sir 44:11, 19, 21; *Jub.* 14:1, 18:5; *Tob.* 4:12). Paul's interpretation follows this stream of thought. In Hester's view, Paul understands the promise of inheritance made to Abraham and his descendants as a tangible land, and thereby employs the inheritance concept in an analogous manner.

Paul, however, does not restrict the inheritance to Canaan. He expands the inheritance to include the entire eschatological world. Hester notes, "The geographical reality of the land never ceases to play an important part in Paul's concept of inheritance. He simply makes the land the eschatological world."[8] In Paul's writings, this is most evidently seen in Romans 4:13, where he states that Abraham "is the heir of the world."

Hester also argues that the expectation of an eschatological inheritance corresponds to what is generally found elsewhere in the NT, namely, the coming kingdom (Matt 25:34; Jas 2:5) in the new heavens and a new earth

---

6. Hester, *Paul's Concept of Inheritance*.

7. Denton, "Inheritance in Paul," 158. This conclusion is also shared by Foreman, *Politics of Inheritance*, 4.

8. Hester, *Paul's Concept of Inheritance*, 82.

(Rev 21). The descendants of Abraham will finally possess this inheritance when their bodies are resurrected at the parousia of Christ (Rom 8:24). So, when Paul speaks of the inheritance, he is referring to the saints' possession of the future kingdom.

Although Hester believes that the focus of the inheritance is in the future, he also contends that this notion is partially fulfilled in the present, because the Christian is already redeemed by Christ and is indwelled by the Holy Spirit (Rom 8; Gal 4). And, "since the life in the Spirit is essentially life lived in the New Aeon, Christ's redemptive work brings the future into the present."[9] So, although the believer eagerly awaits his future inheritance, the fact that he has been redeemed by Christ and is indwelled by the Spirit means that he experiences a present sense of the inheritance. Even so, Christians still look forward to the fullness of their inheritance, and therefore the primary emphasis of this notion is in the future. Simply put, Hester argues that the inheritance is an "already-not-yet" concept, with the primary emphasis on the "not yet."

Overall, Hester's comprehensive treatment of the inheritance in Paul's writings is commendable. He pays close attention to the tangible nature of the inheritance in the OT and points out that this is the primary understanding of this theme in Paul. For Hester, there is no need to completely spiritualize a concept that Paul seems to employ in an analogous manner to OT authors.

While Hester's work fills a lacuna in Pauline studies, I raise the following questions. Does Hester adequately show how the inheritance in the OT is normally accompanied with the notion of the descendants/heirs who will dwell within its boundaries[10] and how Paul may be making the same association? Would not the establishment of such a connection further justify Paul's reference to the inheritance as a physical land? Does the inheritance concept, which revolves around the future possession of land in the OT, also lend itself to a present sense for those who have been redeemed in Christ? Such questions, among others, display the need for a new contribution to the inheritance in Paul.

---

9. Ibid., 91.

10. I will develop this thought throughout this book. For now, it will suffice to say that the offspring of Abraham are intended to inhabit the land. See especially Gen 12:7; 13:15; 15:18; 17:8; 24:7). The offspring-land association is not only evident in Genesis, but also appears to be pervasive throughout the OT, where the people of God are sojourning and then occupying the land (Genesis–Joshua), reigning in the land (Samuel–Chronicles), or exiled from the land and anticipating the inheritance of a better place (Psalms and Prophets). See the similar ideas in Kaiser, "Promised Land," 302–12; Dempster, *Dominion and Dynasty*.

HISTORY OF RESEARCH

While Hester's *Paul's Concept of Inheritance* is the only major study on the inheritance in Paul, there are other works that examine this theme. These are relegated to portions of books or monographs, sections of OT and NT theologies, and journal articles or essays. Commentaries usually provide brief discussions (a paragraph or less), and thus their contributions are less substantial than the aforementioned sources. For example, Douglas Moo, in his commentary on Romans, devotes half a paragraph to the inheritance in Romans 4:13. In his short discussion, he argues that "there are indications that the promise of land had come to embrace the entire world (cf. Isa 55:3–5), and many Jewish texts speak of Israel's inheritance in similar terms."[11] Yet, Moo contradicts this evidence in concluding that "Paul probably refers generally to all that God promised his people."[12] Charles Cranfield, in his two volume Romans commentary, devotes less than a paragraph to the inheritance in Romans 4:13. He argues that "the best comment on the meaning of the promise as understood by Paul is provided by 1 Cor 3:21b–23 . . . It is the promise of ultimate restoration to Abraham and his spiritual seed of man's inheritance (cf. Gen 1.27f)."[13] Given the pithy contributions in commentaries, I will only examine the portions of books or monographs, sections of OT and NT theologies, and journal articles or essays that contribute to a study of the inheritance in Paul since Hester's standard work in 1968.[14] The only exception is Paul Hammer's article, "A Comparison of

11. Moo, *Romans*, 274.

12. Ibid.

13. Cranfield, *Romans*, 1:240. One of the longer comments on the inheritance is provided by Wilckens who dedicates about one page to the inheritance in Rom 4:13 (*Der Brief an die Römer*, 269). In his comments, he notes that, in Rom 4:13, the inheritance is universalized, a thought that he believes is also noted in apocalyptic Jewish texts such as *Jub.* 17:3; 19:21; and Sir 44:21.

14. Dispensationalist sources are also omitted from this history of research, because in the last the last twenty-five years there have been few dispensationalist works that, in some manner, address the promise of inheritance. Before this period, for example, Ryrie and Walvoord argued for a dispensationalist perspective on the inheritance. Ryrie contends that the inheritance is a promise of the Abrahamic covenant and interprets it in the following manner: "Though the nation of Israel occupied part of the territory promised in the covenant, she has never yet occupied all of it and certainly not eternally as the covenant promised. Therefore, there must be a time in the future when Israel will do so, and for the premillennialist this will be in the coming millennial kingdom" (*Basic Theology*, 456–57). Walvoord states that physical Israel will be regathered and will possess the land in the millennial kingdom (*Millennial Kingdom*, 174-82). One would be hard pressed to find such noted dispensationalist viewpoints on the inheritance within the last twenty-five years. This thought, though not explicitly stated, is also evident in Sizer ("Dispensational Approaches to the Land" 142–71). As a result, dispensationalists

KLERONOMIA in Paul and in Ephesians," published in 1958, because D. R. Denton's later article "The Inheritance in Paul and in Ephesians," published in 1982, was written for the purpose of countering Hammer's earlier conclusions. Hence, it is important to examine this earlier work.

In addition, many of the sources in this history of research only survey the inheritance in one of Paul's letters. The examination of such disparate sources, while providing valuable information, also displays the need for an updated study of Paul's view of the inheritance. I will use three common views of the inheritance to group and discuss the relevant works: (1) the inheritance as "already" (realized in the present); (2) the inheritance as "already-not-yet" (fulfilled in the future but partially realized in the present); and (3) the inheritance as "not yet" (fulfilled in the future).

Inheritance as "Already"

Those who contend that the inheritance in Paul's letters has "already" been fulfilled either focus their argument on the notion of being "in Christ" or the indwelling of the "Spirit." For them, the inheritance will not be fulfilled in a tangible, earthly sense. This is the case even though they acknowledge that in the OT this concept is primarily understood as the land of Canaan promised to Abraham and his offspring.

William D. Davies

William D. Davies's *The Gospel and the Land* is one of the most detailed studies on the inheritance of land in the NT.[15] More specifically, Davies is "one of the most influential proponents of . . . a spiritualized reading of land in Paul."[16]

Davies agrees that in the OT this concept is focused on the land promised to Abraham, a thought supported in the Apocrypha and Pseudepigrapha, Qumran, and the rabbinic writings. Even so, he argues strongly that Paul's interpretation of the promise of land is "a-territorial." In his opinion,

---

do not make a substantial contribution to the inheritance in recent history, and thus this history of research will not review the dispensationalist perspectives on the inheritance in Paul.

I have also omitted Hodge, *If Sons, Then Heirs,* from this history of research. While I interact with her work in upcoming chapters, she mainly focuses on the notion of sonship, not inheritance. Thus, I did not feel it was necessary to include her in this section.

15. Foreman, *Politics of Inheritance*, 6.

16. Ibid.

Paul "ignores completely the territorial aspect of the promise," because the promise of land has been fulfilled for those who are "in Christ."[17] His reasoning is evident in his comments on Galatians 3–4 and Romans 4 and 8:

> Salvation was now not bound to the Jewish people centered in the land and living according to the Law: it was "located" not in place, but in persons in whom grace and faith had their writ. By personalizing the promise "in Christ" Paul universalized it. For Paul, Christ had gathered the promise into the singularity of his own person. In this way, "the territory" promised was transformed into and fulfilled by the life "in Christ" . . . In the Christological logic of Paul, the land . . . had become irrelevant.[18]

What is more, the logic of Davies's "landless" view of the inheritance in Paul is also apparent in his view that in the OT the Torah is inseparable from the land. Unlike the OT, Davies contends that in the NT Jesus Christ is the substitute for the Torah. So, when Paul makes Jesus the center of his life rather than the Torah, "he in principle breaks with the land."[19] Being "in Christ" makes Paul "free from the Law and, therefore, from the land."[20] Davies's logic seems to be that if Paul understands that the Law is replaced in Jesus Christ, so too is the land.

In Davies's mind, Paul has a spiritualized understanding of the inheritance. Paul has so "deterritorialized" this notion that there is no sense in which he interprets the promise to Abraham and his descendants as a land they will possess. Instead, Paul views the promised inheritance as already fulfilled and presently experienced "in Christ."

Bruce Waltke

In his *Old Testament Theology*, Bruce Waltke, like Davies, argues that Paul spiritualizes the inheritance as life "in Christ." Although he makes this claim, Waltke, again like Davies, concurs that the inheritance in the OT "retains and refreshes the people's memory of the promises of the land."[21] Waltke also argues that this observation is consistent with what the Second Temple sources, such as the Apocrypha (*1 En.* 90:28–38; *2 Bar.* 4:1–7), Qumran (CD 111:7–10; IQM 1:5), and the Rabbinic literature (*m. Sanh.*

---

17. Davies, *Gospel and the Land*, 178.
18. Ibid., 179.
19. Ibid., 220.
20. Ibid.
21. Waltke, *Old Testament Theology*, 534.

10:1), affirm about this concept.[22] Waltke, therefore, views the inheritance to be the promise of land in both the OT and Second Temple literature.

In the Pauline epistles, Waltke departs from interpreting the inheritance in accord with its physical, territorial sense in Jewish literature, for, as noted above, he contends that the inheritance is spiritualized as "life in Christ." From such passages as Galatians 3:26 and Ephesians 2:11–22 and 3:6, he argues, "the logic of Paul's theology demands that he spiritualize the land promises, but he does so explicitly. The apostle to the nations replaces Abraham's physical seed's attachment to the land with Abraham's spiritual seed attachment to a life in Christ."[23] In addition, Waltke goes on to argue that all of the OT promises find their fulfillment in Christ and therefore any sense of territory is insignificant for Paul. So, when Paul uses the words "in Christ," they represent his understanding of the fulfillment of the promises from the OT, including those of land.

Waltke, then, does not interpret the inheritance in Paul as a tangible promise of land, as is the case in the OT and Second Temple literature. Waltke contends that the inheritance is spiritualized because all the OT promises have been fulfilled "in Christ." As a result, any sense of territory is insignificant for Paul.

Sam Williams

Sam Williams's article "Promise in Galatians: A Reading of Paul's Reading of Scripture" attempts to explain the content of the promise sworn to Abraham in Galatians 3–4. Williams's study is pertinent to this discussion because the notion of promise is often associated with the inheritance.

At the inception of his article, Williams concedes that there is no consensus among scholars regarding the content of the promise. Nonetheless, he points to Galatians 3:14 as the key text to understand the substance of what was promised to Abraham. In this verse, he believes that Paul "virtually defines the promise for his readers" as the Spirit.[24] Thus, whenever Paul mentions the promise in Galatians 3–4, he specifically refers to the Spirit, which, in 3:23, has already been delivered to Christians.[25]

Williams, nonetheless, acknowledges that there may be two other promises in Galatians 3–4: the promise of innumerable descendants in 3:6 and the promise of land in 3:16. He argues that the former is equivalent to

---

22. Ibid., 553–57.
23. Ibid., 578.
24. Williams, "Promise in Galatians," 712.
25. Ibid., 711–12.

the promise of the Spirit, because of Paul's conviction that the Spirit begets the descendants of Abraham. According to Williams, Paul reasons in the following manner:

> Prior to becoming believers, the Galatians—and indeed, by extension, all "sinners from the Gentiles" (2:15)—were enslaved to beings who were not really gods (4:8), and the Jews were in custody, confined, under the law (3:23). But now God is at work claiming his human creatures, Jews and Gentiles, by bestowing sonship upon them (4:4–5). Significantly, at Gal 4:5–6 Paul closely connects the believers' receiving *sonship* with God's sending forth the *Spirit* of his son into their hearts.[26]

The connection between the descendants of Abraham and the Spirit is, per Williams, even clearer in 4:28–29, verses which affirm Abraham is given a son, Isaac, according to the Spirit. Hence, those who, like Isaac, are born of the Spirit are also children of the promise. Williams argues that such a connection between the promise and the Spirit in 4:28–29 lends further support to the idea that the promise in Galatians 3–4 is "nothing other than the promise of the Spirit, the Spirit whose bestowal God was promising when he assured Abraham that he would be the father of many descendants."[27] And, since God keeps his word to Abraham, "the promise of many descendants to Abraham is, at the same time, the promise of the Spirit."[28]

Williams then argues that the promise of a land inheritance in Galatians 3:16 is also equivalent to the Spirit. This verse states that the promise is given to Abraham and "to your seed." The prepositional phrase "to your seed" is directly cited from Genesis 13:5 and 17:8.[29] In each of these passages, Williams recognizes that what is sworn to Abraham and his descendants is the land, a promise that is not limited to Canaan but broadened to include the entire earth. Yet, he argues that "the promise of the world is nothing other than the promise of the Spirit,"[30] justifying this claim by contending that the land promise is fulfilled in that the descendants of Abraham have authority over the world (Gal 4:1–8, 21–31). They are no longer under the authority of the elements of the world, but are now lords over the world (Gal 4:2). Hence, the promise to give the land "to your seed" has been fulfilled.

26. Ibid., 714–15.

27. Ibid., 716.

28. Ibid.

29. Williams contends that Paul is only quoting from Gen 13:5 and Gen 17:8 because, "unlike Alexandrinus, the MT and Sinaiticus read 'to your seed,' omitting *kai*" in Gen 24:7 (ibid.).

30. Ibid., 717.

Moreover, since in Galatians 3–4 Paul affirms that by the Spirit the world is coming under the authority of God's people, the promise of land is equivalent to the promise of the Spirit.[31]

In sum, Williams contends that the promise of numerous descendants and the promise of land both converge into the promise of the Spirit, i.e., the Christian's present inheritance. In Williams's own concluding words, "We can properly appreciate what [Paul] has in mind . . . only from the perspective of 3:6 (which alludes to the promise of numerous descendants) and 3:16 (which alludes to the promise of the world). And these promises, in turn, are to be understood—for so Paul understands them—as the promise of the Spirit (3:14)."[32]

Inheritance as "Already-Not-Yet"

Rather than solely interpreting the Pauline inheritance as a concept that is fulfilled in the present, "already-not-yet" proponents also argue that there will be a future, earthly fulfillment of the inheritance.

Edward Adams

In *Constructing the World*, Edward Adams examines Paul's use of κόσμος and κτίσις in Romans 4:13–17 and 8:17–25. Adams asserts that in Romans 4:13–17 the promise of inheritance to Abraham is encapsulated in the statement τὸ κληρονόμον αὐτὸν εἶναι κόσμου (4:13), the meaning of which is grounded in the land of Canaan promised to Abraham in Genesis (12:7; 13:14–15, 17; 15:7, 18–21; 17:8).[33] In later Jewish tradition, by the time of Paul, the promise of land to Abraham "evolved to cosmic proportions."[34] Two of the Jewish texts that Adams cites are *Jubilees* 17:3, which states that "Abraham rejoiced because the Lord had given him seed upon the earth so that they might inherit the land," and *Jubilees* 32:19, which states that God will give to the seed of Abraham "all of the land under heaven" (Sir 44:21; *Jub.* 32:19; 1 *En.* 5:7; Philo, *Somn.* 1.175; Philo, *Mos.* 1.155).[35] Adams notes that the universalizing of the promise to Abraham is even found in the rabbinic traditions (e.g., *Mek. Exod.* 14:31). These observations suggest that

---

31. Ibid., 717–19.
32. Ibid., 720. Emphasis mine.
33. Adams, *Constructing the World*, 167.
34. Ibid.
35. Ibid., 167–68.

"almost certainly . . . the construction τὸ κληρονόμον αὐτὸν εἶναι κόσμου relates to the reinterpreted promise to Abraham in which the promised inheritance is no longer just the land of Palestine but the whole world."[36]

As well, Adams argues that Paul's choice of κόσμος over γῆ is further evidence of the expansion of the promise to Abraham. The term κόσμος, given its broad focus, "eliminates any suggestion of a reference to Palestine."[37] The word γῆ, on the other hand, having a more limited focus, does not lend itself to an expanded sense.

According to Adams, the thought of a widened inheritance in Romans 4:13–17 is connected to 8:17–23. To make this point, he notes that Hester argues from 8:17–23 that "Paul is concerned to show that creation will be a suitable inheritance for the people of God."[38] As 8:21 makes evident, it is the emancipated κτίσις that Christians, the fellow heirs with Christ, will one day inherit. The connection between 4:13–17 and 8:17–23 leads Adams to conclude that the "association of ideas in 8:17–23 strongly suggests that the inherited κόσμος of 4:13 is to be equated with the emancipated κτίσις of 8:21. If this interpretation is sufficiently accurate, 8:18–23 may, on one level, be understood as an explication of the construction τὸ κληρονόμον αὐτὸν εἶναι κόσμου."[39]

While acknowledging that the inheritance is broadened to include the entire emancipated creation, Adams argues that Romans 8:23–25 is filled with already-not-yet tension, because the Spirit within Christians is a "foretaste" (8:23) of the inheritance they eagerly await.[40] Christians, therefore, presently experience the frustration of receiving in part that which they will one day enjoy in full.

Adams's analysis of κόσμος and κτίσις in Romans 4:13–17 and 8:17–25 contributes to an already-not-yet view of the inheritance in Paul's letters. From these passages, he argues that the inheritance is the renewed cosmos which, in the Spirit, is being partially experienced in the present.

G. K. Beale

In *A New Testament Biblical Theology*, G. K. Beale also understands the inheritance in Paul's letters as an "already-not-yet" concept, which has its roots in the OT. He claims, though, that there is a hermeneutical problem in

36. Ibid., 168.
37. Ibid., 170.
38. Ibid.
39. Ibid., 171. See also 174–84.
40. Ibid., 174.

understanding the OT promise of land in the NT. Such difficulty leads him to ask, "Have the land promises faded from a view of literal, physical fulfillment only to be realized in some spiritual way, so that at best these older promises were typological for inheriting spiritual salvation in Christ?"[41] Beale argues that the OT promises of land will be fulfilled physically in the future. Nonetheless, he concedes that there is a present fulfillment of these promises for those who possess the Spirit.

In affirming that the land promises will be fulfilled in the future, Beale notes that Paul acknowledges Abraham as the heir of the "world," i.e., the heavens and the earth. According to Beale, Paul's universalizing of the Abrahamic land promises probably stems from such passages as Psalm 2:8 and Isaiah 26:19, 27:6, and 54:2-3. In addition, he argues that the thought in Romans 4:13-14 is connected to Romans 8:10-21, since the latter "indicates that the future hope of believers' bodily resurrection and of the renewal of the cosmos is rooted in the promise that Abraham and his seed would be heirs of the world."[42] Other Pauline passages he discusses are Ephesians 1:13-14 and Colossians 1:12-14, both of which assert the believer's inheritance to be the coming world.

As well, Beale argues that in Romans 8:10-21 and Ephesians 1:13-4 there is a sense of present fulfillment of the OT land promises. This is because the Spirit has entered into believers and has begun their end-time renovation (Rom 8:10-21) and because the Spirit himself is "the very beginning of this inheritance and not just the guarantee of the promise of its coming (Eph 1:13-14)."[43] Moreover, the Spirit testifies that those who are in Christ partake of the new creation, which was introduced by Christ at his physical resurrection and will be consummated at his return (John 5:24-29; 20:19-23; Acts 2:29-36).

Beale's interpretation that the presence of the Spirit is evidence of the new creation leads him to conclude that the inheritance is also realized in the present. So, while the inheritance will be consummated in the coming world, it is being realized in the present for those who possess the Spirit.

Paul Hammer

Paul Hammer's article "A Comparison of KLERONOMIA in Paul and Ephesians" is based on his doctoral thesis at the University of Heidelberg,

---

41. Beale, *New Testament Biblical Theology*, 751.

42. Ibid., 761–62.

43. Ibid., 763.

"The Understanding of the Inheritance in the New Testament."[44] The inspiration for this thesis came from "an observation from Professor Guenther Bornkamm that [the inheritance] had never been the subject of a monograph."[45] Hammer's article essentially summarizes his thesis' discussion of the inheritance in Paul and what he calls the "deutero-Pauline letter to the Ephesians." He limits his study to passages such as Galatians 3:15–4:7, 30, Romans 4:13–14 and 8:16, and 1 Corinthians 10:11, rather than those that "repeat traditional formulations,"[46] such as Galatians 5:21 and 1 Corinthians 6:9–10 and 15:50.

Hammer argues from such select passages that the inheritance in Paul is oriented toward the past and present, and its content is Jesus Christ. In Ephesians, however, the inheritance is oriented toward the future and its content is the cosmic unity of the church (Eph 1:10–21, 2:7, 3:6–11). Hammer claims that these differences are neither properly noted in the *Theologisches Wörterbuch zum Neuen Testament* nor "do any of the OT or NT theologies deal extensively with it, even though the term mirrors something of the total theological development in Hebrew and in Early Christian history."[47]

Hammer attempts to validate his claim by citing Galatians 3:18, "For if the inheritance (kleronomia) is by the law, it is no longer by the promise; but God gave it to Abraham by a promise."[48] Here, the words "gave it" seem to suggest that the inheritance is oriented in the past. Then, Hammer also contends that the content of the inheritance is Jesus Christ (Gal 3:14), whose coming indicates that the promised inheritance is now a present reality. In Hammer's own words,

> The past promise is now fulfilled. "The fullness of the time has come" (Gal 4:4) . . . Further Paul can refer to himself and the Corinthians as those "upon whom the end of the ages has come" (1 Cor 10:11). Thus for Paul *kleronomia* is a term that primarily relates the past and the present, and whose content, i.e., "Jesus Christ," is a genuinely eschatological event. In Christ "the end of the ages has come."

In addition, Hammer argues that Christ is not only the content of the inheritance in Paul, but also the heir of Abraham (Gal 3:16). As the heir, he

44. Hammer, "Understanding of the Inheritance."
45. Hammer, "Comparison of KLERONOMIA," 267.
46. Ibid., 268.
47. Ibid., 267.
48. Ibid., 268.

is the means by which believers become fellow beneficiaries of the promise (Rom 4:13–14, 8:17).

In contrast to Paul, Hammer contends that the inheritance in the letter to the Ephesians is oriented towards the future (Eph 1:13–14), and its content is not Christ but the cosmic unity of the church (Eph 3:4). He defines this cosmic unity as the future oneness between Jew and Gentile. As such, Ephesians neither focuses on the past nor present realization of the promised inheritance.

Simply put, Hammer argues that in Paul the inheritance is a promise that is oriented in both the past and the present, and its content is Jesus Christ, who is also the means by which others become heirs. On the other hand, in Ephesians the inheritance is oriented toward the future and its content is the cosmic unity of the church. Since I hold to both the authenticity of the undisputed Pauline epistles and the disputed letter to the Ephesians, I place Hammer's results in the "already-not-yet" understanding of the inheritance in Paul, despite his deutero-Pauline view of Ephesians.[49]

D. R. Denton

D. R. Denton's article "Inheritance in Paul and Ephesians" counters Hammer's claim that there is a difference between "the Pauline concept of inheritance . . . and the understanding of the term in Ephesians."[50] Denton is not interested in addressing the issue of authorship in Ephesians, but only in rebutting Hammer's argument.

Denton points out that Paul's epistles display a future orientation of the inheritance in passages that Hammer ignores, such as Galatians 5:21 and Romans 8:17–23 (cf. 1 Cor 6:9, 10; 15:50; Col 3:24), which are consistent with the eschatological thought of Ephesians 1:13–14. Moreover, the content of the future inheritance, as asserted in Romans 8:17–23, is the future "glory (8:17) and redemption of the body (8:23)."[51] So, the claim that Paul views the inheritance to be in the past, and thus contradicts what Ephesians affirms, is not accurate, for Paul too understands that the inheritance is oriented in the future, namely, the future glory and redemption of the body.

As well, Denton argues that in Paul there is a sense in which the inheritance is experienced in the present. Yet, he makes no attempt to prove this from any text. He simply quotes from Hester that "it is the essence of

---

49. For an argument in favor of Paul's authorship of Ephesians, see the exhaustive work of Hoehner (*Ephesians*, 1–59).

50. Denton, "Inheritance in Paul," 159.

51. Ibid., 160.

the inheritance that it *is*, and yet *is not*,"[52] and then concludes that "Paul's position on the inheritance is one of 'already but not yet,' and both of these elements form an essential part of his teaching."[53]

Following this, Denton compares the "already" sense in Paul to Ephesians 1:13–14 and argues that "the Holy Spirit as the *arrabon* of our inheritance . . . conveys the idea that the Spirit who guarantees our inheritance is also himself part of it, the part which has already been experienced."[54] So, in Ephesians, as in Paul's undisputed letters, there is an "already" understanding of the inheritance, because the Spirit is a present realization of this notion.

In short, Denton argues that the inheritance in Paul and in Ephesians is consistent, because they both give evidence of an "already-not-yet" view of this theme. He thus points out that Hammer's claim—that there is a difference between the inheritance in Paul and in Ephesians—is unsustainable.

Inheritance as "Not Yet"

The proponents of a "not yet" interpretation of the inheritance in Paul assert that this notion will be fulfilled in the coming world. Thus, there is no sense in which the inheritance is fulfilled in the present. This view contradicts the "already" and "already-not-yet" arguments above.

Mark Foreman

In *The Politics of Inheritance in Romans*, Mark Foreman claims that the inheritance in Romans follows the OT's presentation of this concept, i.e., the land promised to Abraham and his seed. Yet, for Foreman, like Hester, the land is not restricted to Canaan, but is broadened to include the entire world (Rom 4:13). He views this world to be the future kingdom in the new heavens and earth, which is consistent with texts such as Revelation 21:1 and Pauline passages such as 1 Corinthians 15:50 and Galatians 5:21. In expanding the promise of inheritance, Foreman believes that Paul stands in continuity with the intertestamental texts that employ this notion, such as *1 Enoch* 5:7: "But to the elect there shall be light, joy, and peace, and they shall inherit the earth," and Sirach 44:21: "Therefore the Lord assured him with an oath that . . . [he would] give them [the descendants of Abraham] an

52. Ibid.
53. Ibid.
54. Ibid.

inheritance from sea to sea and from the Euphrates to the end of the earth."[55] Therefore, Foreman argues that in Romans Paul views the inheritance to be the entire eschatological world, a thought which is found elsewhere in Paul's letters and the intertestamental literature.

In addition, Foreman contends that a study of the relevant inheritance passages in Galatians supports his findings in Romans. For example, from Galatians 3:15–4:7 he contends that the offspring of Abraham will inherit the eschatological world, as in Romans 4:13–25.[56] Beyond Galatians, the inheritance in Romans is also consistent with Ephesians 1:11–14, 18, Colossians 1:12 and 3:24, and other similar passages.

Following his exegetical findings on the inheritance, Foreman notes the political implications of a tangible view of this concept for Paul's readers. He argues that Paul's first-century Roman readers lived a marginalized, urban existence, one in which they constantly dealt with "ongoing troubles of persecution, poverty, and conflict."[57] These people had no land of their own. Such an existence will not be permanent. One-day Christians will have a physical inheritance, for they are the true heirs of the world. As such, Foreman argues, "Inheritance helps the Christians at Rome to perceive society in alternate ways and thus it exposes the supposedly permanent and immutable character of the present order of the world. By evoking a world where land is granted by God . . . the language of inheritance calls into question and subverts the present situation of land in Rome."[58]

In short, Foreman views the inheritance in Romans as the eschatological world. For him there is no sense in which this notion has been spiritualized. Foreman even notes the implication of a tangible understanding of the inheritance for Paul's readers, who, though poor and oppressed, will one day inherit the world. While I will not pursue the political implications of the inheritance, it is valuable to note the hope that a future, physical understanding of this concept might provide poor, oppressed Christians.

Yon-Gyong Kwon

In *Eschatology in Galatians*, Yon-Gyong Kwon opposes the idea that "there is a structure of realized eschatology in Galatians,"[59] for Paul's argument in this

---

55. Foreman, *Politics of Inheritance*, 80–81.

56. Ibid., 172–206.

57. Ibid., 98.

58. Ibid., 100.

59. Kwon, *Eschatology in Galatians*, 120.

letter "is in fact set within a distinctively future eschatological framework."[60] Within this futuristic structure, he argues the inheritance in 3:15–4:7 is the promise of land to Abraham and his descendants, which awaits its fulfillment in the coming world.

Thus, for Kwon the promise of the Spirit in 3:14, regardless of the opinion of some scholars, should not be identified as the inheritance in 3:15—4:7—for Paul takes up a different discussion in 3:15, one that leaves behind the promise of the Spirit in 3:1–14 and begins the argument concerning the promise of land in 3:15—4:7. The strongest evidence that Kwon presents for this claim is that in Galatians 3:16 Paul cites verbatim the phrase καὶ τῷ σπέρματι σου from Genesis 12:7, which refers to the land promised to Abraham and his progeny.[61] According to him, this promise of land in Galatians 3:15—4:7 has not been fulfilled, for the "idea of fulfillment is not in the mind [of Paul] at all."[62]

Kwon goes on to identify the inheritance as the eschatological land, an idea Paul makes evident in Romans 4:13. Nonetheless, there is no need to go outside of Galatians to understand the inheritance eschatologically, for in 5:21 Paul states that οἱ τὰ τοιαῦτα πράσσοντες βασιλείαν θεοῦ οὐ κληρονομήσουσιν. This verse suggests that "the ancient promise of the land is now understood to be the promise of eschatological land . . . i.e., the future kingdom of God and eternal life."[63]

Kwon interprets the inheritance in Galatians as the eschatological land. Like Foreman, he believes that the inheritance will be realized in the future and is thereby not spiritualized in the present.

N. T. Wright

Among his other works, N. T. Wright's essay "New Exodus, New Inheritance: The Narrative Substructure of Romans 3–8" makes a pointed contribution to the present discussion. Here, Wright argues that in Romans 3–8 Paul has the new exodus story in mind. In this new and better exodus, Christians have been delivered from slavery to the Egypt of sin and are being led by the Spirit to the inheritance.[64] Given that the expanded inheritance is the goal of this journey, Wright argues, "The revealing explanation of what God promised to Abraham . . . is a clear indication that he already has in view

---

60. Ibid.

61. Ibid., 120–22.

62. Ibid., 122.

63. Ibid.

64. See discussion in Wright, "New Exodus, New Inheritance," 25–30.

the way in which God's fulfillment in Christ and by the Spirit will result in God's renewed people receiving as their inheritance not merely one piece of territory but the whole restored cosmos" (Rom 4:13–17, 8:16–27).[65]

Wright's closing comments stress the importance of the cosmic inheritance in Romans to understand rightly the Christian's eternal hope:

> It is not sufficient, that is, to speak of "eternal life," on the basis of, e.g., Romans 5:21 and 6:23, and to assume that this refers to a generalized "heaven" such as characterizes much common Christian tradition. Paul's expectation was more specific: "the life of the coming age" . . . was to be enjoyed, not in "heaven" as opposed to "earth," but in the renewed, redeemed creation, the creation that has itself shared the Exodus-experience of the people of God.[66]

Wright affirms that Christians are the new exodus people sojourning to their inheritance, i.e., the renewed cosmos. His argument does not spiritualize the promise to Abraham—for he expects that Christians will inherit the tangible, restored world when they complete the Spirit-led new exodus.

Summary of the History of Research

The sources in this history of research, though not comprehensive in scope, display that there are three common views of the inheritance in Paul: (1) the inheritance as "already"; (2) the inheritance as "already-not-yet"; and (3) the inheritance as "not yet." These three perspectives will now be used to situate the thesis of this book.

THESIS

In this book, I will argue that Paul's view of the land inheritance promised to Abraham and his descendants is not restricted to Canaan but is expanded to include the entire renewed world where God will establish his permanent kingdom. The present work thereby differs from the "already" and "already-not-yet" views in that it argues that the promise of inheritance to Abraham's offspring will be fulfilled solely in the future worldwide monarchy. The inheritance is therefore a concept that has "not yet" been realized.

Unlike Hester, I will demonstrate the OT connection between the inheritance and descendants who will dwell within its boundaries, which Paul

---

65. Ibid., 31.
66. Ibid., 35.

employs. Doing so will underscore that the inheritance will only be realized when Abraham's offspring possess the future territory sworn to them. As well, Hester's study is almost exclusively focused on the *hauptbriefe*, otherwise called the undisputed letters of Paul. My study will encompass all the relevant texts in Paul—both disputed and undisputed—providing a better understanding of the apostle's concept of inheritance.

PREVIEW

Chapter 2 will provide a brief overview of typology and intertextextuality for understanding the inheritance in Paul. Since the inheritance theme is grounded in the OT narrative, it will be essential to address these hermeneutical concepts before moving forward.

Chapter 3 will show that in the Hexateuch and historical books the central understanding of the inheritance is the land of Canaan promised to Abraham and his descendants (e.g., Gen 15:3–5; 17:8, 21:10), the territory to which Israel sojourned and established a monarchy. But since they did not drive out all the inhabitants, they were not at rest in the land, thereby suggesting that there is a better inheritance that awaits the people of God. As well, the return to the land in Ezra does represent a fulfillment of the promises, for they are still slaves to a foreign ruler (9:9). At best, this is a type of the true return from exile.

Chapter 4 will argue that in the Psalms and Prophets the expectation of an inheritance is enlarged beyond Canaan to include the entire world (e.g., Ps 2; Isa 54, 65–66; Zeph 3:9–10). The eschatological nature of this theme is clarified in that God's people will possess the world when they are resurrected from the dead, at which time David's royal descendent will reign over them forever (Ezek 36–37; cf. Dan 7). So, although the original stay in Canaan did not fulfill the promise to Abraham, God's people have the hope that they will be raised from the grave to inherit an eschatological kingdom.

Chapter 5 will display that the inheritance in Second Temple literature is in line with the presentation of this concept in the Psalms and Prophets, for it expands this theme to include the entire world (e.g., Sir 44:21; *Jub.* 22:14; 32:19), to which God's people will be resurrected to dwell (e.g., *4 Ezra* 7) and over which Messiah will reign (e.g., *1 En.* 51:1–5; 1QH^a 14:29–31).

Chapter 6 will contend that in Galatians Paul follows the interpretation of the inheritance in the OT and Second Temple literature, for he too views this notion to be the renewed world (3:15–29; 4:21–31) where God will establish his lasting monarchy (4:1–7). Beyond this, he also suggests that the Spirit is the guarantee of the believer's future inheritance (4:1–7).

Paul's allegorical interpretation of the Sarah and Hagar story serves to underscore that believers are the true heirs of the promise (4:21–31).

Chapter 7 will examine the inheritance in Romans. Here, Paul clearly affirms the cosmic nature of the inheritance (4:13), confirming the observations about the inheritance in Galatians, which are themselves rooted in OT and Second Temple Jewish literature. Like Galatians, in Romans Paul also suggests that the Spirit will see to it that God's people receive an inheritance (8:14).

Chapter 8 will examine the inheritance in the relevant undisputed and disputed Pauline letters. In these epistles, Paul continues to hold that the coming world is the kingdom to which the Spirit is leading God's people. Though scholars, like Hester, rarely examine Paul's disputed epistles, these letters are credible witnesses to the apostle's view of the inheritance.

Chapter 9 will summarize the argument of this book, displaying that Paul envisions the inheritance to be the renewed earth. The apostle does not see a spiritualized existence as his future hope, for he looks forward to what his forefathers, such as Abraham, Isaac, and Jacob, had anticipated for centuries: a physical, eternal inheritance under the reign of the promised Messiah. This vision is not exclusive to Paul; it is the vision of the saints who came before him.

2

Paul's Typological and Intertextual Use of the Inheritance Theme

SINCE PAUL'S USE OF the inheritance theme is grounded in OT and Second Temple literature, I will examine two hermeneutical concepts that will allow us to see (more) clearly the apostle's use of Jewish texts: typology and intertextuality.[1] I concede that the sea of literature on these concepts is vast— too vast to cover in this chapter. Thus, I will not attempt to wade deeply into these waters. I will limit my discussion to typological and intertextual insights for envisioning Paul's view of inheritance. Here are a couple of examples that underscore the need for a brief chapter on these concepts.

Paul's typological use of the inheritance is evident in Romans 4:13, in which he states that "Abraham is the heir of the world." This verse raises several interpretive questions. Did God not promise to Abraham that he would inherit the land of Canaan (e.g., Gen 13:15; 15:18; 17:8)? How, then,

---

1. Regarding typology, Hamilton contends that without typology "we cannot understand the New Testament interpretation of the Old" ("Typology of David's Rise," 4). With specific reference to Paul, Seifrid states that "Paul's understanding of Scripture is fundamentally typological" ("Gospel as the Revelation," 99). If both Hamilton and Seifrid are correct, then one would not be able to interpret rightly the OT concept of inheritance in Paul's letters without a proper grasp of typology.

Regarding intertextuality, Hays argues that "we will have great difficulty understanding Paul, the pious first-century Jew, unless we seek to situate his discourse appropriately within what . . . enveloped him: Scripture" (*Echoes,* 19). For this reason, Hays argues for an intertextual approach for comprehending Paul's use of the OT. The implication of Hays's argument for my mine is that, since the inheritance is grounded in Jewish literature, an understanding of intertextuality is essential for understanding the inheritance in Paul.

can he now say that "Abraham is the heir of the world?" In other words, how is it that Abraham's inheritance is originally identified as Canaan in the OT and later the world in Romans 4:13? A grasp of typology provides insight into such questions. Typology is not only important for interpreting the inheritance in Romans 4:13, but also for interpreting this concept throughout Paul's letters.

Paul's intertextual use of the inheritance is evident in Galatians 3:16, in which he cites the exact words καὶ τῷ σπέρματι σου from Genesis 13:15, 17:18, and 24:7, which speak of God promising the inheritance to both Abraham and to his offspring. Without an understanding of intertextuality, the following questions remain unanswered. Why does Paul cite καὶ τῷ σπέρματι σου verbatim from passages that discuss the inheritance in Genesis? Should one consider the original context in which these words are found in interpreting Galatians 3:16? Or, should one discard the original OT framework and solely look to the current context? A grasp of intertextuality provides insight into comprehending Paul's use of the OT in Galatians 3:16 and other inheritance related passages.

In view of these examples, I will now discuss the role of typology and intertextuality for interpreting the inheritance in Paul's letters. In the coming chapters, I will use these hermeneutical concepts to shed light on Paul's use of Jewish texts in inheritance related passages.

TYPOLOGY

Typology is found within the OT itself. This is seen "as later OT writers, such as Isaiah, saw the exodus as a paradigm for future acts of divine deliverance."[2] This mode of interpretation, as well as others, was then carried into extra-biblical Jewish literature. Yair Zakovitch contends,

> Post-biblical exegetes did not create new worlds *ex nihilo*. The Bible's textual witness, the Qumran literature, the Apocrypha, New Testament, and, above all, rabbinic literature and Jewish exegesis that fed from it all fastened themselves into the secure foundations of inner-biblical interpretation and proceeded along paths that had already been paved within the Bible.[3]

So, when one comes to the NT, typology already appears to be an accepted practice.

---

2. Harris, "Eternal Inheritance," vii–viii. For more specific examples from the OT, see Baker (*Two Testaments*, 171).

3. Zakovitch, "Inner-biblical Interpretation," 61.

Similarly, E. Earle Ellis claims that "typological interpretation had been employed earlier in Judaism and became, in early Christianity, a basic key by which the scriptures were understood."[4] After making this assertion, Ellis goes on to state that in the NT typology "relates the past to present in terms of historical correspondence and escalation in which the divinely ordered prefigurement finds a compliment in the subsequent greater event."[5] Since God has divinely ordered all types in Scripture, I will primarily address the first two elements of typology outlined by Ellis: historical correspondence and escalation.[6]

Of these two elements, historical correspondence is the first step in validating a typological interpretation.[7] If historical correspondence is present, then the perceived type is legitimate. If it is not present, then the alleged type is consequently "trivial and valueless for understanding the Bible."[8] It is therefore appropriate to say that the validity of a typological interpretation is determined by historical correspondence between events, people, institutions, and places.[9]

4. llis, "Biblical Interpretation," 713.

5. Ibid., 713. Similarly, Leonhard Goppelt, *Typos*, 17–18. Leithart argues thus: "Typological reading is simply reading of earlier texts in the light of later texts and events" (*Deep Exegesis*, 74). Leithart shows how NT authors give new meanings to OT types and figures. He summarizes his argument in the following paragraph: "'Out of Egypt I called my son' takes on new proprieties, new meanings, as Jesus flees from the Egypt of Herodian Israel. 'God spoke and there was light' takes on new meaning once we hear Jesus say, 'I am the light of the world.' Yahweh forming Adam from the dust is a different event once Jesus bends down outside the temple to make clay from dust and spittle" (Ibid.)

6. Typology should not be confused with the kind of allegory described as "a fanciful method of interpretation . . . which is found in many early Christian writings (esp. of the Alexandrian school) and is still used by some interpreters to the present day" (Baker, *Two Testaments*, 170). Because of this description, Baker contends that "some biblical scholars have outlawed typology as a valid way of interpreting the Bible in the modern church" (ibid.). Regardless of what some argue, Baker is right in observing that "the concept of 'typology' comes from the Bible itself and should not be dropped simply because it has been misunderstood in some periods of history" (ibid.).

7. Likewise, Hamilton argues that "it is precisely the historical nature of a type that is essential to it being interpreted typologically" ("Typology of David's Rise," 8).

8. Baker, *Two Testaments*, 180.

9. Gundry notes that the "rule of thumb" is that "a type is a type only when the New Testament specifically designates it to be such." Examples of such designated typological texts are Rom 5:14, which states that Adam is "a type of the one to come" (τύπος τοῦ μέλλοντος; cf. 1 Cor 15), and 1 Cor 10:11, which says that "these things happened to them as types (τυπικῶς) and were written down for us on whom the fulfillment of the ages has come" ("Typology as a Means of Interpretation," 239). Although the "rule of thumb" is that "a type is only a type" when identified in this manner, I contend that a typological interpretation is valid when there is historical correspondence and

Once historical correspondence has been determined, it is then right to decide whether escalation has occurred. For example, in Romans 4:13 Paul says that "Abraham is the heir of the world." There is historical correspondence between Canaan in the OT and the world in Romans 4:13, thereby validating that the former is a type of the later. After making this point, it is then appropriate to state that escalation has taken place, for Abraham's territorial inheritance has been expanded beyond Canaan to encompass the entire world.

In the coming chapters, I will contend that Canaan in the OT is a type of the renewed world in Paul, the true inheritance (Rom 4:13; 8:12–25). Such an understanding of the inheritance, which affirms both historical correspondence and escalation,[10] makes typology an essential hermeneutical concept for understanding the inheritance. Since Paul is a beneficiary of Jewish tradition, I will show how Paul follows a typological interpretation of the inheritance previously established in OT and Second Temple literature.

INTERTEXTUALITY

Richard Hays's *Echoes of Scripture in the Letters of Paul* has led to a paradigm shift in the way scholars interpret Paul's letters.[11] In the last thirty years, Hays's work has aided in shifting scholarly attention from Paul's interaction with Hellenism to his use of Jewish writings, namely, the LXX.[12] Importantly, Hays defines intertextuality as "the imbedding of fragments of an earlier text within a later one."[13] This phenomenon, he says, "has always played a major role in the cultural traditions that are heir to Israel's Scriptures."[14] Since Paul is heir to this stream of tradition, it is no surprise that his letters

---

escalation between a recognized pair. Explicit types provide a model for doing typological exegesis, but typology is not restricted to such examples.

10. Goppelt observes that "typological heightening is obvious to Paul, although . . . it has not been given any special emphasis" (*Typos*, 138).

11. Meek makes the argument that evangelicals who hold to authorial intent should use the label "inner-biblical exegesis" rather than "intertextuality" ("Intertextuality," 280–91). While his argument is valid, I prefer to use the term intertextuality, since authors can allude to or echo texts of which they may not have been conscience. In other words, an interpretation may extend beyond an "author's intent."

12. I must note that Hays's work benefits from the research of scholars such as Schweitzer and Sanders. A "new perspective" counterpart of Hays is N. T. Wright. I choose to interact directly with Hays, because his work focuses on Paul's intertextual hermeneutic.

13. Hays, *Echoes*, 14.

14. Ibid.

contain "paradigmatic instances of intertextual discourse."[15] Such discourse should alert the reader to the fact that Paul's letters often exhibit interplay, whether in the form of an explicit citation or allusion, with previous OT texts and therefore exist "as a node within a larger literary and interpretive network."[16]

When encountering a citation of an OT passage, Hays prefers to call this a recollection.[17] He favors this term because a "recollection . . . is a pure case of echo rather than quotation or overt allusion."[18] An example of this is again in Galatians 3:16, in which Paul cites verbatim the words καὶ τῷ σπέρματι σοῦ from Genesis 13:15; 17:18; and 24:7. In the case of an "allusive echo" (transumption or metalepsis), Hays believes that it "functions to suggest to the reader that text B should be understood in light of a broad interplay with text A."[19] An allusive echo "places the reader within a field of whispered or unstated correspondences," something often encountered in Paul's letters.[20] An example of this phenomenon is found in 1 Corinthians 11:1–10, where Paul does not cite but rather alludes to Genesis 1–2 to support his argument that women are to wear head coverings during worship.[21]

---

15. Ibid. For a discussion of "inner-biblical exegesis" in Jewish literature, which Hays finds insightful for his work on intertextuality, see Fishbane (*Biblical Interpretation in Ancient Israel*, 3–26). See also Henze, *Biblical Interpretation at Qumran*.

16. Hays and Green, "Use of the Old Testament," 228. Beuken and van Wolde helpfully describe the notion of texts as threads, nets, webs, or textures: "Texts refer to each other, chronologically backwards and forwards, semantically inwards and outwards. . . . Texts do not exist without other texts" (Draisma, *Intertextuality in Biblical Writings*, 7). This point also applies to Paul. Paul's texts were written within his first-century Jewish context, which relied heavily on the LXX as a basis for the future hope and salvation in Messiah. Thus, to understand Paul we must strive to understand how he interacts with such texts in his own writings. Of importance for this study is how he engages OT and Second Temple writings that discuss the inheritance theme.

17. Hays, *Echoes*, 20.

18. Ibid.

19. Ibid.

20. Ibid.

21. Hays and Green, "Use of the Old Testament," 228. See also Phil 1:19. Hays affirms that this verse contains an echo of the OT even though there is no explicit citation of a text (*Echoes*, 21). He goes on to state that if one limits the consideration of echoes to explicit citations, the epistle to the Philippians "would appear to contain no Old Testament references at all" (ibid.).

One cannot ignore that subjectivity plays a role in noting such allusions and echoes. While Paul displays creativity in his employment of Israel's Scriptures, how can we be sure that we rightly understand the texts to which he alludes? Thiselton, in view of Culler's *The Pursuit of Signs*, is right to assess that hermeneutics "after Heidegger, from Gadamer onwards, depends not on questions of individual consciousness only, but on inter-subjectivity. Just as hermeneutics depends on the dialectic of the hermeneutical

Since Paul embeds OT texts in his letters, the phenomenon of intertextuality must play a significant role in the interpretation of his writings. Certainly, Paul's letters must not be studied in isolation. The broader "interpretive network" of the Scriptures must be taken into consideration. This is especially important for understanding the inheritance, a concept which can scarcely be understood without grasping its grounding in Jewish literature.

With this in mind, I will use the following terms to specify the ways in which Paul creatively interacts with Israel's Scriptures: direct quotation, allusion, and echo. I follow Hays's understanding of the relationship between these terms: "Quotation, allusion, and echo may be seen as points along a spectrum of intertextual reference, moving from the explicit to the subliminal. As we move farther away from overt citation, the source recedes into the discursive distance, the intertextual relations become less determinate, and the demand on the reader's listening power grows greater."[22] In recognizing these categories of intertextuality, I will mainly appeal to direct citations/quotations and allusions.[23] Since echo is the least determinate category, I will appeal to this classification sparingly.

---

circle, so intertextuality moves between two poles of langue and parole" (*New Horizons*, 497). I raise these concerns because we are not objective interpreters, and we are separated from the apostle's thought and use of language by roughly twenty centuries. As Owens argues: "To engage in an intertextual analysis is admittedly to pursue a somewhat subjective enterprise where plausibility can be in the eyes of the beholder" (*As It Was in the Beginning*, 10). In view of these concerns, it is appropriate to note Hays's seven criteria for evaluating proposed echoes: (1) availability (the echo's availability to the original author and audience), (2) volume (mainly repetition of words and syntactical patterns), (3) recurrence (the frequency of Paul's use of the same scriptural passage elsewhere), (4) thematic coherence (the echo's fit into Paul's argument), (5) historical plausibility (determining whether Paul's readers would have understood the echo), (6) history of interpretation (determine whether other interpreters have heard such echoes), and (7) satisfaction. The satisfaction criterion is the most difficult to summarize, so I will cite Hays: "With or without clear confirmation from other criteria listed here, does the proposed reading make sense? Does it illuminate the surrounding discourse? Does it produce for the reader a satisfying account of the effect of the intertextual relation?" (*Echoes*, 31). Simply put, Hays says that this criterion is "another way of asking whether the proposed reading offers a good account of the experience of a contemporary community of competent readers" (Ibid., 32). While these criteria are not without difficulties, Owens notes that they "have generally been accepted by the scholarly community" (*As It Was in the Beginning*, 11). While not using these exact terms, I will mainly appeal to the first five criteria (availability, volume, recurrence, thematic coherence, and historical plausibility) to discern a legitimate allusion or echo.

22. Hays, *Echoes*, 23.

23. The scope of this work does not allow for thorough interaction with issues related to dialogism, heteroglossia, and polysemy in intertextuality. Thiselton provides an exemplary discussion of such views (*New Horizons*, 471–509). Other helpful volumes on intertextuality (including those who may or may not agree with Hay's conclusions)

In the following chapters, I will employ typological and intertextual observations to interpret inheritance texts. Paul does not operate in an intellectual vacuum. Rather, his hope for the renewal of creation is shaped by Jewish writings. Thus, appealing to his typological and intertextual use of such texts will make (more) certain that the inheritance is not understood in isolation from its proper literary background, that which gave Paul hope for an eternal inheritance for God's people.

---

are Leithart, *Deep Exegesis*; Porter and Stanley, *As It Is Written*; Stanley, *Paul and Scripture*; Ellis, *Paul's Use of the Old Testament*. Watson, *Hermeneutics of Faith*. In Porter and Stanley's volume, Bates contributes an insightful essay ("Beyond Hay's Echoes of Scripture in the Letters of Paul," 263–92) that builds on Hay's work and argues that the interpreter must not only consider *pre-texts* (Paul's use of the LXX) but also *co-texts* (a direct citation of the same text by Jewish or Christian authors) and *post-texts* (a direct citation of the *pre-text* by a later author, such as Irenaeus). While I will not pursue this line of thought, Bates's argument would allow interpreters to discern whether they are correctly evaluating Paul's use of Jewish literature by determining whether there is support in both *co-texts* and *post-texts*, thereby providing another check on their reading of Paul.

3

The Inheritance in the Old Testament
The Hexateuch and Historical Books

IN THE HEXATEUCH AND historical books, the inheritance is primarily centered on the promise of land to Abraham and his descendants.[1] This is the land in which Abraham and his offspring are to experience lasting rest (Deut 12:10, 25; Josh 22:4; 23:1).[2] So important is this hope that the attainment of the inheritance becomes "the goal and desire of the people of God."[3]

The verb נָחַל and the noun נַחֲלָה are the main Hebrew words associated with the inheritance concept in the OT.[4] Closely associated with נָחַל is the verb יָרַשׁ ("inherit"),[5] often taking אֶרֶץ ("land") as its object.[6] OT authors consistently use these terms to show that the inheritance is the land promised to God's people.

The promise of inheritance before the exile is focused on Canaan as God's people are sojourning and initially occupying the land

---

1. I will examine the OT books according to their Christian, rather than Hebrew, order. I agree with Schreiner who argues that the significance of choosing one order over the other is exaggerated (*King in His Beauty*, xv–xvi). In his judgement, "the central themes of OT theology are not affected dramatically whether one follows the Hebrew order or the order used in English translations" (ibid., xvi).

2. Waltke, *Old Testament Theology*, 539.

3. Miller, "Gift of God," 461–65.

4. For a fuller examination of the inheritance concept in the OT, see Appendix A. All Hebrew citations in this chapter are from the *BHS*.

5. Lipinski, "נָחַל," 9:320.

6. Harris, "Eternal Inheritance," 33.

(Genesis–Joshua)[7] and later reigning in the land (Samuel–Chronicles).[8] After the exile, Ezra displays the Israelites' renewed hope of life in Canaan. Closely associated with the promise of inheritance are the promises of descendants and blessing (e.g., Gen 22:15–19), for they are employed in similar promissory contexts. Though these promises are closely related, they are distinct and should not be confused with one another.[9] Thus, the discussion of inheritance here refers specifically to the promise of land and not the promises of descendants and/or blessing.

The first section of this chapter will observe the inheritance in the Hexateuch. Within this corpus, the initial promise of inheritance is made to Abraham and his offspring in Genesis and reaffirmed throughout the Pentateuch. In Joshua, the land is partially occupied, suggesting that there is a better inheritance to come. The second section will examine the inheritance in the historical books. In Samuel, Kings, and Chronicles, the reign in the land is temporary because of Israel's disobedience, insinuating that Canaan is not Israel's lasting inheritance. Nevertheless, there remains the hope that David's royal offspring will establish God's people in the promised land. The return they experience in Ezra does not fulfill this expectation, for it is nothing more than a brief period of refreshment in captivity.

THE INHERITANCE IN THE HEXATEUCH: THE SOJOURN TO THE LAND

The inheritance in the OT is first evidenced in Genesis, where God promises to give the entire land of Canaan to Abraham and his descendants (12:7; 13:15; 15:18; 17:8; 24:7; 22:17; 28:4). Closely associated with the promise of inheritance are the promises of descendants and universal blessing (e.g., Gen 22:15–19). The quest for the inheritance continues from Exodus

7. The traditional grouping of the first five books of the Bible (Genesis, Exodus, Leviticus, Numbers, and Deuteronomy) is called the Pentateuch since the second century CE (Blenkinsopp, "Introduction to the Pentateuch," 1:305). When discussed as a unit, the first six books of the Bible are called the Hexateuch by scholars such as Abraham Keunen and Julius Wellhausen and record the story of Israel's original promise of land (Genesis), their sojourn to the land (Exodus-Deuteronomy), and their entrance into the land (Joshua). I will follow the layout of Hexateuch, for it provides a helpful overview from promise to (seeming) fulfillment.

8. Although Chronicles was written after the exile, it is included in this chapter because the book's narrative is predominantly set during the period of the monarchy.

9. Harris seems to argue that the land, descendants, and God's presence are all part of the inheritance promised to Abraham ("Eternal Inheritance," 31). I prefer to state that these promises are closely associated without being subsumed under the concept of inheritance.

through Deuteronomy, as Israel sojourns through the wilderness with the hope of entering the land of Canaan. The initial sojourning generation, however, never enters the land because of their disobedience and unbelief. The book of Joshua then records that the following generation finally enters and settles in Canaan. Although Israel arrives in the land, the promise of inheritance is not fulfilled, for Canaan is not completely occupied, insinuating that there is better land to come. This section discusses the progression of the inheritance in the Hexateuch, from the initial promise in Genesis to the incomplete settling of the land in Joshua.

Genesis

The promise of inheritance is first articulated to Abraham in the context of Genesis 12:1–9, in which God tells him: "I will give this land to your seed (לְזַרְעֲךָ)" (12:7).[10] This promise is later reiterated in such verses as 15:18, 24:7, and 26:4. Although the promise of land is only made to his progeny in 12:1–9, Abraham himself later receives the promise in 13:15.[11]

When the promise of land is made to the descendants of Abraham in Genesis, as well as when it is affirmed throughout the Pentateuch (e.g., Gen

10. Many scholars hold that Genesis is a composite work, consisting of three interwoven sources (Yahwist, Elohist, and Priestly). This view is primarily attributed to Julius Wellhausen. See the discussion in Wenham, *Genesis 1–15*, xxvii–xxxvi. Recently, this view has come under fire from critical scholars. Fretheim contends: "From the source critical perspective, the nature, scope, and dating of the sources have been regular subjects of debate. Few doubt that Genesis consists of traditions from various historical periods, but there is little consensus regarding the way in which they have been brought together into their present form" ("Book of Genesis," 1:322). Fretheim prefers to hold that "Genesis [is] a patchwork quilt of traditions from various periods in Israel's life" (ibid.). Despite modern critical studies, it is important to note that Jesus affirms Mosaic authorship of the Pentateuch in passages such as Matt 19 and John 5. As well, almost unanimously Christians and Jews held to Mosaic authorship of the Pentateuch until the nineteenth century. In view of both Jesus' testimony and tradition, I am persuaded that Moses wrote the book of Genesis. Thus, my argument in this section assumes his authorship. Waltke makes an insightful point: "As the greatest of Israel's prophets, Moses . . . would have had the ability to draw upon God's omniscience and omnipresence in the retelling of Israel's historical traditions (cf. Num. 11:25; Deut. 34:10–11). With this extraordinary gift . . . he was imminently qualified to usher in his audience into the heavenly court at the time God created the cosmos (Gen. 1) and to reveal what the Almighty and other human beings thought, felt, and intended (6:6, 8; 13:13; 25:24b)" (*Genesis*, 23). I do not deny, however, that Moses used sources in composing his work (ibid.; Gen 5:1; Num 21:14). Luke also claims to have used and investigated sources in composing his narrative (Luke 1:1–2). Hence, Moses' use of sources does not invalidate his authorship of Genesis, as it does not invalidate Luke's authorship of his Gospel.

11. Hamilton, *Genesis*, 377.

15:18; 26:4; 48:4; Exod 33:1), the construction לְזַרְעֲךָ is consistently used to indicate that the promise is given "to the seed of Abraham." The LXX translates לְזַרְעֲךָ as either τῷ σπέρματί σου in Genesis[12] (e.g., 12:7, 15:18) and τῷ σπέρματί ὑμῶν elsewhere in the Pentateuch (e.g., Exod 33:1; Deut 34:4).[13] The only difference between these translations is that in Genesis the final suffix ךָ is rendered as the singular pronoun σου and elsewhere in the Pentateuch it is rendered as the plural pronoun ὑμῶν. Although there is dissimilarity in the translation of ךָ, the LXX consistently renders the prefixed preposition לְ and the noun זֶרַע as τῷ σπέρματι. When Abraham later receives the promise of land in Genesis 13:15 (cf. 17:8, 24:7), the conjunctive particle וְ is prefixed to לְזַרְעֲךָ, written as וּלְזַרְעֲךָ, to indicate that the land is sworn to both Abraham and his offspring. The LXX regularly translates this construction as καὶ τῷ σπέρματί σου. In view of these observations, it is evident that the consistent use of the word formation לְזַרְעֲךָ, translated as either τῷ σπέρματί σου or τῷ σπέρματί ὑμῶν, and וּלְזַרְעֲךָ, translated as καὶ τῷ σπέρματί σου, is not coincidental. Rather, verbatim citations (or recollections) of earlier inheritance texts are embedded within later ones.[14] Thus, the Pentateuch displays an intertextual pattern when the promise of land is given to Abraham's descendants or to both Abraham and his descendants.

Besides God promising Abraham that his offspring will inherit the land, God also promises him numerous descendants and universal blessing (Gen 12:2–3). These are the three main promises sworn to Abraham, which are later expanded and affirmed throughout the Pentateuch (e.g., Gen 15:1–21; 17:1–27; 22:1–19).[15] Of these promises, the OT commonly refers to the land as the inheritance.[16] This idea is apparent in passages such as Genesis 15:7, where God tells Abraham that he will give him the

12. LXX Genesis citations are from Wevers, *Genesis*.

13. All other LXX Pentateuch citations are from Wevers, *Exodus*; Wevers, *Leviticus*; Wevers, *Numeri*; Wevers, *Deuteronomium*.

14. See Hays, *Echoes*, 14. Fishbane notes how verbatim citations, such as in Neh 8:14–16, were recognized by the Israelites, usually with the result that people were moved to action (*Interpretation in Ancient Israel*, 107–11). In the case of Neh 8:14–16, some believe that the Israelites recognized the cited text, perhaps from Lev 23:42 ("you must dwell in booths"), and as a result built booths (ibid., 109–11). See also Leonard, "Identifying Inner-Biblical Illusions," 241–65.

15. Sailhamer insightfully notes: "The preparation of the land and the divine blessing are important to the author of Genesis (and the Pentateuch) because these two themes form the basis of his treatment of the patriarchal narratives and the Sinai covenant. In translating the Hebrew word אֶרֶץ ("earth") in 1:1–2, the English versions have blurred the connection of these early verses in Genesis to the central theme of land in the Pentateuch. . . . Thus from the start the author betrays his interest in the covenant by concentrating on the land in the creation account" (*Pentateuch as Narrative*, 82).

16. Hester, *Paul's Concept of Inheritance*, 24

land as his inheritance (אֶת־הָאָרֶץ הַזֹּאת לְרִשְׁתָּהּ) and in Genesis 28:4, where Isaac prays that God may bless Jacob so that he might inherit the land (לְרִשְׁתְּךָ אֶת־אֶרֶץ). Each of these passages employs the verb יָרַשׁ to indicate that what is inherited is the אֶרֶץ. In Numbers (e.g., 26:52; 34:2) and especially Joshua (e.g., 11:23; 12:6; 13:1; 18:7, 20, 28; 19:1, 8, 9, 10), the אֶרֶץ is apportioned to the tribes of Israel as their inheritance.[17] This individual allotment was part of the larger collective inheritance of land promised to Abraham's offspring. In Deuteronomy (e.g., 12:10, 19:14), the Psalms (e.g. 37:19; 105:11), and the Prophets (e.g., Isa 49:8, 60:21), the land is also referred to as the inheritance of Israel. Even in contexts where it is not called the inheritance, the land is still recognized as "the inheritance of Israel because it was passed down to Abraham's descendants by the promise."[18] This is the same territory that the prophets, such as Isaiah, "reaffirm [as] the land which God promised to Abraham, Isaac, and Jacob [as] the inheritance of their descendants."[19] These observations underscore that the inheritance points to the land sworn to Abraham and his offspring. The promise of descendants and universal blessing, although discussed in similar promissory contexts, should not be confused with nor blended into the notion of inheritance. To do so ignores the fact that the OT identifies the land of Canaan, not the offspring or the blessing, as the inheritance of Abraham's progeny.

Although the inheritance should be distinguished from the promises of descendants and universal blessing, it is important to note that throughout Genesis the themes of inheritance and offspring are closely associated (e.g., Gen 15:1–21; 17:1–27; 24:1–9; 26:1–3; 28:1–5; 35:9–12). A couple of pertinent examples are found in 15:1–21 and 17:1–27.

In Genesis 15:1–21, the promise of an heir appears to be in peril. God, however, reassures Abraham of innumerable offspring (Gen 15:1–6). After doing so, he once more swears to Abraham, "To your descendants (לְזַרְעֲךָ) I will give this land" (Gen 15:18). The surety of this promise is based on the "unilateral, irrevocable covenant" (the Abrahamic Covenant) to give Abraham the land of the Canaanites.[20] This promise is so certain that God pledges to curse himself "if the descendants do not possess the land."[21] God's oath guarantees that Abraham's offspring are destined to inherit the land, giving straightforward evidence of the connection between the concepts of

17. Ibid. So central is the notion of land in Joshua that Waltke argues that it is the central theme of the book (*Old Testament Theology*, 513).

18. Hester, *Paul's Concept of Inheritance*, 24. See also Williamson, "Promise and Fulfillment," 15–34.

19. Hester, *Paul's Concept of Inheritance*, 25. Brackets mine.

20. Waltke, *Old Testament Theology*, 317.

21. Dempster, *Dominion and Dynasty*, 77–92.

inheritance and offspring. In Genesis 17:1–27, after doubting the promise of an heir and having a child with Hagar (Gen 16), God once more assures Abraham of countless offspring who will inherit the entire land of Canaan,[22] doing so in the form of an "everlasting covenant" (17:7). In addition to being numerous, Abraham's descendants will comprise nations and kings who will dwell in the land of Canaan (Gen 17:6). So as with Genesis 15:1–21, it appears that Abraham's offspring are destined to inherit the land. This observation affirms the association between the themes of inheritance and descendants, which is also found throughout the remainder of Genesis (17:1–8; 24:1–9; 26:1–3; 28:1–5; 35:9–12).[23] It is even warranted to say that the concepts of inheritance and descendants, though distinguishable, are tightly connected throughout the entire OT—for Abraham's offspring are intended to dwell in the land.[24]

Subsequently, it is important to mention that the visible assurance that Abraham will have an heir comes about when Sarah gives birth to Isaac (Gen 21:1–2). God reassures Abraham of this promise when he tells him that his offspring will be named through Isaac and not Ishmael (Gen 21:12). Soon after, the promise of an heir seems again at risk, as God calls Abraham to sacrifice his only son (Gen 22:2). The irony here is that the very one who promised an heir to Abraham—God himself—is also the one who places the promise in jeopardy.[25] Yet, at the time of the sacrifice God provides a ram as a substitute for Isaac and then reassures Abraham of innumerable descendants (Gen 22:17). His offspring will be so numerous that "they will be as the stars in the sky and the sand on the seashore" (Gen 22:17). Such an oath guarantees that the promise of descendants who will inherit the land is secure.

Following Abraham's death, God confirms to Isaac, "And to your seed (וּלְזַרְעֲךָ) I will give all this land" (Gen 26:3). This promise is later reassured to Jacob (Gen 28:13–15 and 35:9–12), as once more God promises to give the land of Canaan to him and his offspring (וּלְזַרְעֲךָ). Even as Jacob is leaving for Egypt, God swears to bring him back to the land (Gen 46:4). Although

---

22. Alexander contends that the promise of "multitudinous and international descendants" is evidence that the people of God "require a much larger, indeed a global, inheritance" ("Beyond Borders," 18).

23. VonRad affirms that the themes of inheritance and descendants "run through the whole like a *cantus firmus*" ("Typological Interpretation," 31).

24. Brueggemann argues that this connection is evident throughout the OT, because God does not intend for his people to be permanently displaced but to have a place where they will be safe and secure, "a place with Yahweh . . . filled with memories of life with him and promises from him and vows to him" (*Land*, 1–6).

25. Dempster, *Dominion and Dynasty*, 84.

the promise of a land inheritance is not again affirmed in the remainder of Genesis, Dana Harris contends that Jacob's "dying request to be buried in Canaan (49:29–32) and its fulfillment (50:4–14) indicate his confidence in the land promise."[26] Furthermore, in Genesis 50 Joseph's final request to have his bones buried in Canaan also demonstrates his confidence in the promise of land. And since both Jacob and Joseph, as Abraham's offspring, ask to be buried in the land, their petitions display their assurance that Abraham's offspring are supposed to dwell eternally in the land, thus tying the themes of inheritance and descendants.[27]

Exodus

Exodus begins by recording that the twelve tribes of Israel have settled in Egypt and have become extremely numerous (1:1–7).[28] God's multiplication of the offspring of Abraham implies that he "is keeping the promise he made to Abraham" to greatly multiply his descendants, "and this in spite of the new king in Egypt who does not know about Joseph."[29] God is multiplying Abraham's offspring while they are enslaved under the heavy hand of Pharaoh. If Pharaoh has his way, God's people will remain as slaves in Egypt and will never enter their inheritance.

God will not allow his people to remain in servitude, for he is faithful to the covenant he promised to Abraham. So, he reveals himself to Moses at the mountain of God as "the God of your father (אָבִיךָ),[30] Abraham, Isaac, and Jacob" (Exod 3:6), disclosing that he has chosen him to deliver his peo-

26. Harris, "Eternal Inheritance," 36.

27. In view of passages such as Ezek 36–37 and Rom 8 (which I will discuss in the coming chapters), one can further argue that Joseph's request "to have his bones buried in Canaan" suggests that he believes that his body will be resurrected to dwell in the land.

28. Many scholars also believe that Exodus is a patchwork of sources from the Yahwist, Elohist, and Priestly authors (Noth, *Exodus*, 13.) As in the case of Genesis, I side with the testimony of Jesus and unbroken tradition until the nineteenth century, that Moses wrote Exodus. I will thereby assume his authorship throughout this section.

29. Hamilton, *God's Glory*, 90. Similarly, House contends that "the book's opening verses are to be read as a theological affirmation of God's ongoing faithfulness, kindness, and provision for Abraham, Isaac, and Jacob. The promise-keeping God continues to act across centuries, keeping pledges to men and women long dead" (*Old Testament Theology*, 89).

30. Certainly, the plural form of אָב, rendered as "fathers," would seem to make more sense in Exod 3:6. Nevertheless, Durham argues that this form "is decidedly singular (cf. Gen 26:24; 31:5; 43:23; Exod 15:2; 18:4) despite the various (and unjustified) attempts to make it plural" (*Exodus*, 31). This view is supported by both the MT (אָבִיךָ, "your father") and the LXX (τοῦ πατρός σου, "your father").

ple from the Egyptians to bring them into "a good and spacious land, a land flowing with milk and honey, the land of the Canaanites" (Exod 3:7–10).[31] Since Moses does not feel qualified for such a task, God assures him that he will be with him and will deliver Israel from Egypt (Exod 3:11–18).

Following Pharaoh's denial of Moses' request for three days of liberty to worship God (Exod 5:1–17), God reiterates to Moses that he will give the land of Canaan to his people (Exod 6:2–5). The recurrence of the promise once more assures the offspring of Abraham that they will enter their inheritance, regardless of their difficult circumstances.

After God brings ten plagues upon Egypt, beginning with the turning of water into blood and concluding with the death of the first-born (Exod 7:14–12:36), Pharaoh finally releases the Israelites (Exod 12:31). Before leaving Egypt, Moses assures the people of the promise to bring them into their inheritance (Exod 13:5, 11). This is the final affirmation of the promise before beginning the exodus and setting out toward the land of Canaan.

Shortly after departing, Pharaoh changes his mind and decides to pursue the Israelites (Exod 14:5–9). The pursuit proves to be futile, for God miraculously delivers his people through the Red Sea (Exod 4:15–31). God's powerful deliverance of his people leads them to sing "a song of praise extolling Yahweh's might" (Exod 15:1–18).[32] At the conclusion of the song (Exod 15:13–17), the Israelites sing that God will lead them to his "holy abode" (Exod 15:13) and plant them in the "mountain of his inheritance (נַחֲלָה)" (Exod 15:17). Victor Hamilton believes that God's "holy abode" and the "mountain of his inheritance" may refer to the immediate or distant future.[33] If these phrases refer to the immediate future, they point "to Israel's passing over/through the wilderness and arriving at Mount Sinai."[34] If they refer to the distant future, they point "to Israel's crossing over the Jordan River and entering into and conquering 'the holy land.'"[35] After examining the options,

31. The phrase "a land flowing with milk and honey" depicts Canaan as a plentiful and abundant land. Hamilton observes that "this description of Canaan appears twenty times in the Bible" (*Exodus*, 232–33,). See, for example, Deut 6:3; 11:9; 26:9–15; 27:3; 31:20. Striving to find the ancient near eastern background for this phrase, Hamilton states: "Antedating these twenty references to Canaan's fertility is an Egyptian story, the story of Sinuhe, which dates to the early second millennium BC. After his flight from Libya and Egypt, Sinuhe arrives in Palestine. His description of this land is as follows: 'It was a good land, named Yaa (=Canaan). Figs were in it, and grapes. It had more wine than water. Plentiful was its honey, abundant its olives. Every (kind of) fruit on its trees" (ibid., 55–56). See also Dozeman, *Exodus*, 128–29.

32. Hamilton, *God's Glory*, 96.

33. Hamilton, *Exodus*, 232–33.

34. Ibid.

35. Ibid.

Hamilton concludes that Exodus 15:13–17 focuses on "what is shortly coming down the pike rather than what is centuries away."[36] Although this interpretation is plausible, it is more likely that God's "holy abode" and the
"mountain of his inheritance" point to the more distant future: the entering
in and conquering of the promised land of Canaan. Thus far, the narrative
of Genesis and Exodus has recorded that the offspring of Abraham have
received the promise of inheritance and have been reminded of its contents
on numerous occasions (e.g., Gen 26:3; 28:13–15; 35:9–12; 46:4), receiving
the last reminder just before leaving Egypt and setting out toward Canaan
(Exod 13:5–11). Hence, it is more probable that God's people are anticipating their final arrival in the promised land, rather than their more temporary stay at Mount Sinai.

In the third month of the wilderness journey, Israel arrives at Mount
Sinai (Exod 19:1–2). Here, God announces to Moses his intention to make
Israel "his own possession out of all the people" of the earth and "a kingdom
of priests and a holy nation" (Exod 19:5–6). God's intention to make Israel
"his own possession" displays his aim to bring to himself a people who will
be members of his eternally adopted family (cf. Rom 4:13–17, 8:12–25; Gal
3, 4).[37] God's plan to make Israel "a kingdom of priests and a holy nation"
shows that he aims to do so in the land of their inheritance. Since God desires for his people to dwell eternally in the land, this is the place where
he will establish the kingdom.[38] This is seen, for example, in Deuteronomy
17:14–20, which provides the requirements for the monarchy that will be
instituted in the land, such as the king being appointed by God (17:15) and
his duty to rule over the people in accord with Torah (17:18–20).[39] As well,
the kingdom in the land is where God's son, the offspring of Abraham, will
reign eternally (cf. 2 Sam 7; Ps 2; Rev 21). These observations make evident
that Israel will be a "kingdom of priests and a holy nation" in the land (cf. 1
Cor 6:9–10; 15:50–56; Gal 5:19–21; Eph 5:3–7; Col 1:9–14; 3:18–25).

---

36. Ibid., 232.

37. Stuart, *Exodus*, 422.

38. Merrill notes that at this point in Israel's history (Exod 19–23) they were a nation with a king, "Yahweh himself. . . . All they lacked now was a land to give their
nationhood objectivity and stability. Even this was theirs by promise. Vassal Israel had
only to carry out its divine mandate to seize and occupy the land for Yahweh the King"
(*Kingdom of Priests*, 111). Thus, if Israel is a nation with a king, which will one day occupy a land, then the implication is that they will be a kingdom in the land of promise
under the authority of Yahweh.

39. Ibid., 208.

While still at Mount Sinai, God speaks the Ten Commandments to Israel.[40] Keeping these commandments will ensure that they receive their inheritance and become a kingdom. The remaining laws describe the way the people are to dwell in the land, reflecting the holiness of Yahweh (Exod 21:1–23:19).[41] In short, Exodus envisions a people sojourning to their inheritance to become a holy kingdom, living according to the laws of their God.

Leviticus

Leviticus asserts that the land, although given to Israel as their permanent inheritance (נַחֲל), ultimately belongs to God.[42] This is primarily evidenced in the Holiness Code of Leviticus 19–26. The most emphatic statement of this fact is found in verse 25:23, where God forbids the permanent selling of the individual allotments of the inheritance because the land, he says, "is mine."[43] Moreover, the Holiness Code suggests that those who dwell in the land are to be holy because God, the owner, is holy. If the people fail to live according to his standards, the land will "vomit them out" (Lev 20:22–27).[44] Hence, the implication of God being the true owner of the land is that the

---

40. Harris, "Eternal Inheritance," 38.

41. Ibid., 39.

42. Ibid. Most scholars argue that Leviticus was written in the post-exilic period "in conjunction with the Priestly source" (Kaiser, "Leviticus," 1:996). Kaufmann, however, argues that the Priestly source is pre-exilic, but not Mosaic (Ibid.). Sherwood, leaving much to the imagination, contends that "the whole book of Leviticus is a third-person narrative in which the narrator tells us what the Lord or Moses or Aaron or the people said or did" (*Leviticus, Numbers, Deuteronomy*, 28). Critical Pentateuchal studies thus remain in flux. Kaiser argues: "It is now abundantly clear that there is no sole, higher-critical position; rather, there are a number of quite diverse ways by means of which to understand the origins of the Pentateuch and, hence, Leviticus" ("Leviticus," 1:997). The lack of consensus is unpersuasive. Like Genesis and Exodus, I am persuaded by Mosaic authorship of Leviticus, considering Jesus' affirmation and church tradition. As well, Kaiser observes: "the prominent formula 'The Lord said to Moses,' helps explain why both the synagogue and the church held to the essential unity of this book and to Mosaic authorship until well into medieval times" (Ibid., 995).

43. Hartley, *Leviticus*, 4:437.

44. Martens observes, "Land is a gift from Yahweh, and Israel, throughout preoccupation with it, has her attention continually called to Yahweh. Land requires a specific and appropriate life-style. Responsibilities regarding social behavior are enjoined upon the people for the time when they will occupy the land, and they are warned that disobedience defiles the land and may result in their loss of privilege of tenancy" ("Land and Lifestyle," 240).

people must live in harmony with his holy principles. The failure to do so will result in the forfeiture of their inheritance.

Numbers

Numbers begins with a sense of anticipation. Paul House says that "Hundreds of years have passed from the giving of the Abrahamic promises (c. 2000 B.C.) to the conclusion of Leviticus (c. 1440 or c. 1290 B.C.), and at long last the promised land looms before the freed children of Israel."[45] While still at Mount Sinai, in the second year of the sojourn through the wilderness, God commands Moses to take a census of all the people of Israel (Num 1). The census signifies that the entry into the land is at hand.[46] Shortly thereafter, the people of Israel set out from Sinai and continue their sojourn to the land of Canaan (Num 10:11–12).

Now at the point of entering in the land, Israel sends spies to view the promised land (Num 13:1–27). When the spies return, they report that it is indeed "a land flowing with milk and honey" (Num 13:27). Yet, their report of the intimidating people and the large, fortified cities demonstrates their lack of trust in God's promise to bring them into their everlasting inheritance (Num 13:28–29). Although they are seemingly at the end of their journey, Israel does not trust that God will bring them into the very land that belongs to him (Lev 25:23), was promised to Abraham (Gen 12:1–3; 13:15; 17:8; 24:7), and has been reassured to the subsequent generations of his offspring (Gen 26:3; 28:13–15; 35:9–12; 46:4).

Because of such unbelief, God decides that this generation will be consigned "to killing time, going around and around as on a merry-go-round,

---

45. House, *Old Testament Theology*, 153. Numbers has largely been attributed to the Priestly author. Budd observes: "In the book of Numbers there is very general acceptance of a total priestly contribution in the following chapters—1–9, 15, 17–19, 26–31, 33–36—and a substantial influence in 10, 13–14, 16, 20, 25, 32. The only chapters lacking such influence would appear to be 11–12, 21–24" (*Numbers*, xviii). I remain unpersuaded by such historical critical assumptions, preferring to side with Mosaic authorship based on the testimony of Scripture and church history. Sailhamer provides a succinct, yet convincing and plausible, view of Mosaic authorship for the Pentateuch: "Critical scholarship supposes that writers of a date later than Moses composed the Pentateuch, using various sources that had been perseved among diverse groups within ancient Israel. Some conservative scholars," citing Harrison's *Introduction to the Old Testament*, "suppose Moses used a collection of clay tablets which had preserved the accounts of creation, the flood, and the lives of the patriarchs. Thus, Moses would have written the Pentateuch in much the same way as Luke says he wrote his Gospel (cf. Lk 1:1–4)" (*Pentateuch as Narrative*, 23).

46. Harris, "Eternal Inheritance," 40.

in a meaningless and purposeless existence without ever seeing the land until the despisers die of natural death."[47] Only Caleb and Joshua, who do not doubt that God will conquer the residents of Canaan (Num 14:5–9), will enter the land. The rest will die without ever crossing its borders.

After the unbelieving generation perishes, a new generation is poised to enter the land. Before going in, God commands a new census of the people (Num 26) and gives orders concerning the division of each tribe's inheritance (Num 31–36). Once the people have been accounted and the inheritances have been apportioned, the only task that remains is to occupy the land. The new generation now stands poised to inherit the land that was forfeited by their predecessors.[48]

Deuteronomy

Deuteronomy begins where Numbers ends—with a new generation of Israelites standing at the border of Canaan, in anticipation of receiving their inheritance. So important is the topic of land in this book that "from beginning to end" the land remains a central theme.[49] N. Whybray believes that Deuteronomy has "an obsessive preoccupation with this theme," to the extent that "only in this book is there a fully developed theology of the land in which the entire future of the nation has been concentrated."[50]

Deuteronomy also reminds the Israelites that the reception of the land inheritance is based upon the promise God swore "to Abraham, Isaac, and Jacob, to give (נָתַן) to them and their offspring after them" the land of Canaan

47. Waltke, *Old Testament Theology*, 540.

48. House, *Old Testament Theology*, 165.

49. Dempster, *Dominion and Dynasty*, 118. Critical scholarship mainly attributes Deuteronomy to the Deuteronomistic author with no relation to Yahwist, Elohist, and Priestly authors (von Rad, *Deuteronomy*, 1–23). Space prohibits an extensive engagement with this argument. I still side with Mosaic authorship of all books in the Pentateuch in view of my aforementioned reasons. I also concur with Merrill: "Precritical Jewish and Christian tradition nearly unanimously attributed Deuteronomy to Moses, at least in its basic substance, though there were always dissenters who argued for post-Mosaic interpolations and additions such as the great lawgiver's own death (Deut 34:5–12). . . . The Mosaic authorship tradition finds its initial articulation in Deuteronomy itself, for after the 'title' the text goes on to say . . . literally, 'which Moses spoke,' a statement that attributes the immediately following passage and, by implication, the entire work to Moses. Beginning with Joshua (Josh 1:7–8), the attribution to Moses continues throughout the Old Testament (e.g., Judg 1:20; 3:4; 1 Kgs 2:3; 2 Kgs 14:6; 2 Chr 25:4; Ezra 3:2; and also the New Testament (Matt 19:7; Mark 12:19; Luke 20:28; Acts 3:22; Rom 10:19; 1 Cor 9:9). There can be no doubt that the prophets, Jesus, and the apostles concurred with the witness of Deuteronomy about its authorship" (*Deuteronomy*, 22).

50. Whybray, *Pentateuch*, 98.

(1:8). Throughout Deuteronomy, the verb נָתַן is employed to indicate that the land is a gift from its owner, Yahweh (cf. Lev 25:23; Deut 1:25; 2:29; 3:20; 4:1; 7:1; 11:8; 16:20; 18:9; 23:21; 24:12). The book's further references to the land as נַחֲל serve to solidify this point.[51]

As well, Deuteronomy evidences that Israel is God's "inheritance" (נַחֲל) and "possession" (סְגֻלָּה) out of all the people of the earth (Deut 7:6; 14:2; 26:18).[52] Whereas God intends to make Israel "his own possession" in Exodus 19:5, in Deuteronomy it appears that what was once intended is now being fulfilled, for Israel is now called "God's possession."

Similarly, Israel is compared to a son and God to a father (Deut 8:5; 32:5, 6, 18, 19; cf. 1:31; 8:5; 14:1).[53] As God's son, Israel will receive the land as an inheritance. But the status of sonship requires Israel to reflect God's likeness in obeying the Torah.[54] There will be blessings for Israel's obedience (Deut 28:3–14) and curses for their disobedience (Deut 28:15–69). The ultimate blessing is the possession of the land, while the ultimate curse is exile.[55] It is not enough for Israel to presume that their designation as "son" entitles them to a lasting inheritance, for obedience is required of those who desire to inherit the land.

Joshua

The book of Joshua records Israel's taking (1–12), allotting (13–21), and retaining of the land (22–24).[56] While still viewing the inheritance as the entire land of Canaan (Josh 1–12), the inheritance (נַחֲלָה) in Joshua also refers to the portions of land allotted to the tribes of Israel (Josh 13–21).[57]

51. House, *Old Testament Theology*, 173.

52. See discussion in Harris, "Eternal Inheritance," 42.

53. Dempster, *Dominion and Dynasty*, 119; Harris, "Eternal Inheritance," 42.

54. Dempster, *Dominion and Dynasty*, 119.

55. Ibid.

56. Waltke, *Old Testament Theology*, 513. There is a lack of consensus concerning the date and authorship of Joshua. Scholars attribute the material in Joshua to the Yahwist, Elohist, Deuteronomist, or Priestly authors, or any number of combinations of these authors. Being unconvinced by these arguments and the lack of unanimity, I hold that Joshua wrote the book attributed to him. I concur with Woudstra: "Could not the view of history developed in Joshua have been the product of the days in which Israel, according to the book's own testimony, 'served the Lord' (24:31), i.e., in the days of Joshua himself and of the elders who outlived him? The spirit of joyful optimism which pervades the book by and large could perhaps be accounted for best by that assumption" (*Joshua*, 12–13).

57. E.g., Josh 11:23; 12:6; 13:1; 18:7; 19:1. Isaiah uses similar language in stating that God has "apportioned" the land to his people "with a line" (34:17). Isaiah clarifies that

The tribes are not to settle randomly throughout Canaan. Rather, they must dwell in the portions given to them as an inheritance (נַחֲלָה). The fact that a part of the land is allotted to each tribe displays "an inherent equality in the nation as a whole," because "every Israelite was the child of a heavenly Parent to whom belonged the whole earth, who had chosen Israel out of all the families of the earth (Deut 32:8–9; 9:26, 29; Ps 28:9; 79:1; Jer 10:16) and now distributed, with evenhanded fairness, the land among the people."[58]

With Israel entering and allotting the land, the moment the Hexateuch has been anticipating—from the initial promise in Genesis to its reaffirmation throughout the remainder of the Pentateuch—is seemingly fulfilled. That is, God's people have apparently inherited the land and are experiencing rest (Josh 22:4; 33:1). Yet, the book of Joshua hints otherwise, for pockets of unconquered enemies, such as the Philistines, the Jeshurites, and the Jebusites, remain within the borders of Canaan (e.g., Josh 13:1–7; 15:63; 16:10; 17:12–13).[59] Israel will not rest as long as such enemies dwell in the land. This evidence suggests that Canaan is not the fulfillment of the promise of inheritance to Abraham and his offspring. There must be a better land that awaits the people of God, one in which they will truly experience eternal rest—for Canaan already falls short of this expectation.

Summary of the Inheritance in the Hexateuch

The theme of inheritance, which is identified as the land promised to Abraham and his descendants, is grounded in the narrative of the Hexateuch. The initial promise of inheritance is found in Genesis (e.g., Gen 12:1–9; 17:8). Although the inheritance is found in the same promissory contexts as the promises of blessing and descendants (e.g., Gen 12:1–9; 15:1–21), only the inheritance is understood as the promise of land. Hence, we must neither confuse nor mingle the inheritance with the promises of blessing and descendants. Even so, there is an evident close association between the promises of inheritance and descendants, since the "land" will be occupied by the "offspring" of Abraham—a promise that is reaffirmed to Isaac (Gen 26:3) and Jacob (Gen 28:13–15; 35:9–12).

In Genesis, it is also apparent that, when the promise of land is given to Abraham's descendants, the construction לְזַרְעֲךָ is employed, which the LXX translates as either τῷ σπέρματί σου or τῷ σπέρματί ὑμῶν (e.g., 12:7; 15:18);

God's people "will possess" this land "for eternity; from generation to generation they shall live in it" (34:17).

58. House, *Old Testament Theology*, 209.

59. Merrill, *Kingdom of Priests*, 148.

and when this promise is given to both Abraham and his offspring, the construction וּלְזַרְעֲךָ is used, which the LXX translates as καὶ τῷ σπέρματί σου (e.g., 17:8; 24:7). The embedding of fragments of texts into later ones displays an intertextual pattern in inheritance related passages in the Pentateuch (cf. Exod 33:1; Deut 34:4).

In Exodus, the people of Israel are delivered from exile in Egypt and are sojourning to the land of their inheritance to become a holy kingdom. Once in the land, it is expected that they will live according to God's laws (Exod 21:1—23:19). Leviticus asserts that the land ultimately belongs to God, and thus the failure to live in harmony with his laws will result in the forfeiture of the inheritance (Lev 19–26; cf. 25:23).

Even though God has promised to bring his people into the land, Numbers testifies that the generation that was delivered from Egypt does not believe that God will defeat their enemies and bring them into the land of Canaan. On account of their unbelief, God consigns this generation to wander aimlessly outside of the land, until they perish (Num 14:20–24). Once they die, a new generation stands poised to inherit the land.

With this new generation at the cusp of receiving their inheritance, Deuteronomy stresses that obedience to God's laws is required of the sons who desire to inherit the land. Obedience results in blessing, while disobedience results in curses, the most serious of these being expulsion from the land (Deut 28).

Following years of sojourning, the book of Joshua depicts God's people partially occupying the land of Canaan, for some of Israel's enemies still dwell within their borders (cf. Josh 13:1–7). Israel is not at rest. Thus, there must be a better inheritance that awaits the people of God.

THE INHERITANCE IN THE HISTORICAL BOOKS: THE KINGDOM AND EXILE FROM THE LAND

Before discussing the historical books of Samuel, Kings, Chronicles, and Ezra, it is important to note that the lack of rest that was suggested in Joshua (13:1–7) is confirmed in Judges. Judges displays that God has given the land to Israel (Judg 1:4), but the people have not driven out the inhabitants of Canaan. Consequently, routine cycles of oppression and deliverance from enemies become common (Judg 3:7—16:31). The oppression comes upon Israel when they do evil before Yahweh (Judg 3:7; 12; 4:1; 6:1; 10:6; 13:1), and deliverance arrives when they cry out to God (Judg 3:9, 15; 4:4–9; 10:10–16).[60] Such a cycle displays that the people are not at rest in the land.

60. Hamilton, God's Glory, 155–56.

In addition, the conclusion of Judges records that in those times "there was no king in Israel. Everyone did what was right in their own eyes" (Judg 21:25). This is a far cry from the posture that is expected of Israel in their inheritance (Lev 19–26). This sad state anticipates a time when a king will bring God's people rest in the land[61] and sets the stage for the period of the monarchy in Samuel to Chronicles.

Samuel

Samuel anticipates that God will raise up a king who will deliver his people from their enemies and bring them rest in the land.[62] If rest is achieved, then Canaan is the fulfillment of the lasting inheritance promised to Abraham's descendants. If it is not realized, then the promise of land still remains for the people of God, one that is "permanent, undefiled, and unfading" (1 Pet 1:4). The examination of the inheritance in Samuel will focus on Saul and David, two kings who are expected to bring rest to Israel.

Saul's Reign in the Land

The reign of Saul arises from the people's desire for a king who will deliver them from the Philistines (1 Sam 8:3, 20; cf. 12:12).[63] Samuel views this re-

61. See the similar thought in Butler (*Judges*, 468); Dempster (*Dominion and Dynasty*, 133). von Rad also contends that the rest for Israel is still to come (*Old Testament Theology*, 373–74).

62. The authorship of 1 and 2 Samuel is anonymous. Bergen notes the following: "Although many modern scholars believe Samuel played an important role in recording some of the materials that now comprise the work, the consensus view is that the development of the original canonical (=autographic) form of the book was relatively complex. It is generally conceded that several intermediary steps took place over a considerable period of time leading up to the production of the final form of the book" (*1, 2 Samuel*, 19).

I hold that the final, canonical form of 1 and 2 Samuel should be read as one unit. House states, "Samuel has always been considered one volume in the Hebrew Canon. The book was split in Greek and Hebrew translation, perhaps due to its length or subject matter" (*Old Testament Theology*, 580). Similarly, Klein argues that the division of 1 and 2 Samuel is not very helpful, "and a more traditional unit might simply be Samuel, that is, what we today call 1 Sam 1 to 2 Sam 24. Apparently because of the great length of 'Samuel,' the LXX divided this material into two books, called 1 and 2 Kingdoms or 1 and 2 Reigns" (*1 Samuel*, xxv). These observations make evident that the division between 1 and 2 Samuel is artificial, thus justifying the treatment of 1 and 2 Samuel as one unit.

63. Dempster, *Dominion and Dynasty*, 137.

quest as a rejection of his leadership (1 Sam 8:6).[64] In reality, it is a rejection of God, their true king (1 Sam 8:7). God is the one who delivered Israel from Egypt, led them through the wilderness, defeated their enemies, and settled them in the land. He is the one who has been delivering and leading his people, as is expected of a king. In spite this, the people fail to trust in him for deliverance, thereby rejecting his rule. (1 Sam 8:20).

Even so, Scripture foretells that Israel will have a king (Gen 17:6; 49:9–11; Num 24:7, 17). Deuteronomy 17:14 says that "when you [Israel] come into the land (אֶרֶץ) the Lord your God is giving (נָתַן) you . . . and you will say, 'I will set a king over me as the nations that are around me,' you may appoint a king over you whom the Lord your God will choose."[65] So, it appears that the request for a king is not evil.[66] The closing statement of Judges—"when there was no king in Israel" and "everyone did what was right in his own eyes" (21:25)—provides further evidence that Israel looks forward to a ruler who will bring Israel rest in the land.[67] Therefore, the evil does not lie in the people's petition for a king, but in that they do not ask God for a king (cf. Deut 17:4) through whom he will exercise his power and authority.[68] Instead, they petition Samuel to appoint a king over them "like the nations" (1 Sam 8:5, 19–20). As their ancestors, Israel trusts in someone other than God's anointed (cf. Exod 32), and consequently someone other than God himself, to deliver them.[69] God will allow Samuel to give them their "worldly" kingship, but it will come with harsh "worldly" implications (1 Sam 8:8–18).

Shortly thereafter, Samuel anoints Saul, the son of Kish, to be king over Israel (1 Sam 10:1–16). Saul is described as more handsome and taller than any of the men of Israel (1 Sam 9:2–3). Although he is tall and handsome—things that the surrounding nations value—he is a failure as a ruler. In fact, not long after Saul's coronation, he sins by offering an unlawful sacrifice and is thereby rejected by God (1 Sam 13:8–15). God would therefore remove

---

64. Bergen, *1, 2 Samuel*, 115.

65. Brackets mine.

66. Similarly, Hamilton, *God's Glory*, 163.

67. Webb claims that Judges 21:25 "foreshadows what is to come (the institution of the monarchy), but leaves us wondering, in view of the disasters that have attended kingship in the body of the book, whether, in the end, kingship will fare any better than judgement has done" (*Judges*, 508). While agreeing that this statement looks forward to the monarchy, I contend that it ultimately looks forward to Christ's reign. Whereas Israel's monarchy would encounter many of the same failures as the period of the judges, the Kingdom of Christ will initiate an eternal period of rest and peace that the world has yet to know.

68. Hamilton, *God's Glory*, 163.

69. Ibid.

the kingship from Saul and grant it to a man "after his own heart" (1 Sam 13:14).

Saul's failure as king is also evidenced in that he does not eradicate the Amalekites from the land of Canaan (1 Sam 15).[70] The Amalekites were a threat to Israelite stability, so their annihilation was necessary. As the ruler of Israel, Saul was to eliminate these people in order to bring peace to the land. His failure to do so confirms that he is not the king the people were expecting, the one who would bring them rest in their inheritance.

Since Saul is not fit to be king, God leads Samuel to anoint David as the next ruler of Israel (1 Sam 16:1–13). Following this, the Spirit of the Lord comes upon David (1 Sam 16:13) and departs from Saul (1 Sam 16:14). Saul has failed as king and now David is officially selected to take his place.[71]

The remainder of the account of Saul's life describes his decline and the corresponding rise of David.[72] During Saul's demise, he openly seeks to kill David (1 Sam 19), causing David to flee from Saul's presence (1 Sam 20:1—23:1). In spite of this, David has the courage to encounter Saul in his own camp. There he chastises Saul for pursuing him and proclaims his innocence (1 Sam 26:17–20).[73] He even says to Saul that the wicked men hunting him "have now driven me from a share in the inheritance of the Lord (בְּנַחֲלַת יְהוָה)" (1 Sam 26:19; cf. Lev 19–26), i.e., the land promised to Abraham and his descendants.[74] David would not be separated from his inheritance forever, for Saul and his men would eventually flee in battle from the Philistines and fall slain (1 Sam 31:1–2). When mortally wounded, Saul would take his own life so that the Philistines could not mistreat him (1 Sam 31:4). Saul's death means that David can now return to the land and take his place as king.

What is more, it is important to note that, after the death of Saul and his men, the Israelites who lived beyond the Jordan abandon their cities and

70. Dempster, *Dominion and Dynasty*, 138.

71. McCarter, Jr., *1 Samuel*, 278.

72. Ibid.

73. Klein, *1 Samuel*, 258.

74. Forshey argues that "the inheritance of the Lord" in 1 Sam 26:19 refers to the people of God and not the land of Canaan ("Construct Chain Nahalat," 51–53). This reading, however, does not suit the context. David is now outside the land of promise, and he looks back on what has been assured to his forefathers, the place from which he has been removed. Moreover, after David finishes saying to Saul that he has been driven out of "the inheritance of the Lord," Saul remorsefully responds to David by telling him to "return . . . for I will do you no more harm." It seems that "the place" to which Saul is exhorting David to return is the location from which he has been forced to flee, i.e., the land. Thereby "the inheritance of the lord" is the land of promise rather than God's people.

the Philistines then live in them (31:7). Such events reveal that the situation during the end of Saul's reign is the same as when he was first installed as king—Israel is oppressed by the Philistines. The people wanted a king to deliver them from the Philistines (8:8), but Saul was not the one to accomplish this task. So, the hope of a king who will deliver the people of God and bring them rest in the land is now placed on David. If he brings the people rest, the promise of a lasting inheritance to the descendants of Abraham will be fulfilled. If he does not, the people must look forward to another king who will grant them the respite in the land they desire.

David's Reign in the Land

After Saul's death, David is anointed king of Judah (2 Sam 2:1–7). There then commences a long war between the house of Saul and the house of David for control over the land of Israel (2 Sam 3:1). David eventually conquers the house of Saul and is anointed king (2 Sam 5:1–5). David is now the one to whom the people will look, as they looked to Saul, to conquer their enemies and bring them rest in their inheritance.

One of the first steps in bringing rest to Israel is defeating the Philistines, something which Saul was never able to accomplish. David accomplishes this task early in his reign (2 Sam 5:17–25) and proves that he is the rightful king.[75] He also makes Jerusalem the capital of the nation (2 Sam 5:7) and brings the ark of the covenant within the city (2 Sam 6). Moving the ark to Jerusalem evidences that "David's kingship is subservient to Yahweh's, a fact further expressed by the description of David as Yahweh's 'servant' (2 Sam 7:5, 19–29) and 'ruler' (2 Sam 7:8)."[76]

With the ark now in Jerusalem, Samuel says that "the Lord has given David rest from his enemies around him" (2 Sam 7:1). Does this statement mean that the promised rest from enemies in the inheritance has been realized (Deut 12:10, 25; Josh 22:4; 23:1)?[77] Given that in the Davidic covenant God promises David a future rest from his enemies (2 Sam 7:11), the current affirmation of rest seems temporary and incomplete.[78] As William

---

75. Harris, "Eternal Inheritance," 60.

76. Williamson, *Sealed with an Oath*, 122. Baldwin contends that Israel's true king is God. Her claim is based on the idea that the absence of a coronation ceremony for David was intended to display that God was Israel's true monarch (*1 and 2 Samuel*, 211–12).

77. See the relevant discussion in Anderson (*2 Samuel*, 116); von Rad (*Problem of the Hexateuch*, 94–102).

78. Williamson, *Sealed with an Oath*, 123; Bergen, *1, 2 Samuel*, 335.

Dumbrell states, "On the one hand, rest had been given to David, 7:1, on the other hand, rest is yet to come, 7:11."[79]

In the Davidic covenant, God also promises that he "will appoint a place (מָקוֹם) for my people Israel and will plant them, so that they will dwell in their own place (מָקוֹם) and no longer be troubled" (2 Sam 7:10). The language of "planting" and "dwelling" in their "place" (מָקוֹם) reaffirms the future promise of land[80] and also recalls Exodus 15:17, which similarly states that God will "plant his people in the mountain of [his] inheritance (נַחֲלָה)." Another promise of the Davidic covenant is that God "will raise up [David's] seed (זֶרַע) after [him] . . . who will establish his kingdom,"[81] and that he will set up "the throne of his kingdom forever" (2 Sam 7:12–3). The thought of raising up "seed" (זֶרַע) alludes to God's promise of progeny to Abraham (cf. Gen 15), establishing a link between the Abrahamic and Davidic covenants.[82] This link is further solidified in that David is the offspring of Abraham, and thus his royal offspring is ultimately a descendant of Abraham. Hence, it is David's descendent, who is also the offspring of Abraham, for whom God will establish an everlasting kingdom.

In view of the Davidic Covenant, it is apparent that God will use David's royal offspring (2 Sam 7:12–13) to plant Israel in the land (2 Sam 7:11) and bring them rest (2 Sam 7:10).[83] Whether such a state has already come about or will be realized in the future depends, in part, on the interpretation of the following verbal phrases in 2 Samuel 7:10–12: וְשַׂמְתִּי מָקוֹם (v. 10), וַהֲכִינֹתִי אֶת־מַמְלַכְתּוֹ (v. 12), וַהֲקִימֹתִי אֶת־זַרְעֲךָ (v. 11), וַהֲנִיחֹתִי לְךָ (v.12). Some, such as A.A. Anderson, translate these phrases with a past-time sense.[84] The fact that the verbs in these phrases are in the perfect tense allows for such an interpretation.[85] Each of these verbs, however, is linked by a series of *waw* conjunctions, thus making them *weqatal* verbs, which are normally

---

79. Dumbrell, *Covenant and Creation*, 124.

80. The noun מָקוֹם generally refers to a physical "location, place, homeland, etc." Hence, the reference to מָקוֹם as the land of Israel's inheritance is well within the lexical bounds of this word. For similar territorial uses of this word, see Gen 1:9,30:25; Exod 20:23; Num 24:11, 25. See also *HALOT*, 1:626; Bergen, *1, 2 Samuel*, 399.

81. Brackets mine.

82. Williamson, *Sealed with an Oath*, 124; Bergen, *1,2, Samuel*, 340.

83. Williamson, *Sealed with an Oath*, 126. Jer 33:14–18 assures the fulfillment of the Davidic covenant promise of a king from David's line who will reign in the land and bring safety to God's people (2 Sam 7:10–16). Jer 33:16 ("in those days Judah will be saved and Jerusalem will dwell in safety") testifies that this event will take place in the future.

84. Anderson, *2 Samuel*, 120.

85. Ibid.

translated with a future-time sense.[86] This grammatical point alone provides a valid warrant for translating the *weqatal* chain in 2 Samuel 7:10–12 with a future-time connotation.

The grammatical point is not the only justification for such a rendering. The LXX employs the future tense verbs θήσομαι (2 Sam 7:10), ἀναπαύσω (2 Sam 7:11), ἀναστήσω (2 Sam 7:12), and ἑτοιμάσω (2 Sam 7:12) to translate each of the perfect tense forms in 2 Samuel 7:10–12.[87] So, given the fact that *weqatal* verbs are normally translated with a future sense and that the LXX translates the perfect tense forms in said verbal phrases with future tense verbs, there is sufficient support for understanding the *weqatal* chain in 2 Samuel 7:10–12 with a future connotation. This observation suggests that God has not yet planted Israel in their land and brought them rest. When Israel finally experiences rest in the land, the rest that only God's anointed king will bring about, it will be certain that they are in the promised inheritance.

David's last words reaffirm that this state will be realized in the future (2 Sam 23:1–7), expecting that a righteous ruler will reign over all mankind and reinvigorate the earth (2 Sam 23:3–4; cf. Ps 72:6). Paul Williamson argues that David is in fact looking forward to the one through whom God will establish the kingdom.[88] The fact that such a ruler will come from David's dynasty is grounded in the "everlasting covenant" made with him in 2 Samuel 7 (cf. 2 Sam 23:5). Thus, Israel's future hope lies in a Davidic king who will reign over mankind and bring needed reinvigoration to the earth. Since this expectation is linked to the Davidic covenant, the ruler who will bring refreshment to the earth (2 Sam 23:3–4) is the same one who will plant God's people in the land and bring them rest (2 Sam 7:10–12). At this point, there is already an allusion to the idea that David's royal seed will not only reign over Canaan but the entire earth, and that the land upon which this ruler will bring rest is also not solely Canaan but the whole earth. Yet, the narrative in the Hexateuch and Samuel has yet to explicitly make this point. The remaining discussion in Samuel to Chronicles and the Psalms and Prophets will at some point have to expand the land over which the coming royal descendent of David will have dominion to encompass the

---

86. Williams observes that the *weqatal* verb, otherwise known as the perfect *waw* consecutive, is "traditionally said to refer to an action without having the completion of the action in view, just like an incomplete action imperfect, and to often form a temporal sequence in the future-time narrative" (*Hebrew Syntax*, 76). See also McCarter, *2 Samuel*, 202.

87. LXX 2 Samuel citations are from Ziegler, *Susanna, Daniel, Bel et Draco*.

88. Davidson, *Sealed with an Oath*, 131. See also House, *Old Testament Theology*, 247.

whole earth. Doing so will bring to light what already seems to be implied in 2 Samuel.[89]

In sum, the insinuation of a royal descendent of David who will rule over and bring rest to the entire earth appears to be present in Samuel. That the Davidic covenant and the last words of David are oriented toward the future display that David is not the one to bring about this universal reign and rest. Therefore, the narrative of Samuel to Chronicles will now turn to Solomon in the book of Kings, in expectation that he is the descendent of David who will bring rest to God's people.

Kings

Kings commences with David now advanced in age (1 Kgs 1:1).[90] When near death, he calls on his wife and tells her that Solomon will reign after him (1 Kgs 1:30). The people recognize that Solomon is David's successor when he is anointed king (1 Kgs 1:30–40). Shortly thereafter, David dies and Solomon's reign is officially established (1 Kgs 2:13–46).

Under Solomon's rule, God's people are "as many as the sand by the sea" (1 Kgs 4:20). This statement confirms that the promise of numerous descendants to Abraham is being fulfilled (cf. Gen 12:1–3; 15:1–7; 22:17; 32:17).[91] Also under his rule, the kingdom of Israel extends "over the

---

89. Using later events to clarify earlier ones assumes the Bible is a unified, progressive narrative. While scholars are not in agreement on this perspective, especially postmodern scholars who eschew the very idea of a metanarrative, Bauckham makes the following insightful observation: "While the Bible does not have the kind of unity and coherence a single human author might give a literary work, there is nevertheless a remarkable extent to which the biblical texts themselves recognize and assert, in a necessarily cumulative manner, the unity of the story they tell" ("Reading Scripture," 40).

90. House argues for the anonymous, single authorship of 1 and 2 Kings (*1, 2 Kings*, 39). This view is preferred over the multiple-author position because "scholars advocating multiple authors do not agree on the number, date, or criteria of the proposed redactions. They are forced to posit 'schools' that last for decades to account for the unity of the books, or they must utilize highly selective and sensitive criteria to separate one edition from the other. These tendencies appear to be based more on a preference for a modified source criticism than on the final form of the text itself. Certainly the single-author viewpoint has difficulties of its own, such as accounting for the books' various theological emphasis, but it does deal resourcefully with theological, historical, and literary issues" (ibid.).

I will treat 1 and 2 Kings as one document. Although broken up into *3 Regnum* and *4 Regnum* in the LXX, Kings is one story that details the loss of much of what Moses, David, and Joshua worked so hard to attain. See House, *Old Testament Theology*, 251; DeVries, *1 Kings*, 7–11.

91. Brueggemann, *1 & 2 Kings*, 62; DeVries, *1 Kings*, 72.

kingdoms of the river Euphrates to the land of the Philistines to the border of the Euphrates" (1 Kgs 4:21), a dominion that "encompasses the boundaries of the land promised to Abraham" (cf. Gen 12:1–3; 15:1–7).[92]

While the promise of descendants is being fulfilled, the realization of the promise of a land inheritance is still uncertain, since the inheritance is supposed to be "everlasting" (Num 13:28–29) and a place of "permanent rest" (Deut 12:10, 25; Josh 22:4; 23:1). We must examine the remainder of Solomon's reign in order to determine whether under his rule God's people have settled into their "everlasting inheritance" and are experiencing "permanent rest."

Kings goes on to depict Solomon's building of the temple (1 Kgs 6–7). Once the temple is constructed, the ark of the covenant is brought into the inner sanctuary (1 Kgs 8).[93] With the temple finalized and the ark resting in the most holy place, there is at least "temporary rest" in the land.

Later in the narrative, God appears to Solomon and tells him that if he will walk in integrity before him, as his father David, he will establish his throne forever (1 Kgs 9:3–5). But if Solomon, or his children, turns away from God, then he "will cut Israel off from the land" (1 Kgs 9:6–9). Despite this threat, Solomon marries multiple foreign women who turn his heart to other gods (1 Kgs 11:1–8). The judgment that follows leads to the fracturing of the kingdom after his death, splitting Judah in the south from the tribes in the north (1 Kgs 11:30–40) and beginning the plunge into exile that was promised in Deuteronomy 28:15–69 and 1 Kings 9:6–9. Since the course towards exile is set in motion, it is apparent that Solomon is not the promised king who will establish Abraham's offspring into their "everlasting inheritance" and give them "permanent rest." Despite his disappointing reign, there remains the hope that a royal descendent of David will plant Israel in the land and bring them relief from their enemies (2 Sam 7:10–12; cf. 23:1–7). Until that time, Israel will continue to look for such a king.

Chronicles

The Chronicler composes his narrative centuries after the exile has taken place.[94] One of his aims is to reassure the exiles that God will use the royal

92. Dempster, *Dominion and Dynasty*, 148.

93. See Hens-Piazza, *1–2 Kings*, 78–79.

94. See Hamilton, *God's Glory*, 339. The anonymous author known as the "Chronicler" composed 1 and 2 Chronicles, using Samuel and Kings as his main sources (Thompson, *1, 2 Chronicles*, 23). Chronicles will also be treated as a literary unit. In support of this view, Klein argues, "In Jewish tradition 1 and 2 Chronicles were

seed of David to plant his people in the land and give them rest from their enemies (2 Sam 7, 23). The chronicler intends to remind the exiles that God has not forgotten the promises God made to his people.

Evidence of the Chronicler's aim is found in his restatement of the Davidic covenant in 1 Chronicles 17:1–15 (cf. 2 Sam 7:10–16), which recounts God's promise to plant his people in their place (מָקוֹם) and bring them rest (1 Chr 17:8–9; 2 Sam 7:10–11; cf. Ex 15:17). It also promises that God will raise up David's offspring (זֶרַע) and will establish his kingdom (1 Chr 17:11; 2 Sam 7:12–3).[95]

Besides restating the Davidic covenant, the Chronicler also recounts Solomon's instillation as king (2 Chr 1) and his building of the temple (2 Chr 2–5). Solomon was the royal descendent of David expected to usher in the state of lasting rest in Israel. He was even considered to be the wisest king in all the earth (2 Chr 9:22). Despite his wisdom, 1 Kings 11:30–40 records that the Lord would split the kingdom and initiate the road to exile, because he turned away from the Lord. Fittingly, the remainder of the Chronicler's account traces the mostly wicked kings of Judah down the path to exile (2 Chr 10–36).

At the end of Chronicles, the people are in exile, looking for the royal Davidic descendent who will bring them into their permanent inheritance and give them rest. For all his God-given wisdom and splendor, Solomon fell short of this expectation. Yet, Israel is not without hope, for the Chronicler restates the Davidic covenant to remind the exiles that God will use a royal descendent of David to plant them in the land inheritance and bring them respite from enemies (1 Chr 17).

Ezra

At the inception of Ezra, Israel is in exile under Persian rule. Yet, there appears to be a ray of hope. In Ezra 1:1–4, King Cyrus receives a word from

considered one book with the *masorah finalis* appearing only at the end of what we call 2 Chronicles. A marginal note at 1 Chr 27:25 . . . 'half of the book in verses,' indicated the midpoint of this one book. The division of the book into two by LXX eventually found its way into Hebrew Bibles, but that is not attested before 1448" (*1 Chronicles*, 1).

95. The Chronicler was no slavish copier of materials. The traditions that he chooses to recount, such as those regarding the promises to David, make evident that he has a definite theological agenda: to give the exiles hope. Childs observes that the Chronicler "has chosen to omit the history of the Northern Kingdom and focus solely on the history of Judah. Again, the central role of David is everywhere evident, and one sees his concern to legitimate the cultic office of David as a guardian of Israel's messianic hope" (*Biblical Theology*, 159).

the Lord and issues a decree: Israel may return to their land and rebuild the Temple.[96] Ezra 2 records the names of those who returned to Judah, accompanied by "Zerubbabel, Jeshua, Nehemiah, Seraiah, Reelaiah, Mordecai, Bilshan, Mispar, Bigvai, Rehum, and Baanah" (v. 2). Ezra 3 then provides an account of how the Israelites rebuilt the altar (vv. 1–7) and laid the foundation for the Temple (vv. 8–13). At first glance, it seems that God is at last establishing Israel in the land inheritance, keeping his promise to Abraham and David and bringing the exile to an end.[97]

All is not as it appears. In the midst of celebration, Ezra 3:12–13 records:

> But many of the priests and Levites and heads of father's houses, old men who had seen the first house, wept with a loud voice when they saw the foundation of this house being laid, though many shouted for joy so that the people could not distinguish the sound of joyful shouting from the sound of the weeping of the people, for the people shouted loudly, and the sound was heard at a distance.

Many in the crowd know that this is a far cry from Solomon's Temple. Their weeping beckons the following questions. If the promises are being fulfilled, should there not be a unanimous sense of joy? Are the people's tears insinuating that, since this Temple does not compare to Solomon's, there must be a better land with a better Temple to come?[98] Mervin Breneman argues: "Joy was mixed with sadness, as their enthusiasm was mixed with fear (3:3), suggesting that as wonderful as the experience of grace is, there is yet more

---

96. In the MT, Ezra is part of Ezra-Nehemiah. The LXX divides these volumes into Ezra and Nehemiah. The authorship of Ezra is unknown. Hill and Walton hold that an anonymous Chronicler wove the memoirs of Ezra, and other reliable sources, into a single volume, much like the process Luke undertook to write his gospel (*Survey of the Old Testament*, 229–30). This process, they argue, in no way invalidates the inspiration and historical accuracy of Ezra.

97. In discussing Ezra 2, Waltke observes: "The claim of its families to the land is based on impeccable family records on their ancestral home. They are not cut off from the promise of Canaan to Abraham and are the raw material of Abraham's posterity from which God will continue salvation history" (*Old Testament Theology*, 777). Waltke seems to be arguing that the promise of land, in some sense, is being fulfilled in the return of exiles to the land. Hamilton seems to contend that the return to the land means that the exile has come to an end: "Now that the people have returned to the land, having been restored through the judgement of exile, they glorify God, seeking his mercy as they enter into covenant" (*God's Glory*, 338).

98. The focus of this book prohibits me from entering into a discussion of Temple in the Bible. See Beale, *Temple*; Hamilton, *God's Indwelling Presence*.

to come."[99] The picture in Ezra 3 should lead one to speculate whether the promise of land is indeed being fulfilled.

Later in the narrative, the Israelites complete the Temple (Ezra 6:14–15). The people celebrate the dedication of the Temple and "set the priests in their division and the Levites in their divisions, for the service of the God in Jerusalem, as it is written in the Book of Moses" (Ezra 6:17–18). Despite the exuberance, it is important to note that, when God establishes Israel in the land, David's son will rule over them and they will experience rest (Deut 12:9; 25:19; 2 Sam 7:10–16). At this point in the OT narrative, Darius, a pagan king from a foreign nation, is ruling over the Israelites, suggesting that they are his slaves. Consequently, they have no righteous king and no rest. Ezra's prayer in 9:8–9 makes this evident:

> From the days of our fathers to this day we have been in great guilt. And for our iniquities we, our kings, and our priests have been given in the hand of the kings of lands, to the sword, to captivity, to plundering, and to utter shame, as it is today. But now for a brief moment favor has been shown by the Lord our God, to leave us a remnant and to give us a secure hold within this holy place, that our God may brighten our eyes and grant us a little reviving in our slavery. For we are slaves.

Clearly, Ezra's prayer reveals that the Israelites are slaves, still oppressed by a foreign ruler. The return to the land they are experiencing is nothing more than a brief time of "refreshment" in captivity.

Ezra's prayer in Nehemiah 9 makes a similar affirmation: "Look, we are *slaves* this day; in the land that you gave to our fathers to enjoy its fruit and its good gifts, behold, we are *slaves*. And its rich yield goes to the kings whom you have set over us because of our sins. They rule over our bodies and over our livestock as they please, and we are in great distress" (vv. 36–37). N. T. Wright argues that Ezra's prayer reveals a dilemma. Speaking from the perspective of the Israelites, he underscores: "The prophecies have let us down, and though we are back in our own land the promises about being blessed in that land have not yet come to pass."[100] Being under the thumb of foreign rule could not have been what Moses and David had mind. Nor, as I will argue later, what the Psalms and Prophets envision. The notion of still being in slavery in Ezra 9, and correspondingly in Nehemiah 9, reveals that Israel is still "in need of an exodus, a fresh act of liberation, a new Moses, a victory over the pagan tyrants who oppress them."[101] When

99. Breneman, *Ezra, Nehemiah, Esther*, 96.

100. Wright, *Paul and the Faithfulness of God*, 1:151.

101. Ibid. Wright also helpfully notes: "As noted often enough, both Ezra and

such an even occurs, the Israelites will finally experience rest in the land[102] under the promised Davidic king.

I contend, then, that the book of Ezra does not represent the fulfillment of the inheritance promise. I argue for this point because Israel's resettlement in the land is not accompanied by peace under the rule of David's son. What Ezra does confirm is that Israel is still in exile, showing that the promise of inheritance remains unfulfilled. The reentry into the land is nothing more than brief refreshment in captivity. The prayer in Ezra 9 (cf. Neh 9) is a point of tension for those who argue that the book of Ezra depicts the fulfillment of the land promise—for here is the clearest evidence that Israel has reentered the land as slaves of a pagan king. If Ezra suggests anything about Israel and the land promise, it is this: Israel is still in exile, still looking forward to entering a land under the rule of a better king, where they will experience a better rest.[103]

Summary of the Inheritance in the Historical Books

The book of Samuel begins with the people rejecting God by petitioning Samuel for a king (1 Sam 8:1–20). They hope that such a king will deliver them from Philistine oppression. The king they receive is Saul—who is not the one to bring them liberation. His reign concludes with Israel still oppressed by the Philistines and anticipating rest in the land. As a result, the promise of a king who will deliver the people of God and bring them rest in their inheritance is placed on David.

Second Samuel 7:1 says that the Lord has given David "rest from his enemies around him." Such respite is temporary and incomplete, for there is still the expectation that David's royal offspring (2 Sam 7:12–3) will plant

---

Nehemiah, in their great prayers, very similar to Daniel 9, speak of a continuing state which is hardly the great liberation the prophets had promised" (ibid.). Dempster contends: "If Ezra is a second Moses, he, like the first Moses, has not produced and cannot produce a change in the heart of the people. That awaits some future day. The exile continues even though Israel is in the land" (*Dominion and Dynasty*, 224). To conclude the section on the exile in the land, he argues: "Clearly, the people are still in exile at the end of the Tanakh, with emancipation and restoration a prospect. A long exile still awaits before the Messiah comes and restores all things" (Ibid., 225).

102. Though I disagree with Davies's spiritualized view of the land promise, this point is worth noting: "Deuteronomy makes it clear that there is still a future to look forward to: the land has to achieve rest and peace. . . . Promise and fulfillment inform much of the Old Testament, and the tradition, however it changed, continued to contain the hope of life in the land" (*Gospel and the Land*, 36).

103. For further discussion on the theme of exile in the OT, see Scott, *Exile*; Halvorson-Taylor, *Enduring Exile*; Scott, *Restoration*. Ben Zvi and Levin, *Concept of Exile*.

Israel in the land (2 Sam 7:11) and bring lasting rest (2 Sam 7:10). Moreover, there is also the suggestion that David's royal seed will not only rule over Canaan but the entire earth and that this ruler will not solely bring rest to Canaan but also to the whole earth (2 Sam 7:10–12; 23:3–4; cf. Ps 72:6). Given what has been said about David, I argue that David's offspring, not David himself, will establish the people of God in the land and bring them rest. As a result, the expectation of a Davidic ruler who will accomplish this task falls on Solomon.

At the beginning of his reign, Solomon builds the temple of the Lord and Israel experiences a temporary period of respite (1 Kgs 6–8). Shortly thereafter, the Lord promises Solomon that, if he will walk in integrity as his father David, he will establish his throne forever (1 Kgs 9:3–5). But, if he or his descendants turn away from the Lord, he will cut them off from the land (1 Kgs 9:6–9; cf. Lev 22:2–7; Deut 28:15–69). In the face of this threat, Solomon turns his heart to foreign gods (1 Kgs 11:1–8). Consequently, the Lord promises to split the kingdom after his death (1 Kgs 11:30–40), beginning the plunge into exile that was promised in Deuteronomy 28:15–69 and 1 Kings 9:6–9. Solomon is not the king who would establish God's people in their "everlasting inheritance" and give them "permanent rest." There, nevertheless, remains the hope that a Davidic king will plant Israel in the land and bring them respite from their oppressors (2 Sam 7:10–12; 23:1–7).

Centuries after Israel has been taken into exile, the Chronicler writes to the people of Israel. One of his reasons for writing to them is to reassure the exiles that God has not forsaken his promises to his people. The way he does so is by restating the Davidic covenant in 1 Chronicles 17:1–15, which notes that God will plant his people in their place (מָקוֹם) and bring them rest, and that God will raise up David's offspring (זֶרַע) and establish his kingdom. Subsequently, the Chronicler discusses Solomon's establishment as king (2 Chr 1) and his building of the temple (2 Chr 2–5). The Chronicler then spends the remainder of his narrative following the wicked kings of Judah into exile (2 Chr 10–36), a trajectory that was initiated because Solomon turned away from Lord (1 Kgs 11:1–8). Despite Solomon's failure, I contend that the Chronicler's restatement of the Davidic covenant gives the exiles hope that they will enter their restful inheritance upon the arrival of the promised Davidic king. While some argue that the promise was realized in Ezra, I contend that Israel is still in slavery, still waiting to enter the land, for they are ruled by a foreign king and thereby not experiencing the rest under the righteous rule of David's son.

CONCLUSION

In examining the inheritance in the Hexateuch and historical books, I have shown that God's people are hoping to inherit the land. Even in exile, they do not give up on this expectation. Nor do they believe that the promises have been nullified (1 Chron 17). Although their time in Canaan fell woefully short of their expectations, and the return they experienced in Ezra was nothing more than a brief moment of refreshment in captivity, the Israelites anticipate the appearance of a Davidic monarch who will plant them in the land permanently and establish the kingdom (2 Sam 7). Israel's continuing expectation of an inheritance makes evident that they do not look forward to an "other worldly" or "heavenly" existence. Rather, they long for the tangible fulfillment of the promises to the fathers (e.g., Gen 15; 2 Sam 7). This anticipation is also carried into the Psalms and Prophets. In these corpuses, it becomes apparent that the land God's people will inherit, over which the king will rule, is far better than Canaan.

4

The Inheritance in the Old Testament
Psalms and Prophets

THIS CHAPTER WILL EXAMINE the inheritance in the Psalms and Prophets. Much of the content in these corpuses reassures Israel that God has not forgotten the promises he made to Abraham (e.g., Gen 12, 15) and David (e.g., 2 Sam 7, 23). Among these promises is the land inheritance—the place to which David's royal descendent will bring Israel and establish the kingdom (2 Sam 7:10–17).

Since the hope of an inheritance is carried into the Psalms and Prophets, it is no surprise that the terminology of the inheritance remains the same. As a result, the verb נָחַל and the noun נַחֲלָה are still the primary Hebrew words associated with the inheritance (e.g., Ps 2:8; 132:8, 14).[1] The verb יָרֵשׁ is used as a close synonym of נָחַל, since it too is associated with the concept of inheritance (e.g., Isa 54:3; 57:13; 69:36).

The first section of this chapter will focus on the Psalms. Here, the inheritance undergoes a significant expansion beyond the borders of Canaan and the heir narrows down to one individual, the Davidic king. The second section focuses on the Prophets. Within this corpus, the expanded inheritance is identified as the new heavens and new earth, thus clarifying the eschatological nature of the inheritance. Furthermore, since the genuine heir of this place has been identified as the Davidic king, those who desire to be his fellow-heirs must put their trust in him (Isa 57:1–13). The discussion of the inheritance in the Psalms and Prophets will not be exhaustive, but limited to pertinent inheritance related passages.

1. All Hebrew citations in this chapter are from the *BHS*.

THE PSALMS

Psalms 2, 16, 72, and 95 are especially relevant for understanding the inheritance.[2] Psalm 2 clarifies that the true heir of the promise is the Davidic king. Psalms 2 and 72 both communicate to the exilic community that the land over which the Davidic king will rule—his inheritance—is not restricted to Canaan but is expanded to include the entire world. Psalm 16 shows that the world will be apportioned as an inheritance at the return from exile. Lastly, Psalm 95 supports the notion that the inheritance is where God's people will experience lasting rest.

Psalm 2

In Psalm 2, the Lord declares that he has installed his king in Zion (2:6).[3] The Lord then proclaims the following about the king: "You are my son; today I have begotten you" (2:7). Peter Craigie notes that in this context a decree is "a document given to a king during the coronation ceremony (cf. 2 Kgs 11:12); it is his personal covenant document, renewing God's commitment to the dynasty of David."[4] Psalm 2:6–7 thus brings to mind the Davidic covenant, which promises that God will permanently establish the kingdom of David's offspring (2 Sam 7:10–17). Also in this covenant, God declares that the Davidic king "shall be my son" (2 Sam 7:14), which is strikingly similar to the sonship language in Psalm 2:7. In view of these observations, Psalm 2 should be understood in light of the Davidic covenant in 2 Samuel

---

2. The authorship and dating of the Psalms, like most every other OT book, is highly debated. Wilson provides a reasonable perspective on this issue: "The book of Psalms then represents the end result of a long history of transmission, collection, and arrangement. . . . It is, like so many of the Old Testament books, a collection of compositions by many different authors in many different times and settings. . . . Psalms 3–42 surely represent an earlier collection of Davidic Psalms, as their headings attest. Psalms 120–34 all share the common heading 'Psalm of Ascent,' probably a much later collection of Psalms sung by pilgrims on their way to Jerusalem. The Asaph psalms (50; 73–83) and the psalms of the Sons of Korah (42; 44–49; 84–85; 87–88) probably represent the remains of collections of songs written by these two guilds of temple singers" (*Psalms*, 20). In its final composition, I hold that the Psalms provided the exiles the hope that God had not abandoned them. The promises made to their fathers would be fulfilled (e.g., Ps 2, 37, 72).

3. Craigie, *Psalms 1–50*, 66.

4. Ibid., 67.

7:10–16.[5] This suggests that the king whom God has appointed (Ps 2:6) is none other than the promised Davidic king, God's son (Ps 2:7).[6]

As God's son, the king "has the legal right to inherit."[7] Psalm 2:8 declares that the nations are his "inheritance" (נַחֲלָה) and the ends of the earth are his "possession" (אֲחֻזָּה). I have already noted that in the OT the inheritance is understood as the land of Canaan (Gen 12:7; 13:15; 15:18; 17:8; Num 33:54; Josh 15:20; 18:28; Judg 20:6). The reference to the inheritance in Psalm 2:8 is unlike earlier OT texts, for here this concept is significantly expanded beyond the borders of Canaan. The Psalmist specifically says that "the nations" (גּוֹיִם) are the inheritance of God's royal son. As a result, the Davidic king's rule will stretch far beyond the original promised land.

The idea that the Davidic king will receive an expanded inheritance is even clearer when examining Psalm 2:8 in view of its parallel structure:

the nations your inheritance (גוֹיִם נַחֲלָתֶךָ)
and the ends of the earth your possession (וַאֲחֻזָּתְךָ אַפְסֵי־אָרֶץ).[8]

The second line (וַאֲחֻזָּתְךָ אַפְסֵי־אָרֶץ) clarifies the first one (גוֹיִם נַחֲלָתֶךָ),[9] demonstrating that the nations over which the king will rule include "the people who live in the ends of the earth."[10] In other words, the king's inherited territory "will extend through all the lands to the most remote regions."[11] It is also important to note that in this parallelism נַחֲלָה corresponds to אֲחֻזָּה, identifying the inheritance as the king's possession. Psalm 2 therefore asserts that the promises of the Davidic covenant (2 Sam 7:10–17) will still be fulfilled. There will come a king from the royal offspring of David (cf. 7:11–14), whose reign will extend to the ends of the earth.

The expansion of the king's inheritance confirms the insinuation in 2 Samuel 23:1–7, that David's royal heir will reign over the entire world. Hence, that which is implicit in 2 Samuel 23:1–7 is made explicit in Psalm 2:8. The reaffirmed and expanded nature of the promise in Psalm 2:7–8 assures Abraham's descendants of a time when David's son will reign over the world.

---

5. Ibid. VanGemeren, "Psalms," 5:66–70.

6. Goldingay, *Psalms 1–41*, 100–101.

7. Harris, "Eternal Inheritance," 83.

8. Ross, *Psalms*, 209.

9. See the relevant discussion in Chisholm (*Exegesis to Exposition*, 142–45).

10. Ross, *Psalms*, 209.

11. Ibid.

In addition, Psalm 2 narrows the scope of the heir of the promised inheritance to one individual, God's royal son.[12] As Harris notes, "Whereas the historical books trace the expansion of the heir of the Abrahamic promise from Isaac to the nation of Israel, Psalm 2 represents the crystallization of the heir into a single individual, the chosen king, understood as God's son."[13] This king is the true beneficiary of the promised inheritance, which now encompasses the entire world. Moreover, since the heir of the promise has been narrowed to one individual, those who desire to dwell in the land, and thus be fellow heirs with God's son, must honor him as king. Those who refuse to honor him will perish (Ps 2:12), while those who submit to his rule will surely be blessed (Ps 2:12).[14] So, even at this point there seems to be no other way to the land than by honoring the son (cf. Gal 3–4; Rev 20–22).

Since the Davidic king will inherit the world, it is apparent that the OT presents the inheritance as a typological concept. This observation is evident in that there is historical correspondence between Canaan in Genesis and the world in Psalm 2:8. Escalation is also present, since Canaan is enlarged significantly to include the entire earth. Historical correspondence and escalation are the two most common elements of a typological interpretation, therefore justifying Canaan as a type of the world, the true inheritance (cf. Rom 4:13–17; 8:12–15; cf. also Rev 21).

Psalm 16

Having expanded the land to cosmic proportions, the Psalmist affirms his trust in God (Ps 16:1). Shortly thereafter, he shifts his attention to "the saints who are in the land (בָּאָרֶץ)," claiming that "they are the excellent ones, in whom is all my delight" (Ps 16:3). Craigie argues that "the psalm, with its respect to its initial meaning, is neither messianic nor eschatological in nature."[15] Then, he proceeds to say that the earliest Christian communities gave this Psalm an eschatological/messianic sense not recognized by the original audience (Acts 2:25–28 and 13:35).[16] While I concur that the Christ event has recontextualized the OT, it is important to note that the Psalms

---

12. Harris, "Eternal Inheritance," 84.

13. Ibid.

14. Craigie notes that in Ps 2:12 "kissing the son" is "a sign of homage and submission (cf. 1 Sam 10:1; 1 Kgs 19:18). Failure to submit to God through his king would result in disaster, for God's hasty wrath would culminate in their destruction (v. 12)" (*Psalms 1–50*, 68).

15. Craigie, *Psalms 1–50*, 158.

16. Ibid.

were intended to shape the readers' vision of what the world will one day be like under Messiah's reign.[17] In this light, we can see that, even before early Christianity, the context of Psalm 16 is eschatological, providing the exiles hope for what is to come. In view of its futuristic context, John Goldingay is correct in arguing that the Psalm implies "a return from exile" and "a rejoicing in the land . . . the people in the land (v. 3) are then people here as opposed to being in exile."[18]

The eschatological sense of Psalm 16 puts verse 6 into perspective: "The lines have fallen for me in pleasant places; indeed I have a beautiful inheritance (נַחֲלָה)." The Psalmist recalls the measuring of the land allocations in Canaan (Num 33:54; Josh 15:20).[19] Only here the allocation is eschatological. As such, the Psalmist envisions that God will apportion a cosmic, eschatological inheritance to his people when the Israelites return from exile. Only then will they receive what has been promised to them.

Psalm 72

Psalm 72 coheres with Psalm 2 in that it extends the rule of the Davidic king to the ends of the earth.[20] This notion is explicitly found in 72:8, where the Psalmist says of the Davidic king: "May he rule from sea to sea, and from the river to the ends of the earth (אֶרֶץ)." There is no need to restrict the reign of the Davidic king from one sea to another or from a certain river to a remote location of the earth, for the idea here is "a universal rule, encompassing seas, rivers, and lands."[21] A. F. Kirkpatrick states, "Extension, not limit, is the idea conveyed. The world belongs to God: May he confer on His representative a world-wide dominion!"[22] Psalm 72 therefore reiterates the idea that the Davidic king will rule over the earth, expanding the notion of the inheritance beyond the borders of Canaan. This point again confirms

17. Wright notes: "Paul referred to several Psalms and wove them in quite a sophisticated way into his remarkable theology. But beyond those explicit references there stands, I believe, an entire world in which Jewish people were singing and praying the Psalms day by day and month by month, allowing them to mold their character, to shape their worldview, to frame their reading of the rest of Scripture, and (not least) to fuel and resource the active lives they were leading and burning hopes that kept them trusting in their God, the world's creator, even when things seemed bleak and barren" (*Case for the Psalms*, 14–15).

18. Goldingay, *Psalms 1–41*, 231.

19. Ibid.

20. VanGemeren, "Psalms," 472.

21. Ibid.

22. Kirkpatrick, *Psalms*, 420.

the typological sense of the inheritance and clarifies that the true heir of Abraham is God's kingly son.

One further observation is that in Psalms 2 and 72 David's son will rule over his land inheritance, the implication being that notion of inheritance is also associated with kingdom. This connection may also be seen in earlier OT texts. For example, in Exodus 19:5–6 God announces to Moses his intention to make "a kingdom of priests and a holy nation" in the land. Deuteronomy 17:14–20 sets forth God's prescriptions for the monarchy that will be established in the land. And, of course, throughout the majority of Samuel to Chronicles there is a kingdom in the land of promise. Thus, the association between inheritance and kingdom in Psalms 2 and 72 follows an established OT pattern.

Psalm 95

Psalm 95 begins with an invitation to worship God (vv. 1–7a). This joyful summons is immediately followed by a severe warning about the wilderness generation (vv. 7b–11)[23] whom God loathed (v. 10):[24] "They are a people who go astray in their hearts and have not known my ways. Hence, I swore in my anger, 'They will not enter my rest'" (Ps 95:10–11). Although the OT does not record the specific words in Psalm 95:7b–11,[25] "they effectively embody the substance of what was said again and again."[26]

The phrase "they will not enter into my rest (מְנוּחָה)"[27] is associated with not entering the land inheritance.[28] The wilderness generation failed

---

23. Mays, *Psalms*, 305. The shift in tone from Ps 95:1–7a to Ps 95:7b–11 is summarized succinctly by Schaefer: "Psalm 95 opens in a festive mood, with procession and joyful praise. The scene is set suddenly, then God, who is being celebrated, speaks and chills the festive air. Thus ends the Psalm" (*Psalms*, 236).

24. VanGemeren argues that the lord's anger toward the wilderness generation was more than occasional (*Psalms*, 619). He claims that the Lord "was so greatly disturbed with the negative reaction from his people that he 'loathed' them, even as a man under God's judgment may come to loath his own corruption (cf. Ezek 6:9; 20:43; 36:31) and as a righteous man may loath sin (cf. 119:158; 139:21)" (ibid.). See also *HALOT*, 1:1083, which notes that the word קוּט in Ps 95:11, often translated as "loath," may best be rendered here as "feel disgust." If that is the case, then it may be said that the wilderness generation's sin resulted in God being "disgusted" with them.

25. Harris, "Eternal Inheritance," 85.

26. Leupold, *Psalms*, 678.

27. Tate asserts that Ps 95:11 recalls the announcement of judgment on the wilderness generation in order to encourage God's people "to hear the message of Yahweh and avoid the mistakes of the past" (*Psalms 51–100*, 502).

28. VanGemeren, *Psalms*, 619.

to experience rest in their inheritance because they refused to trust in the Lord. The connection between "rest" and "inheritance" is especially evident in Deuteronomy 12:9, which records that Israel has yet to enter their "rest" (מְנוּחָה) and "inheritance" (נַחֲלָה; cf. Ps 132:8, 14).[29] Furthermore, the phrase "Today (הַיּוֹם) if you hear his voice" in Psalm 95:7 "has a forward looking orientation," suggesting a future anticipation of rest in the land.[30] As noted in Psalms 2 and 72, the inheritance that awaits those who honor God's royal son has been significantly expanded beyond the borders of Canaan to include the whole earth. Those who refuse to honor the king will not receive an inheritance but will be crushed (Ps 2:12).

Summary of the Psalms

The Psalms reassure God's people of the promise of inheritance. Beyond this fact, Psalm 2 specifies that the true heir of the promise is the Davidic king. Those who do not honor him have no hope of an inheritance. Psalms 2 and 72 explain that the inheritance is not restricted to Canaan but is enlarged to include the entire world. Psalm 16 shows that the world will be apportioned as an inheritance at the return from exile. Lastly, Psalm 95 clarifies that God's people will experience rest when they enter their inheritance. These observations display that the inheritance that awaits God's people is far more glorious than original land to which they sojourned. Following the Psalms, we now turn our attention to the prophets.

THE PROPHETS

Isaiah and Ezekiel make the most significant contributions toward understanding the inheritance in the prophetic corpus. The relevant chapters in Isaiah are 54, 57, and 65–66. Isaiah 54, like Psalm 2, reiterates the idea that the inheritance has been enlarged to include the entire world. Isaiah 57, as suggested in Psalm 2, asserts that those who will dwell in the land along with God's son are those who trust in him. Isaiah 65–66 further clarify that the future worldwide inheritance for God's people is the new heavens and new earth. The pertinent chapters in Ezekiel are 36–37. Here, Ezekiel crystalizes the eschatological nature of the inheritance by promising that God's

---

29. Ibid. See Kaiser, "Promise Theme," 135–50, for a study of "rest" in Scripture. See also Braulik, "Das Land oder der Tempel?," 33–44.

30. Laansma, *I Will Give You Rest*, 45.

people will inherit the land when they are resurrected from the dead. When this finally takes place, a Davidic monarch will reign over them forever.

Isaiah 54

Isaiah 54:1 calls the barren woman to break forth in singing and crying, for she will soon bear children (v. 1).[31] The image of a barren woman appeals to the account of Sarah in Genesis 21:1–7, which portrays her as "barren and without hope and then, by the goodness of God, [she] is given a child and an heir."[32] The allusion to Sarah in Isaiah 54:1 refers to Israel, "whose bareness signifies the hopelessness of exile."[33] The fact that the barren woman will bear children means that God is keeping his promise to multiply the seed of Abraham. This promise is directly tied to the hope of an inheritance (cf. Gen 15, 17, 24), for the offspring of Abraham will dwell eternally in the land (cf. Deut 12:10, 25; Josh 22:4; 23:1). Such a connection suggests that the barren woman will give birth to children who will occupy the land. Isaiah's use of "bareness-birth" imagery therefore symbolizes the hopelessness of Israel's exile and the anticipation of dwelling in the promised land.[34]

Isaiah then commands the following to the barren woman: "Enlarge the place (מְקוֹם) of your tent, and let the curtains of your habitations be stretched out" (54:2).[35] Isaiah's command to "enlarge the place (מְקוֹם) of your tent" gives the indication that a large amount of exiles will enter the land, therefore necessitating the expansion of the מְקוֹם.[36] The מְקוֹם, in light

31. Most scholars hold to multiple authorship of Isaiah, dividing the book into either two parts (chapters 1–39 [Isaiah] and 40–66 [Deutero-Isaiah]) or three parts (chapters 1–39 [Isaiah], 40–55 [Deutero-Isaiah], and 56–66 [Trito-Isaiah]). Oswalt points out that "the multiple authorship of Isaiah is one of the most generally accepted dogmas of our day" (*Isaiah 1–39*, 17). Despite the consensus, I concur with his perspective: "It is my conviction that the essential content of the book has come to us through one human author, Isaiah the son of Amoz. It is he who received the revelations from God and who directed the shaping of this book" (ibid., 25). See also Watts, *Isaiah 1–33*, xliii–lxxx.

32. Brueggemann, *Isaiah 40–66*, 151. Brackets mine. In Gal 4:27, Paul uses Isa 54 in reference to barren Sarah, which supports the idea that the barren woman in Isa 54:1 is an allusion to her. Contra Smith, who, without consulting Paul's use of said text, rules out the "barren woman" as a reference to Sarah (*Isaiah 40–66*, 477).

33. Brueggemann, *Isaiah 40–66*, 151. See also Oswalt, *Isaiah 40–66*, 416.

34. See Brueggemann, *Isaiah 40–66*, 151.

35. Baltzer argues that the imperative in Isa 54:2 is the opposite of what Israel and the land have experienced, according to Jer 10:20: "My tent is destroyed. . . . My children have gone from me. . . . There is no longer someone to spread my tent, and to set up the covering of my tent" (*Deutero-Isaiah*, 436).

36. Smith rightly says that "the general imagery of expanding a tent should be

of similar uses in Exodus 3:8; Numbers 32:1; and 2 Samuel 7:10, is a reference to the land.[37] While David's tent may also be in view,[38] the emphasis is on the expansion of the concept in the head noun מָקוֹם. The tent of David will certainly be expanded, but it necessitates the expansion of the place/land on which it rests.

Isaiah 54:3 affirms that the reason why (כִּי) the barren woman is to stretch out the place of her tent is because she will "spread all around to the right and to the left." In other words, her descendants will be so numerous that they will spread out in all directions. This pronouncement alludes to the oath that God made to Jacob in Genesis 28:14, that his offspring would spread out "to the west, east, north, and south" (Gen 28:14).

Furthermore, the woman's countless "descendants will inherit[39] the nations" (וְזַרְעֵךְ גּוֹיִם יִירָשׁ, Isa 54:3). Isaiah's use of the noun זֶרַע alludes to the fulfillment of the promise of innumerable offspring in Genesis (e.g., 13:6; 15:5). Isaiah also uses the verb יָרַשׁ, which normally takes אֶרֶץ as its object in inheritance related passages (e.g., Gen 15:7; Deut 1:8). Here, however, the object of יָרַשׁ is גּוֹיִם, establishing that the woman's offspring will inherit all the domains occupied by the nations of the world. The expansion of the inheritance in this passage is in line with what is found in 2 Samuel 23 and Psalm 2, and once more signifies that Canaan is a type of the cosmic inheritance.

Later 54:17, Isaiah declares, "This is the inheritance of the servants of the Lord" (זֹאת נַחֲלַת עַבְדֵי יְהוָה). The demonstrative pronoun זֹאת functions either anaphorically or cataphorically.[40] Since in the following sentence the particle of interjection הוֹי signifies a transition to a new subsection,[41] זֹאת

---

broadly applied to the picture of preparing for a rapid expansion of additional people in Zion" (*Isaiah: 40–66*, 479).

37. Baltzer, *Deutero-Isaiah*, 436.

38. Ibid., 436–37.

39. See Wright, "יָרַשׁ," 3:547; *HALOT*, 1:441–42. Many translations, such as the NAS, NET, NRS, and ESV, render יָרַשׁ as "possess" in Isa 53:3. "Inherit" is a more viable translation in this passage. This is mainly due to the following: (1) the promise of offspring (זֶרַע) is often coupled with the promise of an inheritance (Gen 12:7; 15:18; 26:4; 48:4; Ex 33:1); (2) these promises are reaffirmed in 54:2, since Isaiah notes that the barren women will bear numerous descendants and that the land inheritance will be enlarged; and (3) the conjunction כִּי connects Isa 54:2 and 54:3, thus making the thought in both verses consistent. Given these reasons, it is more suitable to render יָרַשׁ in Isa 54:3 as "inherit."

40. Williams, *Hebrew Syntax*, 49; Waltke and O'Connor, *Hebrew Syntax*, 309.

41. The MT begins a new section in Isa 55:1 with the word הוֹי. This marker commonly indicates the inception of a new subsection or section. One may call this a transitional signal. For a discussion of הוֹי and other such markers, see Waltke and O'Conner (*Hebrew Syntax*, 632–36). Oswalt contends that the presence of הוֹי in Isa 55:1 "along

must function anaphorically, suggesting that Isaiah describes "the inheritance of servants of the Lord" in the preceding context of 54:1–17a. According to these verses, the inheritance will be a place where God's "steadfast love" (חֶסֶד) will not depart (v. 10), where the foundation will be laid with sapphire and the walls built with precious stones (vv. 11–12). In this place, the barren woman's children will be taught by the Lord and they shall experience peace (v. 13). They will also be established in righteousness and will be far from oppression (v. 14). Given that the verbs throughout this passage, such as יִירָשׁ (v. 3) and תִּכּוֹנָנִי (v. 14), all carry a future sense, God's people will possess the inheritance in the eschaton.[42]

Following this affirmation, Isaiah goes on to state, "and their righteousness is because of me" (וְצִדְקָתָם מֵאִתִּי, Isa 54:17b).[43] This clause is often translated with the previous clause as, "This is the inheritance of the servants Lord and their righteousness from me.[44] This translation gives the impression that וְצִדְקָתָם מֵאִתִּי is part of the demonstrative statement that points back to the inheritance in Isaiah 54:1–17a. While the conjunction וְ may refer to the previous context, in this passage it joins the final two clauses

---

with five imperatives in this verse gives a strong sense of urgency and importance of what follows. The reader knows that what is being said here is not simply a prosaic continuation of a previous discourse" (*Isaiah 40–66*, 435).

42. Smith argues that the "concept of inheritance was traditionally connected with receiving the land of Palestine as their possession" (*Isaiah 40–66*, 492). However, now in Isa 54 "the heritage of the nation includes children (54:1), an enlarged tent to the left and to the right (54:2) . . . God's compassion (54:8), God's unfailing love and covenant peace (54:10), a bejeweled city (54:11–12), sons taught by God (54:12), and divine protection (54:14–17)" (ibid.). As noted throughout the OT, the children are not the inheritance but they will receive the inheritance. Also, notions such as God's compassion and unfailing love (54:8–10), a place built with jewels (54:1–12), etc., are all things that will characterize life in the land inheritance. Thus, it is not valid to contend, as Smith, that Isa 54 now defines the inheritance as something other than the land. It has certainly been expanded (2 Sam 23; Ps 2; Isa 54:2–3), but it is still fundamentally the land promised to Abraham and his descendants.

43. The construction מֵאִתִּי is best translated as "because of me" rather than "from me." This rendering is both consistent with the semantic range of the preposition מִן and the expectation in the Hebrew Scriptures that righteousness will be brought about on account of God's work. Seifrid makes the following important observation: "The Hebrew Scriptures operate with the simple but profound assumption that 'righteousness' in its various expressions is ultimately bound up with God and his working. As a state of the affairs in the world, 'righteousness' cannot be accomplished or even rightly conceived apart from its enactment by God. . . . The ultimate hope of the Hebrew Scriptures, we may suggest, is that 'righteousness'—presently still unseen—shall be realized ultimately by God" ("Righteousness Language," 44). Such insightful comments certainly lend credence to the translation of מֵאִתִּי as "because of him," since God is the only one who will bestow righteousness on his people.

44. See NIV, ESV.

in 54:17 without suggesting that וְצִדְקָתָם מֵאִתִּי is part of the demonstrative statement. The LXX supports this reading, for it translates the two phrases as ἔστιν κληρονομία τοῖς θεραπεύουσιν κύριον, καὶ ὑμεῖς ἔσεσθέ μοι δίκαιοι.[45] The LXX uses the conjunction καί to connect the two clauses, in order to add that the people "will be righteous (δίκαιοι) on account of the Lord."[46] These observations demonstrate that ן joins 54:17a and 54:17b to connect entering the inheritance (54:1–17a) with being righteous on account of God (54:17b).[47]

Isaiah 57

Isaiah 57:1–13 describes the fate of the ungodly and the reward for those who place their faith in Lord (vv. 3–13). The ungodly are identified as sorcerers and adulterers (Isa 57:3), who worship idols by engaging in un-orthodox cultic activities, such as slaughtering their own children and participating in illicit sexual rituals (57:4–11). They will cry out and will not be delivered by their gods, for these lifeless idols have no power even to save themselves (57:12–13). In contrast to the wicked (ן),[48] those who trust in the Lord will inherit the land (יִנְחַל־אֶרֶץ) and will possess God's holy mountain (וְיִירַשׁ הַר־קָדְשִׁי, 57:13). The use of the qal imperfect verbs יִנְחַל and יִירַשׁ indicate that believers will receive their recompense in the future.

It is important to point out that Isaiah 57:13 claims that those who trust in the Lord are the heirs of the land, which seems to contradict the

45. LXX Isaiah citations are from Ziegler, *Isaias*.

46. The dative pronoun μοι in Isa 54:17, as with מִן above, is taken with a sense of cause, for the following reasons. (1) The dative may carry a causal sense with an impersonal verb. See Eph 2:8. (2) The LXX translates מֵאִתִּי with μοι to indicate cause, since this function is consistent with both forms. See *HALOT*, 1:597–98; Smyth, *Greek Grammar*, 348–49. See also Job 14:9; Exod 28:18. (3) God is the one who declares people righteous. See Rom 3:20–26; 5:6–21; Gal 3:6–24. (4) The notion of righteousness is a fundamentally eschatological verdict that will be pronounced by God. See Gal 2:17; 5:15.

47. The word צֶדֶק in Isa 54:17b (δίκαιος LXX) refers to God's legal verdict of "right standing" with him. See Seifrid, "Righteousness Language," 415–52. See also Avemarie, "Bund als Gabe und Recht," 163–216; Ringgren and Johnson, "צָדַק," 7:239–69. The legal understanding of צֶדֶק as "right standing" appears to be supported by the futuristic context of Isa 54:1–17 and the fact that God's final verdict of righteousness will come about in the eschaton (cf. Gal 2:7; 5:15). So, the type of righteousness God's people will experience in their inheritance is one in which they will be legally "in the right" before their creator. Brueggemann sees that the "use of judicial language" in Isa 54:1–17 was taken up by Paul in his notion of sure "justification" (=vindication) in the gospel (*Isaiah 40–66*, 158). That same assurance belonged to Judaism before Paul wrote.

48. The conjunction ן in Isa 57:13b has a contrastive function.

assertion in Psalm 2 that the sole beneficiary of the land is God's son, the Davidic king. Rather than bringing contradiction, reading Isaiah 57:13 in view of Psalm 2 clarifies that those who will dwell in the land along with God's kingly son (Ps 2) are those who put their faith in him (Isa 57:13). This contrasts with the wicked who put their faith in inanimate idols (Isa 57:1–13a), and thus have no hope of being heirs with the king.

Isaiah 65–66

Isaiah 65:1–25 reinforces that the wicked will have no place with God's people (65:1–8; cf. 11:1–15). Instead of receiving an inheritance, they will experience God's righteous judgment (65:11–15).

Also in this chapter, the Lord proclaims that "the one who is blessed in the land (בָּאָרֶץ) will bless himself (יִתְבָּרֵךְ) in the God of truth, and the one who takes an oath in the land (בָּאָרֶץ) will swear (יִשָּׁבַע) in the God of truth; because the sorrows of the past have been forgotten and hidden from my eyes" (65:16). This state is reserved for the servants of the Lord (65:15b).[49] They are the ones who will live in a land devoid of sorrows,[50] which will be unlike anything they have ever experienced.[51] Moreover, since the verbs יִתְבָּרֵךְ and יִשָּׁבַע carry a futuristic sense, it is apparent that the Lord's servants will inherit the land in the future.

Subsequently, Isaiah 65:17–25 describes (כִּי)[52] the future land inheritance as the "new heavens and a new earth," a place where "the former things shall neither be remembered nor called to mind" (v. 17) and where God's people will "be glad and rejoice forever in that which [he] will create" (v. 18). It will be a place where they will enjoy "the blessings of . . . security, longevity, and the prosperity to enjoy one's children and labors without fear"[53] (vv. 19–25). This will be a real, physical place, for people will build and inhabit houses (v. 21), and plant and not labor in vain (vv. 22–23). This description of the new heavens and new earth makes evident that the curse brought about in Genesis will be reversed, for the former things, such as tragedy,

49. The antecedent of the relative pronoun אֲשֶׁר is אֲדֹנָי יְהוָה in Isa 65:15, making evident that the "servants of the Lord" are those who dwell in the land.

50. See similar ideas in House, *Old Testament Theology*, 296; Brueggemann, *Isaiah 40–66*, 244.

51. Brueggemann, *Isaiah 40–66*, 244.

52. Ibid. The conjunction כִּ establishes that 54:17 is built upon the preceding context. For a study of this particle, see Follingstad, *Deictic Viewpoint*. See also Gesenius, *Hebrew Grammar*, 305.

53. Harris, "Eternal Inheritance," 96.

pain, and death, will be forgotten, and God's people will experience gladness and prosperity forever. In other words, it will be a return to life in Eden.[54]

Isaiah 65:17–25 demonstrates that the land God's people will inherit is the new heavens and the new earth (cf. Rev 21–22). This underscores that the inheritance is an eschatological concept, solely to be realized in the future. In addition, Isaiah 66:22–23 goes on to mention that the new heavens and new earth will exist perpetually before the Lord and the offspring of Abraham will remain upon it forever. These verses recall the promise to Abraham that his offspring will inherit the land as their permanent, physical dwelling (Gen 17:1–8; 24:1–9; 26:1–3; 28:1–5; 35:9–12; Deut 12:10, 25; Num 13:28–9; Josh 22:4; 23:1). In view of Psalm 2 and Isaiah 57:1–13, those who will dwell in the new heavens and new earth (i.e., the future reconstituted world, cf. Rom 8:18–25), and thereby will be fellow heirs with God's son, are those who trust in the Lord. Only such people will dwell in the future inheritance and have no memory of the former pains and troubles, for the curse will be reversed and mankind will live as in the days Eden.

Ezekiel 36–37

Ezekiel's contribution to the concept of inheritance is that he solidifies the eschatological nature of this notion.[55] In order to appreciate his input into the discussion, it is important to note that the Psalms and Prophets have thus far asserted that the inheritance has been enlarged beyond the boundaries of Canaan to include the entire coming world (Ps 2, 72, 95; Isa 54:1–17). This future world is further identified as the new heavens and new earth (Isa 65:1–25; 66:22–23), giving a distinctly eschatological character to the inheritance. This idea is only accentuated by Ezekiel, as he holds out the hope that God's people will enter the eschatological land (Ezek 33–48; cf. 11:15).[56] Since this is most clearly seen in Ezekiel 36–37, the focus of this section will be on these chapters.

---

54. House, *Old Testament Theology*, 296.

55. I hold to the unity of Ezekiel. Cooper provides some valid reasons for holding to this view: "First, it is a well-organized unit that has a balanced structure. There are no breaks in the flow of the messages and arrangement of the text of chaps. 1–48. Second, there is a uniformity of language and style that is characteristic of books with a single author. At least forty-seven phrases have been identified that recur throughout the book. This phenomenon seems to suggest a unity of authorship" (*Ezekiel*, 31). For further support, see pp. 31–37 in Cooper's *Ezekiel*.

56. See Hummel, *Ezekiel 1–20*, 10.

Ezekiel 36

In Ezekiel 36, God says to Israel, "I will take (וְלָקַחְתִּי) you from the nations and gather you (וְקִבַּצְתִּי) from all the lands (מִכָּל־הָאֲרָצוֹת) and bring you (וְהֵבֵאתִי) into your own land (אֶל־אַדְמַתְכֶם)" (v. 24).[57] The verbs וְלָקַחְתִּי, וְקִבַּצְתִּי, and וְהֵבֵאתִי carry a future sense, indicating that the gathering of Israel into the land inheritance will be forthcoming. Ezekiel 36 also says that Israel will enter a fruitful and tilled land, as the Garden of Eden (vv. 22–36; cf. Isa 65:17–25).[58] The thought that Israel will inherit an edenic land "looks forward to the eschatological state, when God's redeemed shall inhabit a new but greater Eden-like paradise."[59] Such a thought is also consistent with Revelation 21–22, which speaks of God's people receiving the new heavens and new earth.[60]

Ezekiel 36 thereby reaffirms the eschatological nature of the inheritance that has been witnessed thus far in the Psalms and Prophets. The eschatological understanding of Israel's inheritance will now be solidified in Ezekiel 37.

Ezekiel 37

Ezekiel 37:1–14 describes a vision of a valley of dry bones. In this vision, God causes the bones to come together, applies sinews, flesh and skin, forming a body, and then breathes life into them. The way in which God breathes life into the body is reminiscent of Genesis 2:7, where "the human being was first given shape . . . and then received from God himself animating breath . . . 'the breath of life.'"[61] Ezekiel's vision of God bringing to life bodies that were once nothing more than dry bones is an allegorical representation of the bodily resurrection of Israel.[62] God will breathe life into the bodies of

57. The word אֲדָמָה, like אֶרֶץ, may also refer to the land of Israel or the land of promise (e.g., Num 11:12; 32:11; Deut 4:40; 5:16; 11:9; 26:5; Amos 2:10; 3:2). So Plöger, "אֲדָמָה," 1:96–98. Note the use of Exodus-like terminology in Ezek 36:24 (cf. Exod 3:10–12; 6:6–7), "which occurs nine other times in Ezekiel (once, in 29:13, for the Egyptians), and becomes most prominent in the context of restoration oracles in chapters 34–39" (ibid).

58. Zimmerli, *Ezekiel 25–48*, 251.

59. Hummel, *Ezekiel 21–48*, 1060.

60. Ibid.

61. Allen, *Ezekiel 20–48*, 185. Hummel also sees this connection (*Ezekiel 21–48*, 1068). More specifically, he says that "'breath' resonates with the verb וּפְחִי . . . 'breath, blow' (Ezekiel 37:9), the same verb used for God 'breathing' the breath of life into man in Gen 2:7." See also *HALOT*, 1:708.

62. Isa 53; Dan 12. See also Wright, *Resurrection*, 121–27; Dempster, *Dominion*

his people—i.e., he will resurrect them—the same way he breathed life into Adam. So, not only does God promise to bring his people into an eschatological land (Ezek 36), but he also promises to raise them from the dead (Ezek 37:1–14).

The fact that Ezekiel follows the discussion of Israel's entrance into the land (36:22–37) with the vision of dry bones being raised to life (37:1–14) means that these two events will happen in succession, perhaps even simultaneously. This point is clearly summarized when Ezekiel prophesies, "Thus says the Lord: 'Look, my people! I will open your graves and raise you from the grave, and I will bring you into the land of Israel' (אֶל־אַדְמַת יִשְׂרָאֵל)" (37:12). Ezekiel then immediately restates this fact: "And I will put my Spirit within you, and you will live, and I will place you in your land (עַל־אַדְמַתְכֶם)" (37:14). Therefore, it is apparent that the "resurrection" is tied to the reception of the "inheritance," for God's people will inherit the land when God raises them from the dead. As well, the link between these themes suggests that, since the resurrection is an eschatological event, so too is the inheritance of the land.[63] Ezekiel 36–37 thereby serves to crystalize that the inheritance is an eschatological concept to be fulfilled when God's people are resurrected to dwell in the land.

When the people at last inherit the land, Ezekiel asserts that "they and their sons and the sons of their sons will dwell their forever (לְעוֹלָם), and my servant David will be their ruler" (37:25; cf. 37:24–28). The promise that Israel will dwell perpetually in the land is a characteristic of their true inheritance. Also, Ezekiel's assurance of an eternal Davidic ruler, or an "eschatological David," is most likely an allusion to the prophecy in 2 Samuel 7:10–16, where God promises that a descendent of David will rule over God's people forever (cf. Ps 2, 72, 95).[64] His reign in the land will be the long-awaited eternal kingdom in the inheritance (cf. 1 Cor 6:9–10; 15:50–56; Rev 21).

Although neither an eternal stay in the land nor a perpetual Davidic ruler has been witnessed to this point in the OT, Ezekiel 36–37 promises that Israel will inherit the land forever when they are resurrected from the

---

and Dynasty, 170. In defending his interpretation of Ezek 37:1–14 as an account of the future resurrection of Israel, Wright argues that "this is not a mere resuscitation, like miracles performed by Elijah and Elisha. The fleshless bones can only be brought to life by a new and unprecedented act of the creator god" (*Resurrection*, 120). The interpretation of this as a resurrection text is seen as early as the rabbinic period "in textual marginalia from early manuscripts and in the remarkable paintings found at Dura-Europos" (ibid.).

63. Cf., Isa 53; Dan 12; 1 Cor 15; Rev 20–22.

64. Hummel, *Ezekiel 20–48*, 1098.

dead; when this event finally comes about, a Davidic king will reign over them. These chapters confirm that the inheritance is an eschatological concept, only to be fulfilled in the future. To say that the inheritance has been either fully or partially fulfilled does not consider Ezekiel's assurance that God's people will inherit a reconstituted land, which Isaiah clarifies as the new heavens and new earth (65:1–25; 66:22–23), when their dead bodies are raised from the grave (cf. Rev 20–22).

Summary of the Prophets

In the Prophets, Isaiah 54:1–17 reiterates the idea that the inheritance has been enlarged to include the entire world. Isaiah 57:1–13 affirms that those who desire to be fellow-heirs of the land along with God's son are those who trust in him (cf. Ps 2). Isaiah 65:1–25 and 66:22–23 further clarify that the future world that God's people will inherit is the new heavens and new earth, underscoring that the inheritance is a distinctly eschatological concept. Subsequently, Ezekiel 36–37 solidifies the eschatological nature of the inheritance by displaying that God's people will inherit the land when they are resurrected from the dead. When this occurs, a royal descendent of David will reign over them forever. The Prophets therefore underscore that the inheritance is a "not yet" concept, only to be fulfilled in the future.

CONCLUSION

The Psalms and Prophets make a valuable contribution to the interpretation of the inheritance concept—for both corpuses testify that the inheritance has been expanded beyond Canaan to encompass the entire eschatological world (i.e., the new heavens and earth, Isa 65–66), the place over which the Davidic king will reign. Like the Hexateuch and historical books, God's people do not anticipate entering heaven. Instead, they look forward to dwelling in the world to come when their bodies are raised from the grave (Ezek 36–37), an event that will signal the end of exile (Ps 16). No longer will God's people live outside the cosmic territory that has been promised to them. Nor will they be oppressed by enemies.

In the following chapter, I will show that Second Temple literature displays remarkable continuity with the vision of the inheritance in the Psalms and Prophets. This corpus will continue to establish that the Jews—among whom is Paul—expected to receive an eschatological inheritance that stretches from one side of the world to the other.

5

The Inheritance in Second Temple Literature

SECOND TEMPLE LITERATURE SPANS roughly six and a half centuries of Jewish history (587 BC–AD 70). Many of the texts written during this period provide significant insight into the understanding of the inheritance. This chapter will survey the relevant texts in the Apocrypha, Pseudepigrapha, and Dead Sea Scrolls.[1] Second Temple corpuses do not display major developments in the OT understanding of the inheritance. Rather, they, like the Psalms and Prophets, generally view this concept to be the eschatological land promised to Abraham and his offspring.

LXX translators commonly employ κληρονομέω, κληρονομία, and κληρονόμος in rendering OT inheritance terms.[2] This point mainly applies to the Apocrypha and Pseudepigrapha. The Dead Sea Scrolls, like the OT, are written in Hebrew, using the verbs נָחַל and יָרַשׁ and the noun נַחֲלָה when referring to the inheritance theme. With these things said, I will now examine the aforementioned Second Temple corpuses.

---

1. I try to follow the chronological order of Second Temple texts within their corpuses. I will discuss Second Temple texts that are generally noted in the inheritance works of Harris, "Eternal Inheritance"; Hammer, "Understanding of the Inheritance"; Hester, *Paul's Concept of Inheritance*. Of these works, Harris's "Eternal Inheritance" is by far the most systematic and thorough treatment of the inheritance in Second Temple literature. Even in places where I have not cited her, the reader may hear "echoes" of her work.

2. For a fuller examination of inheritance terms in the LXX, see Appendix B.

THE INHERITANCE IN THE APOCRYPHA

The apocryphal books of Tobit, Judith, Sirach, and 1 and 2 Maccabees are the focus of attention in this section. Each of these books asserts that the inheritance is the land that Israel will possess in the future. Tobit, Judith, and Sirach even present a distinctly eschatological understanding of this concept.

Tobit

The book of Tobit is "a rich and complex literary work" that depicts the initial suffering and eventual healing of two diaspora Jews, righteous Tobit and innocent Sarah (Tob 1–12).[3] After Tobit and Sarah's healing, the book's final discourse reassures the readers that, although Israel has suffered on account of being scattered among the nations, God is true to his promise to bring Israel out of exile and into the land (Tob 13–14).[4] The final discourse may suggest that the story of the two main characters' suffering and restoration is a reflection of Israel's present and future states.[5]

Although the assurance of Israel's future entrance into the land is not specifically expressed until Tobit 13–14, the anticipation of the fulfillment of this promise is stated in 3:1–6. In this passage, grief stricken Tobit prays to be delivered from the distress of this life and "set . . . free into the eternal place (εἰς τὸν αἰώνιον τόπον)."[6] This desire reflects Tobit's confidence in the

---

3. Nickelsburg, "Stories of Biblical and Early Post-Biblical Times," 41. Most scholars believe Tobit was composed between 250 and 175 BCE (Moore, *Tobit*, 40–42).

The book of Tobit survives in two different Greek recensions. deSilva notes that "Codices Vaticanus and Alexandrinus (B and A) preserve the shorter edition, while Codex Sinaiticus (‭א‬) preserves the longer edition. Although in most cases it is easier to understand how a longer version is derived from a shorter through scribal expansions and clarifications, with Tobit priority is to be given to the longer text. . . . The discovery of dozens of fragments of five separate manuscripts of Tobit at Qumran has served to confirm the priority of ‭א‬, the longer Greek version, over A and B" (*Introducing the Apocrypha*, 67). Given this reasoning, I will follow the longer version of Tobit. All quotations from the Apocrypha rely heavily on Pietersma and Wright, *New English Translation of the Septuagint*. Any deviations from this translation are my own.

4. Moore, *Tobit*, 6.

5. Davies, "Didactic Stories," 108–13; Harris, "Eternal Inheritance," 106.

6. The definite article in the phrase τὸν αἰώνιον τόπον suggests that the "eternal place" is "well-known" among Tobit's contemporaries. Such a use of the article, in conjunction with the OT expectation of a future land for God's people, further strengthens the notion that the "eternal place" is the inheritance of Israel. See Wallace, *Greek Grammar*, 225. Köster says that the term "place" in Jewish usage denotes "the 'place' which Yahweh has appointed for his people, Ex. 23:20; cf. Nu. 10:29; 2 S. 7:10; 1 S. 12:8. It is

Davidic covenant promise—which is grounded in the Abrahamic covenant (Gen 15)—that God "will appoint a place" for Israel "and will plant them, so that they will dwell in their own place and no longer be troubled" (2 Sam 7:10). The "place" to which both Tobit and David refer is the inheritance of Israel (cf. Num 13:28–29; Deut 12:10, 25; Josh 22:4, 23:1). Tobit's desire to be delivered into this abode reveals his hope in the fulfillment of the promise of land.[7]

After being restored from his distress, Tobit affirms his initial expression of hope in the "eternal place." He does so by confessing that, although God has scattered and afflicted Israel, "Jerusalem will be built as a city, as a house for all the ages" (Tob 13:16); its gates "will be built with lapis lazuli and emerald"; its towers "will be built with gold"; and its streets "will be paved with ruby and stone of Saphire" (Tob 13:16). The language here alludes to Isaiah 54:11–12, which describes the future inheritance of Israel with similar imagery.[8] Moreover, the fact that Tobit states that the nations will come to the rebuilt Jerusalem reflects the "eschatological visions of Isaiah 2 and Micah 4"[9] (cf. also Zech 8:22; Ps 86:9; 96:7–8).

It is also important to mention Tobit's final profession that God will gather his people and they will "live forever in the land of Abraham with security, and it will be given over to them" (Tob 14:7). This proclamation reflects Tobit's anticipation of the fulfillment of the future land inheritance promised to Abraham and his offspring (cf. Gen 12:7; 13:15; 15:18; Num 13:28–29; Deut 12:10).[10]

In short, the book of Tobit acknowledges that God will gather scattered Israel and bring them into the land. The forthcoming nature of this event is confirmed by the eschatological rebuilding of Jerusalem (Tob 13:6)

---

par to נַחֲלָה" ("τόπος," 2:195). Tobit also reflects this understanding, underscoring that the "eternal place" is indeed the inheritance of Israel. All LXX Tobit citations are from Hanhart, *Tobit*.

7. Contra Moore, who claims that Tobit has no hope of "some form of immortality of the soul or resurrection of the body (as in Dan 12:1 or 2 Macc 12:43–44)" (*Tobit*, 140). He also claims that Tobit has neither hope in the coming life nor hope after death, "all of which makes Tobit's plight seem all the more tragic" (ibid.). Moore's comments seem to ignore that Israel's consistent hope throughout the OT is that God will bring them into the promised land and give them eternal rest from their enemies. Such an event will occur when Israel is resurrected from the dead (Ezek 36–37). This narrative, then, is most likely implicit in Tobit.

8. So also Harris, "Eternal Inheritance," 107. See also the similar imagery in Rev 21:10–21.

9. Ibid.

10. Di Lella argues that Tobit's portrayal of the future restoration of Israel is grounded in Deuteronomistic theology ("Deuteronomistic Background," 380–89).

and the future giving of the land to Israel (Tob 14:7). Tobit's understanding of the land promise unmistakably demonstrates that he expects Israel to inherit a future eschatological land.

Judith

The tale of Judith begins with Nebuchadnezzar's desire to conquer the entire known world (Jdt 1:1–12).[11] The Israelites, however, refuse to assist him in his endeavor, for "they did not fear him; to them he was but one man" (Jdt 1:11). Israel's noncompliance provokes Nebuchadnezzar to order a military campaign, which places them on an apparently inevitable path toward destruction.[12] In the face of annihilation, Israel calls upon God, so that he might not "hand over the cities of their inheritance (τὰς πόλεις τῆς κληρονομίας αὐτῶν) to oblivion" (Tbt 4:12).[13] Such collective petitioning does not compare to the prayer of the heroine Judith (Jdt 9).[14] She faithfully calls upon the "God of the inheritance of Israel (θεὸς κληρονομίας Ισραηλ)" (Jdt 9:12) and wins his help.[15] Israel then proceeds to triumph over Holofernes, displaying that God answered Judith's prayer (Jdt 13–15).[16]

11. The book of Judith was written during the Hasmonean period, probably around 107 BCE (deSilva, *Introducing the Apocrypha*, 92). Its historicity, however, is seriously in question. deSilva believes that the "attempt to defend the historicity of Judith, either at face value or in terms of veiled history of the later period, presents insurmountable obstacles because, in fact, the book combines allusions with events that transpire over five centuries of 'real life history'" (ibid.). He then states that "no single period could possibly contain all the people, movements, and events. The work is better read as a piece of historical fiction—an attempt to write a nonhistorical story in the midst of known historical personages and dynamics" (ibid.). Although Judith is most likely a work of historical fiction, Nickelsburg argues that the book "presents a condensation of Israelite history, which has paradigmatic quality. It demonstrates how the God of Israel has acted—and continues to act—in history, and it provides models for proper and improper human actions and reactions vis-à-vis this God. The God of Judith is the deliverer of his people, yet he remains sovereign" ("Stories of Biblical and Post-Biblical Times," 49). For a more extensive discussion of the historicity of Judith, see Enslin, *Judith*, 38–49.

12. Davies, "Didactic Stories," 113.

13. Enslin claims that Judith displays an "unshakable confidence" that God will preserve the inheritance promised to the Patriarchs (*Judith*, 83). He believes that this view is "basic to Jewish thought" (ibid.). All LXX Judith citations are from Hanhart, *Iudith*.

14. deSilva argues that Judith is a "personification of pious Jews, bravely and successfully resisting the foreign invader" (*Introducing the Apocrypha*, 94).

15. Nickelsburg, "Stories of Biblical and Early Post-Biblical Times," 47.

16. Ibid.

After the conclusion of the tale, Judith bursts into a song in which she praises God for the victory, narrates his achievements, and acclaims him as the ruler of all creation (Jdt 16:1–17).[17] In the latter part of the song, Judith warns that God will punish the nations who plot against her people "in the day of judgment" (Jdt 16:17). This statement looks forward to the future eschatological retribution of those who oppose Israel. During the coming judgment, God will "send fire and worms for their flesh, and they will wail in full conciseness forever" (ἕως αἰῶνος, Jdt 16:17). The eschatological imagery of fire and worms alludes to Isaiah 66:24,[18] which is set in the context of God's promise of a new heavens and new earth (i.e., Israel's inheritance) in chapters 65–66. This observation suggests that the broader framework of Isaiah 65–66 provides the whispered context for interpreting Judith 16:17. Consequently, the eternal judgment of fire and flesh-eating worms in this verse will take place when Israel receives their eschatological inheritance.[19] At that time, God's people will finally receive rest from enemies and enter the land promised to Abraham. Thus, the conclusion of Judith points to a time when Israel will be in their future inheritance and their enemies will receive the retribution they so deserve.

Sirach

The book of Sirach is distinguished among Jewish wisdom literature in that it identifies its actual author, Jeshua Ben Sira.[20] In this book, Ben Sira confirms the hope of an enlarged eschatological inheritance. Sirach 36:8–16 and 44:20 most clearly bear witness to this hope. In 36:8–16, Ben Sira pens the following:

> Raise up anger and pour out wrath; destroy an adversary, and crush an enemy. Hasten the time and remember your determination, and let them recount your mighty acts. In wrath of fire let him who survives be consumed and may those who harm

17. Davies contends that "the concluding song in Judith . . . recapitulates scriptural songs by two women: the 'song of Deborah' in Judg 5, mostly in its second part, and the song of Miriam (Moses), in its first part (the victory song)" ("Didactic Stories," 116).

18. Enslin, *Judith*, 175.

19. It is important to restate that Hays claims that an echo "places the reader within a field of whispered or unstated correspondences" and "functions to suggest to the reader that text B should be understood in light of a broad interplay with text A" (*Echoes*, 20).

20. Collins, *Jewish Wisdom*, 23–24. The original Hebrew text of Sirach was written between 196 and 175 BCE and later translated into Greek around 132 BCE (deSilva, *Introducing the Apocrypha*, 158). See also Stone, *Jewish Writings*, 290–92.

your people find destruction. Crush the heads of hostile rulers who say, "There is no one except us!" Gather all the tribes of Jacob, and give them an inheritance (κατακληρονόμησον αὐτούς), as from the beginning.[21]

Here, Ben Sira asks God to bring retribution upon Israel's enemies and to deliver Israel into the land inheritance. The notions of "vengeance upon Israel's adversaries" and "entrance into the inheritance" are eschatological ideas coupled in Isaiah 65–66 and later alluded to in Judith 16:17 (cf. Rev 20–22).[22] This thought underscores that Sirach 36:8–16 expresses hope in an eschatological inheritance for God's people, one in which their enemies will not take part, but will be destroyed.

Subsequently, Sirach 44:20 confirms the vastly expanded nature of the inheritance by asserting that God promised to Abraham's seed (τὸ σπέρμα αὐτοῦ) "that he would give them an inheritance (κατακληρονομῆσαι αὐτούς) from sea to sea and from the river to the end of the earth." This verse resonates closely with Psalm 72:8 and is in broad agreement with the cosmic expansion of the inheritance in the Psalms and Prophets (Ps 2, 72, 95; Isa 54:1–17, 65:1–25, 66:22–23). Taking Sirach 36:8–16 into consideration, it is apparent that the expanded inheritance presented in Sirach 44:20 will be received in the future, thus confirming the enlarged eschatological view of the inheritance.

1 and 2 Maccabees

First Maccabees portrays Matthias and his five sons as divinely appointed agents who delivered "Israel from the threat posed to the Jewish way of life by Antiochus IV" and restored "political independence to Israel after four and a half centuries of foreign domination."[23] First Maccabees also depicts Israel and its fathers as the rightful heirs of the land (e.g., 1 Macc 2:51–60, 4:6–11, 15:33–34). One of the heirs is David, who inherited the throne of the kingdom forever (ἐκληρονόμησεν θρόνον βασιλείας εἰς αἰῶνας, 1 Macc 2:56).[24] This statement alludes to the Davidic covenant promise in 2 Samuel

21. LXX Sirach citations are from Ziegler, *Sapientia Iesu Filii Sirach*.

22. MacKenzie makes the observation that Sir 36:1–17 "looks forward to a dramatic divine intervention on behalf of Israel: what is usually called the Messianic hope" (*Sirach*, 137).

23. deSilva, *Introducing the Apocrypha*, 244. First Maccabees was written late in the reign of John Hyrcanus or shortly after his death, placing the composition of 1 Maccabees roughly between 104–63 BC (Attridge, "Historiography," 171).

24. LXX 1 Maccabees citations are from Kappler, *Maccabaerorum Liber I*.

7:10–16 and David's last words in 2 Samuel 23:1–7, which together affirm that a descendent of David will reign over the land inheritance.[25]

Second Maccabees also tells the story of the successful resistance movement against Antiochus IV and the subsequent reestablishment of Jewish political independence.[26] Second Maccabees likewise gives evidence that the land is the rightful inheritance of Israel. This point is most evidently seen in 2 Maccabees 2:17, asserting that God has "given the inheritance to all his people" (ἀποδοὺς τὴν κληρονομίαν πᾶσιν).[27] The hope that God will eventually bring his people into the inheritance is found in the corporate prayer of 2 Maccabees 1:29: "Plant your people in your holy place" (καταφύτευσον τὸν λαόν σου εἰς τὸν τόπον τὸν ἅγιόν σου)—which recalls Israel's similar request in Exodus 15:17 (cf. 2 Sam 7:10). Both 1 and 2 Maccabees thus display the hope that God's people will one day inherit the land that rightly belongs to them.

---

25. Fuller interestingly notes that there are echoes of an expansive kingdom in 1 Macc 3:9; 14:5–7, 10 (*Restoration of Israel*, 124–25). Goldstein argues that the author of 1 Maccabees believes that the prophecy of the Davidic king/messiah has been nullified by sin (*1 Maccabees*, 241). As a result, Goldstein contends that the author in 1 Macc 2:57 "need not give further explanation of why the kingship of the later Hasmoneans was no usurpation of the kingship of the house of David. The house of David no longer had royal rights" (ibid.). Goldstein's claim that David's house forfeited its royal rights selectively cites random texts from the OT, such as 1 Kgs 2:4; 1 Chr 28:7, 9; Ps 132:11–12; Sir 49:4–5, without explaining how they support his point and also makes unsubstantiated assumptions about the author of 1 Maccabees. Goldstein ignores all the passages that point to a Davidic ruler who will rule over the inheritance of Israel, such as Dan 2, 7; Isa 54, 66, and 67, in addition to those that specifically mention this promise in 2 Sam 7:10–17 and 23:1–7. Furthermore, the statement in 1 Macc 2:57, that David has inherited the kingdom, is placed in the context of Matthias's final charge to his sons, where he tells them of the faithfulness of patriarchs such as Abraham, Joseph, Joshua, and Daniel, and the rewards they received. It is unlikely that the author of 1 Maccabees would place the statement about David inheriting a perpetual kingdom within this extortive context, yet think that the promise to David has been made null. Goldstein's pithy explanations do not even address such issues. Consequently, his comments about David's house are erroneous. One of the main Jewish hopes throughout the OT is that a royal descendent of David will establish an everlasting kingdom in the land, as noted specifically in 2 Sam 7:10–17 and 23:1–7. Thus, it seems there is more warrant for understanding that such passages are in the background of 1 Macc 2:57.

26. deSilva, *Introducing the Apocrypha*, 267. Second Maccabees was probably written between 125–63 BCE (Attridge, "Historiography," 177). LXX 2 Maccabees citations are from Hanhart, *Maccabaeorum Liber II*.

27. Schwartz, *2 Maccabees*, 162, 168. Goldstein argues that "it is not conceivable" that this text says that the inheritance has been restored to Israel (*II Maccabees*, 188).

Summary of the Apocrypha

The apocryphal writings of Tobit, Judith, Sirach, and 1 and 2 Maccabees primarily view the inheritance to be the land that Israel will receive in the future. In particular, Tobit describes the land inheritance to which Israel will be gathered (Tob 14:7) with the eschatological imagery of Isaiah 54:11–12 (Tob 13:6). Judith anticipates a time when Israel will be in their future inheritance and their enemies will be repaid for oppressing them (Jdt 16:17). Sirach claims that Abraham's descendants will inherit the eschatological world (Sir 38:8–16; 44:20). Lastly, 1 and 2 Maccabees anticipate the day when Israel will receive their rightful inheritance (e.g., 1 Macc 1:29). Whereas all of these writings display a future territorial understanding of the inheritance, Tobit, Judith, and Sirach most evidently present the inheritance as an eschatological concept, similar to the Psalms and Prophets.

THE INHERITANCE IN THE PSEUDEPIGRAPHA

This section will survey the pseudepigraphal books of *1 Enoch, Jubilees, Psalms of Solomon, 4 Ezra,* and *2 Enoch*. These books envision the righteous to be the inheritors of the eschatological world. Such a view of the inheritance, like the Apocrypha, is consistent with the interpretation of this concept in the Psalms and Prophets.

1 Enoch

Here, I will focus on the three sections of *1 Enoch* in which the theme of inheritance is most prevalent: The Book of Watchers (*1 En.* 1–36), the Epistle of Enoch (*1 En.* 91–108), and the Similitudes of Enoch (*1 En.* 37–71).[28] Each of these books will be examined in turn.

---

28. Harris also follows this arrangement of *1 Enoch* ("Eternal Inheritance," 111). According to Isaac, *1 Enoch* is a composite work, representing various texts from different authors ("1 Enoch," 1:5–7). See also Knibb, *Essays on the Book of Enoch,* 36–76. In regard to the dating of the three sections of *1 Enoch* that will be discussed in this section, Nickelsburg contends that the Book of Watchers may have been completed by the mid-third century, the Epistle of Enoch in the second century, and the Similitudes of Enoch (The Book of Parables) in the late first century BCE (1 Enoch 1, 7–8). This section will follow the translation of Isaac, ("1 Enoch," 5–100).

The Book of Watchers (1 Enoch 1–36)

The Book of Watchers emphasizes the judgment that is coming upon the earth because of sin.[29] Within this discussion, the clearest affirmation of the inheritance is found in *1 Enoch* 5:5–10, which proclaims that in the coming judgment sinners will not receive an inheritance but will "perish and multiply in eternal execration; and there will not be any mercy unto" them (*1 En.* 5:6). To these there will also "be a curse" (*1 En.* 5:7). Yet "to the elect there shall be light, joy, and peace, and they shall inherit the earth (αὐτοὶ κληρονομήσουσιν τὴν γῆν)" (*1 En.* 5:7).[30] The themes of "suffering" and "curse" for sinners but an "inheritance" for the elect echoes Psalm 37. An even closer resonance for these ideas is located in the eschatologically rich chapters of Isaiah 65–66, which declare that the wicked will be judged, but God's chosen ones will inherit the new heavens and new earth (cf. also Sir 44:20).[31] The textual reverberations in *1 Enoch* 5:5–10 make it likely that the author thinks that the elect have not yet inherited the land,[32] for, as confirmed in Isaiah 65–66, an expanded eschatological inheritance awaits them.

Subsequently, *1 Enoch* 24–27 focuses on a vision of the long and blessed life that the righteous will enjoy upon the earth. On this future earth, there will be a mountain "whose summit resembles the throne of God" and "is [indeed] his throne, on which the Holy and Great Lord of Glory, the Eternal King, will sit when he descends to visit[33] the earth" (*1 En.* 25:1–3). The throne that Enoch describes is the one on which God will sit at the final judgment. After God judges the wicked, the elect will be presented with the tree of life, whose fruit will enable them to live a long life upon the land (*1 En.* 25:5–6). The mention of extended life in the land recalls the similar motif in Isaiah 65:17–22.[34] Moreover, the similarity between *1 Enoch* 25:5–6 and Isaiah 65:17–22 suggests that the land on which the elect will live is the new heavens and new earth.

In sum, the Book of Watchers presents the inheritance as the enlarged eschatological earth, i.e., the recreated world (*1 En.* 5:5–10; 25:1–6).

---

29. Nickelsburg, *1 Enoch 1*, 7.

30. Greek citations for *1 Enoch* are from Knibb, *Ethiopic Book of Enoch*.

31. Ibid., 160–62.

32. Ibid.

33. The term "visitation" in *1 En.* 25:1–3 refers to the day of God's eschatological judgment and punishment. See Deut 28:25; Wis 14:11; Sir 23:24. This notion in the LXX is also carried into the NT, where "the day/time of visitation" is also understood as "God's judgment." See Luke 19:4; 1 Pet 2:12. Beyer, "ἐπισκέπτομαι," 2:606–07.

34. Nickelsburg, *1 Enoch 1*, 315.

Although God's elect have yet to inherit this place, they will do so in the future (1 En. 5:6). Their stay will not be temporary, but they "will live a long life in the land" (1 En. 25:5–6). This is another way of saying that the elect will live forever in their eschatological inheritance. On the other hand, sinners will experience God's judgment, having no portion with God's people (1 En. 5:5–10; 25:1–6).

The Epistle of Enoch (1 Enoch 91–108)

The Epistle of Enoch presents a series of woe-oracles against sinners and denunciations of their actions, interspersed with statements that assure the righteous of the eschatological world that awaits them.[35] The main reference to the inheritance in this letter is found in one of the woes in which Enoch says that sinners "will have no rest," for they "reject the foundations of the eternal inheritance" of their ancestors (1 En. 99:14). The "eternal inheritance" is a reference to the everlasting land promised to the patriarchs, among whom are Abraham (Gen 12:7; 13:15; 15:18; 17:8; 24:7), Isaac (Gen 26:3) and Jacob (Gen 28:13–15; 35:9–12; 46:4).[36] Like the OT, 1 Enoch 99:14 confirms that the inheritance is the place where Israel will experience everlasting rest (cf. Deut 12:10, 25; Josh 22:4, 23:1).[37]

What is more, Enoch contends that sinners "have forfeited any possibility of falling heir to his community's eschatological inheritance,"[38] therefore having no hope of experiencing rest. The righteous, on the other hand, will receive an eternal inheritance in the future (1 En. 107:12–13; 108:13–15).

On the whole, the Epistle of Enoch, like the Book of Watchers, provides hope that the righteous will receive an eschatological inheritance. Sinners will not enjoy rest in the land, but will arouse God's anger and be destroyed (1 En. 99:16; cf. 107).

---

35. Stuckenbruck, 1 Enoch 91–108, 3.

36. Stuckenbruck argues that "whereas in the biblical texts the phrase 'inheritance of the fathers' refers to the material heritage (property or possessions) passed down from one generation to the next, it is used here metaphorically in a way that betrays the sapiential character of the document. . . . It is the tradition of wisdom which the writer believes his community should, but do not, share (ibid., 423)." Although he provides very little (if any) justification for his position, Struckenbruck does concede that "the inheritance of land may be implied by the author" (ibid., 423).

37. The notion of inheritance also appears to be present in 1 En. 93:7: "After the fifth week, at the completion of glory, a house and a kingdom shall be built." Black argues that this verse may refer to the perpetual sovereignty of David's house in 2 Sam 7:16 (1 Enoch, 290).

38. Stuckenbruck, 1 Enoch, 91–108, 423.

Similitudes of Enoch (1 Enoch 37–71)

The Similitudes of Enoch consist of three apocalyptic parables, whose narratives concern themselves with "transcendent realities that are both temporal (envisioning eschatological judgment, salvation, and damnation) and spatial (involving another, supernatural world)."[39] Essentially along the lines of the Book of Watchers and the Epistle of Enoch, the Similitudes present the inheritance as the future eschatological world of the righteous. The wicked, however, will not inherit the earth, but will experience due judgment for their deeds. Simply stated, the righteous will receive an eschatological inheritance, while the wicked will receive judgment.

PARABLE 1 (1 ENOCH 38–44)

In the first parable, Enoch says that when the righteous ones appear, "sinners will be judged for their sins" and "they shall be driven from the face of the earth" (*1 En.* 38:1). Such a statement insinuates that after the judgment sinners will not dwell together with the righteous upon the earth. Enoch affirms this point with a rhetorical question: Since "the righteous and elect will dwell upon the earth, where will the dwelling of sinners be?" (*1 En.* 38:2).[40]

Enoch also declares that when the messianic figure, "the Righteous one," appears, "he shall judge sinners" and drive them from the presence of the righteous and the elect. From that time on, "those who possess the earth will be neither rulers nor princes" (*1 En.* 38:3–4). Enoch's proclamation aligns "sinners" with "rulers and princes," and assumes that they are in control of the world and oppress the righteous. In the eschaton, however, there will be a reversal of roles: the righteous will possess the earth, whereas the oppressive rulers and princes will be driven out. This assertion suggests that "those who possess the earth will be neither powerful nor exalted"[41] and recalls the Sermon on the Mount, which asserts that the meek "will inherit the earth" (κληρονομήσουσιν τὴν γῆν). Thus, *1 Enoch* 38:1–4, like Matthew 5:5, expects that a great reversal of roles will take place in the future—one that will be so drastic that the former kings and rulers will be judged at the hands of the holy and righteous heirs of the earth (*1 En.* 38:5–6).[42]

39. Nickelsburg and VanderKam, *1 Enoch 2*, 10.

40. Ibid., 101.

41. Bauckham, "Apocalypses," 150.

42. Nickelsburg and Vanderkam, *1 Enoch 2*, 106.

The rest of the first parable mainly elaborates on the home of the righteous and secrets of the cosmos (1 En. 39–44). Enoch's vision of the heavenly throne room is nestled within this discussion (1 En. 40:1–10). Here, he sees four Angels: Michael, Raphael, Gabriel, and Phanuel, the last of whom "is set over all actions of repentance of those who would inherit eternal life (τῶν κληρονομούντων τὴν αἰώνιον ζωήν)" (1 En. 40:9). This is the first reference that links a guarantor to the inheritance. Also, the phrase "inherit eternal life" may best understood in light of the similar rabbinical expression—"to inherit life in the world to come"[43] strengthening the claim that the Similitudes present the future eschatological world as the inheritance of the righteous (cf. 1 En. 38:1–4).

PARABLE 2 (1 ENOCH 45–57)

The second parable discusses the fate of the righteous and sinners in much the same way as the first parable: the righteous/elect will receive an eschatological inheritance, whereas sinners will be judged. This idea is evident in the eschatological vision of 1 Enoch 45, which, echoing Isaiah 65:17 and 66:22, proclaims that God will transform heaven and earth for the righteous (1 En.45:4).[44] A similar thought is found in 1 Enoch 72:1, which speaks of the anticipation of the "new creation which abides forever" (cf. 1 En. 91:16). Thus, the vision in 1 Enoch 45:4, and similarly 72:1, closely follows the Isaianic idea that the righteous will inherit a new heavens and new earth. Sinners, on the other hand, "will not set foot on her" and "will be destroyed from the face of the earth" (1 En. 45:6).

Enoch then proclaims that when the dead are resurrected, God "will choose the righteous and the holy ones from among (the risen dead) . . . and the earth shall rejoice; and the righteous ones shall dwell upon her and the elect ones shall walk upon her" (1 En. 51:1–5). Mathew Black contends that "the elect are to go through the length and breadth of the land as did the old Israel when it entered the land of promise. The prophecy about 'inheriting, possessing' the land is now to be fulfilled for the elect of the new Israel; cf.

43. Black, *Book of Enoch*, 201. See similar notion in *Pss.Sol.* 14:6.

44. Ibid., 205. Black contends that the Hebrew source for the notion of a "New Creation which embraces the universe and mankind . . . is obviously Second Isaiah, at Is. 43:19 . . . but more especially Is. 65:17 ff. and 66:22 (cf. also Ps. 102:26)" ("The New Creation in I Enoch," 14). Black also contends that Isa 65:17 is perhaps "the *locus classicus*" for the notion of a new heavens and earth for the righteous "and might well be held to warrant most of the later tradition in the Apocrypha and Pseudepigrapha and rabbinical sources" (ibid.).

Ps. 37.3, 9, 11, 29, 34, Mt. 5.5.”[45] What is more, *1 Enoch* 51:1–5 importantly asserts that God's people will be resurrected to dwell in the renewed eschatological world (cf. Ezek 36–37).[46] N. T. Wright rightly observes that in this passage there is the explicit expectation that the “future resurrection . . . [is] set within the promise for all creation to be renewed.”[47]

As with other material in the parables, Enoch contends that sinners will not inherit the eschatological earth along with the righteous. Instead, after the resurrection, “sinners shall be destroyed from before the face of the Lord of the Spirits—they shall perish eternally” (*1 En.* 53:2). This pronouncement is in line with the theme of the first two parables: the righteous will inherit the eschatological world, while sinners will only experience judgment—with no hope of dwelling in the land.

PARABLE 3 (1 ENOCH 58–69)

The third parable continues to focus on the fate of the righteous and sinners (*1 En.* 58–69). The righteous, Enoch states, will receive a “lot” that “will be glorious” (*1 En.* 58:1).[48] In keeping with the eschatological theme of the parables, the “lot” preserved for the righteous will be “their future compensation in the world to come” (cf. *1 En.* 48:7).[49] Additionally, the “lots of the righteous”[50] will be measured by a group of angels (*1 En.* 61:1–3). Black argues that this passage refers to “the future heritage of the righteous, the ‘measured portion’ of each one.”[51] He also contends that “the author may have in mind the allocation of the promised land in paradise as corresponding to the dividing out of the allotted portions of the land of Canaan at the time of the conquest (Num. 33.54, Jos. 13.6, 19.1f).”[52] So, in accord with Black, the eschatological inheritance will be apportioned to the righteous in the manner in which Canaan was distributed to the tribes of Israel.

The third parable also affirms that sinners (the kings and rulers of the present world) will not receive a “lot” in the future inheritance, but will be filled with shame and driven from the presence of the Son of Man (*1 En.*

45. Black, *Book of Enoch*, 214.

46. Harris, “Eternal Inheritance,” 118.

47. Wright, *Resurrection*, 155. Brackets mine.

48. I am following the translation of Black (*Book of Enoch*, 224).

49. Barrett contends the “lot” in *1 En.* 58:1 is the same “lot” that will be preserved for the righteous by the Son of Man figure in *1 En.* 48:1 (*The Book of Enoch*, 211, 224).

50. I am following the translation of Black (*Book of Enoch*, 231).

51. Ibid., 231.

52. Ibid., 231–32.

63:11–12). This, Enoch declares, is the judgment prepared for them "before the Lord of the Spirits" (1 En. 63:12; cf. 1 En. 62). The third parable, then, as with the previous parables, views the righteous to be the heirs of the coming world. Sinners, on the other hand, will be judged, having no portion in the world to come.

In all, the Similitudes describe the inheritance in a manner consistent with the rest of 1 Enoch. That is, the righteous are the heirs of the eschatological world, while sinners will receive judgment. One further point is that 1 Enoch, like Ezekiel 36–37, displays that God's people will receive their inheritance when they are resurrected from the dead (1 En. 51:1–5; cf. Ezek 36–37).

Jubilees

Jubilees is a rewritten account of Genesis 1–Exodus 14.[53] Although it generally follows the order of the biblical text, Jubilees recasts the chronological structure "into weeks and jubilees of years, dating events in Israelite history to specific times in these cycles."[54] Throughout this chronology there are several important passages pertaining to Israel's inheritance.

The first of such passages is Jubilees 1. Here, God tells Moses that the people of Israel will be taken into exile because of their disobedience (1:7–14). Yet, when they turn to God, he will gather them from the nations and bring them into the land (Jub 1:15–18; cf. Jer 29:13; 33:15). At that time, God "shall descend and dwell with them for all the ages of eternity" (Jub 1:26). The place in which God will dwell permanently with Israel is described as "the new creation when the new heaven and earth . . . shall be renewed according to the powers of heaven and according to the whole nature of the earth" (Jub 1:29), closely echoing Isaiah 65:17 and 66:22.[55] Though Jubilees 1 describes Israel's inheritance as the new heavens and earth, the remainder of Jubilees does not again identify the inheritance in this manner. What it does clearly and consistently state is that the inheritance is the future land that Israel will possess forever (cf. Num 13:28–29; Isa 55–56; Ezek 36–37).

53. Nickelsburg, "Bible Rewritten," 97. English translations for Jubilees are from Wintermute, "Jubilees," 2:34–142. Wintermute contends that Jubilees was written in the second century BC (ibid., 32.).

54. Nickelsburg, "Bible Rewritten," 97.

55. Kugel, Walk through Jubilees, 28. VanderKam assumes that "eschatology is not a dominant concern in Jubilees as it is in some of the Enoch literature, but two important passages—1:7–29 and 23:11–31—focus on the subject" (Walk through Jubilees, 132–33). In these passages, the author is giving "a glimpse into the future that awaits the chosen people" (ibid., 132).

This idea is articulated in *Jubilees* 14:7–8, a text which follows Genesis 15:7–8 and says that Abraham will possess the land as his inheritance "forever."[56] While *Jubilees* 14:7–8 asserts that the land will be Abraham's eternal possession, it is important to note that this idea is not entirely affirmed in Genesis 15:7–8, for these verses state that the land is Abraham's "to possess," without mentioning that he will do so perpetually. Regardless of the author's intent in giving Abraham's possession of the land a lasting quality not found in Genesis 15:7–8, it is clear that *Jubilees* 14:7–8 views the nature of the inheritance to be everlasting.

Another text that mentions the eternal quality of the inheritance is *Jubilees* 15:10. This passage, while alluding to the words of Genesis 17:8,[57] says that Abraham and his descendants "will possess forever" the land.[58] In making such a statement, the author also insinuates that the possession of the land is forthcoming.

Jubilees 22:14 comes close to asserting that the inheritance is the restored world when Abraham prays that Jacob "may inherit all of the earth" (*Jub* 22:14). He then goes on to declare that Jacob's descendants "will remain in all the history of the earth" (*Jub* 22:24).[59] However, the wicked—described as those who worship idols and are hated—will have no lasting heritage with Jacob's offspring, for they will be "uprooted" and "blotted out from the earth" (*Jub* 21:20–22). They will be so utterly removed from the earth that not even their memory will remain (*Jub* 21:22; Cf. *1 En.* 45:6; 53:2). This is in contrast to Jacob's descendants, who will remain upon the earth forever.

At the close of *Jubilees*, Moses assures Israel of a future entrance into the land (49:18–21). When they are at last dwelling in it, there will be no "Satan or any evil (one). And the land will be purified from that time and forever" (*Jub* 50:5). Never again will Israel be influenced by evil, for sin will

56. What text of Genesis, if any, the author of *Jubilees* may have employed is the subject of debate. It is possible that the author may have had both the LXX and Samaritan Pentateuch before him as he wrote (VanderKam, "Origins and Purposes of Jubilees," 5). For a more complete discussion of this issue, see pp. 3–16 in the above source.

57. van Ruiten, *Abraham in Jubilees*, 145–47. van Reuten also provides a careful analysis of how *Jub* 15:3–24 follows closely, sometimes even verbatim, the text of Gen 17 (ibid., 141–44).

58. Unlike Gen 17:8, *Jub* 15:10 does not state that land is given "to Abraham" and "to his seed." Nevertheless, Wintermute restores these phrases based on Gen 17:8 ("Jubilees," 86). van Reuten contends that this restoration is possible because "either the author of *Jubilees* made a mistake when he read his vorlage, or the mistake occurred later in the textual tradition" (*Abraham in Genesis*, 142).

59. I am following the translation of van Ruiten (*Abraham in Jubilees*, 306).

be eradicated from the land. Hence, Israel has the prospect of an idealized future in the inheritance.[60]

In sum, *Jubilees* 1 identifies the inheritance as the new heavens and new earth. Though the remainder of *Jubilees* does not describe the inheritance in exactly this way, it does affirm that the inheritance is the future land—or future earth (*Jub* 22:14)—that Israel will possess forever. Since Israel will dwell perpetually in a land that will be eradicated from evil (cf. *Jub* 50:5), it is apparent that *Jubilees* confirms that Israel is looking forward to an eschatological land.[61]

Psalms of Solomon

The *Psalms of Solomon* are a composition of eighteen songs that display "important evidence for the Jewish eschatological hopes" in the first-century BC.[62] The inheritance is discussed in the context of such eschatological aspirations.

One of the most distinctive aspects of the inheritance in the *Psalms* is that eternal destruction will be the sinner's future inheritance (13:11–12, 14:9, 15:10). In particular, *Psalms* 3:11–12 states that "the destruction of the sinner is forever . . . This is the portion (μερίς) of sinners forever." Though the noun μερίς is not morphologically related to the κληρονομία word group, it is a close cognate of μέρος, which may refer to a "share" or "portion" in the land inheritance of Israel (Josh 18:20; cf. Ezek 47:20).[63] Thus, "the portion" or "the share" (μερίς) of the sinner's inheritance is eternal destruction (cf. Rev 21:7).

Although the notion of the sinner inheriting destruction is implicit in *Psalms* 13:11–12, it is explicit in 14:9 and 15:10. *Psalms* 14:9 states that the sinner's "inheritance (κληρονομία) is Hades and darkness and destruction." *Psalms* 15:10 says that "the inheritance (κληρονομία) of sinners is destruction and darkness." These two passages affirm that the inheritance of sinners is eschatological obliteration. They also give further credence to the similar theme insinuated in 13:11–12.

---

60. VanderKam, *Jubilees*, 84.

61. This point may also be seen in that *Jub* 1 and 50, the first and last chapters of *Jubilees*, clearly describe the inheritance as an eschatological land. Thus, these "bookends" may provide the hermeneutical key for understanding the inheritance in the chapters that lie between, suggesting that, if the inheritance in *Jub* 1 and 50 is an eschatological land, so too is the inheritance in chapters 2–49.

62. Flusser, "Psalms, Hymns and Prayers," 573.

63. Schneider, "μέρος," 4:598. See Atkinson, *Intertextual Study*, 67.

The inheritance of sinners is contrary to that which awaits God's people. In *Psalms* 12:6, the author prays that "the devout of the Lord inherit the promises of the Lord (κληρονομήσαισαν ἐπαγγελίας κυρίου)." The inheritance of the "promises of the Lord" is likely the attainment of that which God promised to his people on numerous occasions: the land (Gen12:7; 13:15; 15:18; 26:3; 28:13–15; 35:9–12; 46:4). Galatians 3:21 also asserts this notion by using the plural form of ἐπαγγελία to refer to the various instances in which the land was promised to God's people.[64] Such evidence therefore makes it likely that *Psalms* 12:6 declares that the Lord's devout ones will inherit the land repeatedly promised to God's people.[65]

As well, *Psalms* 14:10 asserts that the devout ones "shall inherit life (κληρονομήσουσιν ζωὴν) with joy." Though it may seem that this passage points to the inheritance of an abstract spiritual realm, both the OT and Second Temple literature affirm that Israel hopes to inherit the restored physical world (cf. Isa 65–66). Thus, "inheriting life" does not point to the possession of a non-physical, abstract abode, but refers to the inheritance of life in the coming world—as in the case of the similar phrase, "of those who inherit eternal life," in *1 Enoch* 40:9.

The *Psalms* anticipate that the promise of life in the coming world will be fulfilled with the appearance of a Davidic Messiah (*Pss.Sol.* 17:21). When this figure arrives, he will "drive out sinners from the inheritance (ἀπὸ κληρονομίας)" (*Pss.Sol.*17:23). He will also gather "a holy people," known as "God's sons," and "distribute (καταμερίσει)[66] them according to their tribes upon the land" (*Pss.Sol.* 17:26–28).[67] At that time, Israel will enjoy eternal life in their inheritance. Since the Messiah's role in fulfilling this promise recalls 2 Samuel 7:10–17 and Psalm 2:8,[68] *Psalms* 17 insinuates that the Messiah will bring his people into an eschatological inheritance.

In short, the *Psalms of Solomon* affirm that there will be an inheritance for both sinners and God's people. The inheritance of the former will be destruction, while the inheritance of the latter will be the eschatological

64. See my argument in chap. 6. See also Hong, *Law in Galatians*, 132.

65. Atkinson provides further support for the land promises being in view in *Pss. Sol.* 12:6 by contending that Ps 37:11—which states that "the meek shall inherit the land" and points to the fulfillment of the land promise—provides an intertextual resonance for *Pss.Sol.* 12:16 (*Intertextual Study*, 248–49).

66. The future tense verb καταμερίσει makes evident that the apportioning of God's sons into their tribal allotments is still forthcoming.

67. Atkinson writes that "the prophet Ezekiel wrote of a similar distribution of land, my princes shall no longer oppress my people; but they shall let the house of Israel have the land according to their tribes" in Exod 45:8 (*Intertextual Study*, 353). See also Schüpphaus, *Die Psalmen Salomos*, 69–70.

68. Harris, "Eternal Inheritance," 123.

world.[69] Furthermore, it is suggested that a Davidic messiah will bring God's people into their eschatological inheritance (cf. 2 Sam 7:10–17; Ps 2:8).

4 Ezra

Fourth Ezra is an apocalypse consisting of seven visions that mainly describe the transition from the present to the coming world.[70] Like much of Second Temple literature, *4 Ezra* describes the inheritance as the world to come.[71]

This notion is initially found in *4 Ezra* 6:55–59. In this passage, the nations are ruling and domineering over Israel (6:57; cf. 5:28–29). These circumstances lead Ezra to ask the following questions: "If the world has indeed been created for us, why do we not possess our world as an inheritance? How long will this be so?" (6:59; cf. 7:11).[72] Such questions reveal that Ezra assumes the world to be the inheritance of Israel.[73] Since the OT Psalms and Prophets assert the cosmic expansion of the inheritance (e.g., Ps 2, 77; Isa 65–66; Ezek 35–37), Ezra is warranted to question why Israel does not currently possess the world that rightly belongs to them.

In response to Ezra's questions, the angel Uriel acknowledges that the world was made for Israel and claims that Adam's sin prevented them from possessing it (*4 Ezra* 7:1–16). The angel then chastises Ezra for focusing on his current circumstances, rather than considering "what is to come" (*4 Ezra* 7:16). In the context of *4 Ezra*, "what is to come" is Israel's "portion" and "inheritance" (e.g., 7:11), otherwise known as the coming world. Ezra is not to be concerned about the injustices and imbalances of the present earth, for Israel will inherit the world to come, while the wicked will undergo difficulties "and will not see the easier future world" (*4 Ezra* 7:17–18).[74]

---

69. Other verses in the *Psalms* that give the inheritance a distinctly territorial sense are 7:2 and 9:1.

70. See discussion in Stone (*Features of Eschatology*, 44–96). Fourth Ezra was likely written toward the end of the first century AD, "approximately thirty years after the Roman destruction of Jerusalem" (Nickelsburg, *Jewish Literature*, 287–88). This may be evidenced in that "many images, themes, traditions in *4 Ezra* have counterparts in Biblical Antiquities of Pseudo-Philo and 2 Baruch, and its outline and structure parallel 2 Baruch at many points" (ibid., 288).

71. *Fourth Ezra* also refers to God's people as "his inheritance" (cf. *4 Ezra* 15–16, 44–45). This use is less frequent than the coming world as Israel's inheritance.

72. English translations for *4 Ezra* are from Metzger ("4 Ezra," 525–59).

73. Stone asserts that the world "is designated as an inheritance, as was the land of Israel in Num 33:54; 34:13; Jos 14:2" (*Fourth Ezra*, 189).

74. Ibid., 193.

Subsequently, Ezra is told about a time when "the city which now is not seen shall appear, and the land now hidden shall be disclosed" (*4 Ezra* 7:26).[75] The "unseen city" refers to the New Jerusalem (cf. *4 Ezra* 10:27, 42, 44, 54), whose pre-existence is clearly implied.[76] This city, as in *4 Ezra* 13:36, will be revealed in the eschaton.[77] The fact that the city is currently located in heaven does not mean that it is a spiritual abode.[78] Instead, the idea is that it will appear when the "hidden land" is revealed (cf. Rev 21:1–2).[79]

Though the term "hidden land" does not have a parallel in comparable literature, there is still a plausible explanation for this expression. The word "hidden" is best explained by "the apocalyptic penchant for speaking of things which are to be revealed at the time of the eschaton."[80] So, it is likely that the "hidden land" in *4 Ezra* 7:26 is the recreated earth on which the New Jerusalem will exist, which will be revealed in the eschaton (cf. 2 *Apoc Bar* 59:10).

Ezra is told that the Messiah will appear after the revelation of the "unseen city" and the "hidden land" (*4 Ezra* 7:28). This will mark the inception of a four-hundred-year messianic kingdom.[81] Regardless of the length of Messiah's rule, it is important to note that in *4 Ezra* 7:26–28 the New Jerusalem and the future land are associated with a messianic kingdom (cf. Rev 20–22).

75. Stone argues that *4 Ezra* 7:26–44 contains the "fullest description of the eschatological events given in the book. It is of advantage, then, to use it as a basis for the study of the descriptions of the new world" (*Features of Eschatology*, 98). In regard to the "city," he makes the important observation that it is often described in *4 Ezra* as the heavenly Jerusalem or Zion. Moreover, in *4 Ezra* the "new Jerusalem is connected specifically with the Messianic kingdom. It is pre-created, has a special holiness and will appear at the end" (ibid., 102).

76. The notion of the ideal "future Jerusalem has its origins in the Hebrew Bible, and it is widespread in the Apocryphal and Pseudepigraphal literature. It is also found in the New Testament, in the Dead Sea Scrolls, in the Rabbinic literature, and in later Jewish apocalyptic" (ibid., 101). E.g., Isa 52:1; 54:11; Ezek 40–48; Zech 2:5–9; *Apoc Bar* 4:2–4; Rev 22:1–2.

77. Ibid.

78. Ibid. See the similar idea in *4 Ezra* 8:52, where the "hidden city" is also associated with the tree of life, the future age, and rest.

79. Another relevant discussion is found in *4 Ezra* 9:38—10:57. Here, Ezra notices a woman mourning and weeping for the loss of her only child (9:38—10:4). He then chastises her because everyone is morning for Zion, "the mother of us all" (10:7). As Ezra is speaking, the woman is transformed into "an established city . . . the place with huge foundations" (10:27). The appearance of an "established city" with huge foundations is a reference to the New Jerusalem, the pre-existent city that will be manifest at the coming of the Messiah (*4 Ezra* 7:26).

80. Ibid., 102. See also Stone, *Fourth Ezra*, 214.

81. See Stone, *Features of Eschatology*, 101.

Following Messiah's appearance, the Most High will come and execute judgment (4 Ezra 7:33–44). Ezra responds to the Most High's coming with the following observation: "And now I see that the world to come will bring delight to few, but torments to many" (4 Ezra 7:47). The Most High then replies: "Listen to me, Ezra, and I will instruct you . . . For this reason the Most High has made not one world but two" (4 Ezra 7:49)—the present world being prescribed for the ungodly many and the coming world for the righteous few (4 Ezra 8:1).[82] The Most High's instruction is intended to cause Ezra to take his eyes off the present world, for, as one of the righteous, he "shall inherit what is to come" (4 Ezra 7:96).

The apocalyptic book of 4 Ezra provides compelling evidence that the inheritance of God's people is the coming world. This is consistent with the discussion of the inheritance in the Second Temple texts that have been examined to this point. What is more, 4 Ezra also associates the notions of the New Jerusalem, future land, and messianic kingdom (cf. Rev 20–22).

2 Baruch

Second Baruch is an apocalyptic document that was written after the fall of Jerusalem in AD 70.[83] Like other Second Temple literature, 2 Baruch presents the inheritance as the world to come.[84] As 4 Ezra, 2 Baruch sharply differentiates between the ungodly present world and coming world for the righteous.[85] This book also links keeping the Law with receiving the promised inheritance.

Second Baruch first mentions that the inheritance is the coming world in chapter 14. Here, Baruch is told that the righteous "will leave this world without fear and are confident of the world" which the Lord "has promised to them with a full expectation of joy" (14:13). Clearly, Baruch claims

82. See also the brief discussion in Nickelsburg, *Jewish Literature*, 290.

83. Klijn, "2 (Syriac Apocalypse of) Baruch," 615. All English translations for 2 Baruch come from pp. 621–52 of this source.

84. Ibid., 619.

85. Murphy provides a survey and evaluation of the "two-world" concept in 2 Baruch. He contends that the author "places great emphasis on the radical discontinuity between this world and the future one (*Second Baruch*, 31–70). They are ontologically different" (ibid., 67). Even so, Murphy concludes that the future world is not physical but heavenly. The "non-physicality" of the coming world, in his opinion, is "a major step in the direction of Gnosticism" (ibid.). Murphy's conclusion ignores the explicit expectation of a renewed physical world, for example, in 2 Bar. 57. It also ignores the fact that in Second Temple literature the future world is a restored physical place (cf. 1–2 Maccabees, *Jubilees*, 4 Ezra, etc.). God's people are not looking forward to a non-physical reality, but life in the renewed world, a hope that is arguably grounded in Isa 65–66.

that the world to come is the promised inheritance of righteous (cf. *4 Ezra* 7:1–25).[86] In so doing, he also makes a connection between the themes of "promise" and "land." Genesis initially associates these two themes as God "promises" to give "the land of Canaan" to Abraham and his descendants (Gen 15:18; 24:7; 26:4; 48:4; cf. Exod 33:1).[87] *Second Baruch* 14:13, however, no longer restricts the land promise to Canaan, for it shifts the "promise" from Canaan to the "coming world"—a maneuver which neither the OT nor previously examined Second Temple literature so clearly performs (cf. 21:5).[88] This shift in *2 Baruch* 14:13 is later seen in 51:3, when Baruch is told that the righteous "will receive the undying world which was promised to them."

Although he is told that the promised inheritance is the future world, Baruch is mindful that the present corrupt earth was originally created for the Lord's people (14:19; cf. 15:7–8). This world, however, has been a struggle and much trouble (15:8). Such difficulty in the present cosmos redirects Israel's hope to the immeasurable world which they will "inherit" (16:1).[89] According to Liv Ingeborg Lied, "the idea that the other, future world is also the inheritance . . . of the righteous (16:1; 44:13) strengthens Israel's claim on that world."[90]

The coming world is once again mentioned when Baruch delivers a testamentary speech in chapter 44. Before speaking of what is to come, Baruch tells his listeners that everything associated with the present evil time will be destroyed and subsequently forgotten (44:2–9). Nevertheless, there is "a period coming which will remain forever; and there is a new world which does not carry back to corruption" (44:12). Those who persevere in the Torah "will inherit the time of which it is spoken, and to these is the heritage of the promised time" (44:13). Lied makes the claim that "time" and

86. Lied, *Other Lands of Israel*, 274. Lied also clarifies that the land is the inheritance of Israel (ibid.). See also Sir 46:1; 2 Macc 2:4.

87. Dunn makes the important observation that, although the word "promise" had no equivalent in Hebrew, "the sense of 'promise' for ἐπαγγελία . . . emerged into prominence in wider Greek usage in the second century B.C.E." (*Romans 1–8*, 212). Subsequently, he says that "even if the formal category (promise) appears only late on the scene, the fact that God had made such a commitment was a basic element of Israel's faith (see, e.g., Exod 32:13; 1 Chron 16:14–18 . . . Ps 105:6–11; Sir 44:21)" (ibid.).

88. Even *Pss.Sol.* 12:6, which insinuates that the "devout ones" will inherit the promises of land, never shifts the land promise from Canaan to the coming world. Although this may be the author's underlying assumption, given that the future world is the fulfillment of the land promise (cf. 2 Sam 7:10–17; Isa 65–66; Rom 4, 8). Nevertheless, he never explicitly identifies the "promise" as the "coming world."

89. Lied, *Other Lands of Israel*, 274.

90. Ibid.

"space" are interchangeable in 2 *Baruch* (cf. Sir 44:19–2; 4 *Ezra* 6:59; 7:26; 8:52–53).[91] This appears to be the case as the "time" of which Baruch speaks (44:13) is equivalent to the "new world" (44:12).[92]

In 2 *Baruch* 44:12–13, Baruch's listeners are told that keeping the Torah leads to an in inheritance in the "new (eschatological) world."[93] This idea is similarly expressed in 51:3, which asserts that "those who are proved to be righteous on account of my Law" will be transformed, so that they may receive the promised future world.[94] *Second Baruch* 44:12–13 and 51:3 therefore clarify that the righteous heirs of the coming world mentioned in 14:3 and 51:3 are those who persevere in the Torah. On the other hand, those who do not walk according to the Law, but despise it and refuse to listen to its wisdom, "will go away to be tormented" (51:5).

At the end of the book, Baruch writes a letter to the nine and a half tribes in Babylon (2 *Bar*. 78–85). Here, he calls on his readers to focus on the inheritance promised to them, the coming world, rather than the difficulties of the present life (2 *Bar*. 83:4–6; 84:7; 85:5, 1). Baruch also exhorts, "If you trespass the law, you shall be dispersed. And if you shall keep it, you shall be planted" (2 *Bar*. 84:2). Baruch's comments echo the core teaching of Deuteronomy 4 and 30, that violating the Law results in exile, while keeping the Law leads to being established in the land.[95] Baruch's letter to the nine and a half tribes therefore confirms that only those who persevere in the Torah will inherit the future world. All others have no hope of life in the world to come.

Overall, 2 *Baruch* views the inheritance to be the future world of the righteous, a notion that is consistent with other Second Temple literature. The future world is sharply differentiated from the difficult present world. *Second Baruch* also shifts the "promise" of land from Canaan to the "coming world" (cf. Rom 4:13) and links Torah observance with inheriting the world to come. Although God is faithful to his people, 2 *Baruch* envisions that "it

---

91. Ibid. See also Delling, "Die Weise," 305–21.

92. Henze notes that the language of time and the eschaton are closely linked (*Jewish Apocalypticism*, 289). A prime example is Baruch's second public address (11:9–15), in which the following short phrases are clustered together: "the world to come," "the renewed world," "the end of days," "the end," "the consummation," "the consummation of time," "the consummation of the times," "the consummation of the ages," etc. (ibid.).

93. Sayler, *Have the Promises Failed?*, 28.

94. Harris, "Eternal Inheritance," 131.

95. *Second Baruch* 84:2 may also be alluding to Exod 15:17, which speaks of the Lord "planting" Israel on his mountain.

is imperative that Israel keep the Law in order to benefit from the covenant promises."[96]

Summary of the Pseudepigrapha

The Pseudepigrapha asserts that the inheritance of the righteous is the eschatological world. *Jubilees* affirms this notion in identifying the inheritance of Israel as the new heavens and earth. Besides teaching that the inheritance is the eschatological world, each pseudepigraphal book makes a unique contribution to the notion of inheritance. *First Enoch* pairs the possession of the inheritance with the resurrection of the dead (51:1–5). The *Psalms of Solomon* assert that sinners will inherit eternal destruction. The *Psalms* also contend that the future world is the place to which the Davidic king will bring his people (cf. 2 Sam 7:10–17 and Ps 8.). *Fourth Ezra* closely associates the themes of the New Jerusalem, future land, and messianic kingdom (cf. Rev 20–22). Lastly, *Second Baruch* shifts the "promise" of land from Canaan to the "coming world" (cf. Rom 4:13–17) and associates Torah observance with inheriting the eschatological world.

THE INHERITANCE IN THE DEAD SEA SCROLLS

There is a variety of literature associated with the Dead Sea Scrolls, most of which is theological and religious in nature.[97] An extensive examination of the inheritance in all the varied Qumran texts is beyond the scope of this book. This section will therefore examine the inheritance in four selected sectarian texts, the *Rule of the Community* (1QS), the *Damascus Document* (1CD), the *Hymn Scroll* (1QH), and the *War Scroll* (1QM), followed by the *Psalms Pesher* and the *Genesis Apocryphon*. The analysis of the inheritance in these texts will show that the inheritance theme in the Dead Sea Scrolls is similar to what is found in the Apocrypha and Pseudepigrapha.

Rule of the Community (1QS)

Rule of the Community (1QS) presents the regulations of conduct, rules for admission, and beliefs of the Qumran sect.[98] Much of this content contains

96. Bauckham, "Apocalypses," 167.

97. Dimant, "Qumran Sectarian Literature," 487.

98. Ibid., 497–98; Bockmuehl, "IQS and Salvation at Qumran," 387. Nickelsburg argues that 1QS was written between 100 and 75 BC (*Jewish Literature*, 132).

a strong eschatological tone (e.g., 1QS 8:1–16 and 9:3–10:8).[99] An example of this quality is found in *Rule* 4:24, which says that God has sorted men "into equal parts until the appointed end and the new creation."[100]

In such futuristic discussions, *Rule* often uses inheritance language to portray the destinies of individuals.[101] For example, *Rule* 4:16, in expectation of God's visitation (i.e., judgment), states that humans have been placed into divisions depending on their "inheritance (נחלת) . . . great or small, for all eternal times."[102] The language of inheritance here is perhaps taken from Numbers 26:56, which describes the allotted portions of land to Israel's tribes.[103] Also in this context, *Rule* 4:24–26 says that man will be righteous "in agreement with his inheritance (נחלת) in the truth," and he shall act wickedly "in accordance with his share (וכירשתו) in the lot of injustice," until the end of time and the new creation (cf. 1:9–10; 2:17).

In the futuristic passages of 8:1–16 and 9:1–11, *Rule* speaks of making atonement not solely for the land of Israel but for the whole "earth" (הארץ).[104] The purification of the earth may reflect the idea that the entire world is the inheritance of Israel (cf. *4 Ezra* 6:59 and 7:11).

At the conclusion of *Rule*, the author pens a hymn concerning God's chosen ones (11:7–8): "To those whom God has selected . . . he has given them an inheritance (נחל) in the lot (בגורל) of the holy ones."[105] This passage confirms that God has predestined some to receive an inheritance among his holy people, using the language of "apportioning" or "allotting" of the land often found in Numbers (e.g., 26:56; 33:54) and Joshua (e.g., 15:20; 18:28). Such echoes provide evidence that the inheritance in *Rule*

---

99. Nickelsburg, *Jewish Literature*, 132–33.

100. Unless otherwise specified, English citations for the Dead Sea Scrolls are from García Martínez, *Dead Sea Scrolls*. All Hebrew citations are from García Martínez and Tigchelaar, *Dead Sea Scrolls*.

101. Harris, "Eternal Inheritance," 135.

102. It is best to translate נחלת as "inheritance." See Knibb, *Qumran Community*, 102. García Martínez prefers to render this word as "birthright" (*Dead Sea Scrolls*, 7). Given the echo of Num 26:56, I prefer the translation "inheritance."

103. Knibb, *Qumran Community*, 102. An examination of the use of Scripture at Qumran is beyond the scope of this book. For helpful discussions on this topic, see Flint, *Bible at Qumran*; Wenthe, "Use of the Hebrew Scriptures," 314; Lim, *Scripture in Qumran Commentaries*.

104. Although ארץ may refer to the "land" of Israel, I agree with García Martínez's translation of this noun as "world." This rendering is preferable both in light of the Jewish eschatological expectation of an expanded inheritance for Israel and the futuristic elements in IQS 8–9.

105. I am following the translation of García Martínez and Tigchelaar (*Dead Sea Scrolls*, 1:97).

is primarily focused on the territorial promise to Abraham (1QS 8:1–16). Thus, it appears that "key convictions" in this document are "still oriented toward the land itself."[106] These convictions are likely focused on the world, given that *Rule* speaks of making atonement for the entire earth (8:1–16; 9:1–11).

Damascus Document (CD)

The *Damascus Document* (CD) presents the thought of the sectarian community "through their eschatological perspective."[107] The community believes that they are destined to be the "shoot from which the new eschatological world will spring."[108] They identify themselves as the "sprout of Israel" and "a shoot of planting" from Aaron "to possess his land" (את ארצו לירוש) (CD 1:7–8). These thoughts allude to Isaiah 60:21, which affirms that Israel, the "shoot of God's planting," will "possess the land forever" (אֶרֶץ לְעוֹלָם יִירָשׁוּ).[109] The community therefore appears to assume that they are "a remnant under God's covenant to inherit the land."[110] Philip R. Davies contends that the eschatological dimension in this context, "which is hardly prominent and almost entirely implicit," consists of the longstanding expectation of the restoration of the land to the remnant of Israel.[111]

The *Damascus Document* also affirms that, for those who sought God "with a perfect heart," he raised up a Teacher of Righteousness "to direct them in the path of his heart" (CD 1:11). However, those who strayed from the path of the Teacher (CD 1:13–17) are likened to the pre-exilic Israelites who diverged "from tracks of justice" and removed "the boundary with which the very first had marked their inheritance (נחלחם)" (CD 1:13).[112] Removing the ancient inheritance land marks is explicitly forbidden in Deuteronomy 19:14.[113] So, while pointing to the future hope of inheriting

106. Harris, "Eternal Inheritance," 136.

107. Dimant, "Qumran Sectarian Literature," 493. The *Damascus Document* may be dated between 100–75 BC (ibid., 490).

108. Ibid., 493.

109. Knibb, *Qumran Community*, 21; Campbell, *Scripture in the Damascus Document 1–8, 19–20*, 61.

110. Davies, *Damascus Covenant*, 66.

111. Ibid.

112. Davies mentions the possibility that CD 1:12b–18a speaks of the pre-exilic generation, which is later described in CD 5:20 (ibid.,70). Similar to CD 1:13, CD 5:20 states: "And in the age of devastation of the land (הארצ) there arose those who shifted the boundary and made Israel stray."

113. Knibb, *Qumran Community*, 24.

the land (CD 1:7–8), the *Damascus Document* compares those who dis-obeyed the Teacher to the pre-exilic Israelites who violated the inheritance laws (CD 1:13).

Damascus Document 2:8–9 then says that God "hid his face from the land (ארצה), from Israel, until their extinction," and looks back on the punishment of Israel at the time of the exile (cf. Ezek 29, 39).[114] Even still, God "raised up men of renown for himself, to leave a remnant for the land (ארץ) and in order to fill the face of the world (תבל)" (CD 2:11–12). This passage infers the fulfillment of Isaiah 54:1–3, which promises that Israel's offspring will be so numerous that they will receive a worldwide inheri-tance. Although God has hidden his face from Israel, *Damascus Document* 2:8–12 envisions that God's remnant will one day inherit the entire world, fulfilling Isaiah 54:1–3.[115]

Subsequently, *Damascus Document* 3–4 focuses on pre-exilic Israel's history, from their mandate to possess the land, citing Deuteronomy 9:23 (CD 3:7), to their forfeiture of the land because of their disobedience. De-spite Israel's sin, those who remain faithful to God's covenant "will acquire eternal life, and all the glory of Adam is for them" (CD 3:20). The "glory of Adam" refers to the bodily resurrection, for it is paired with the hope of "eternal life."[116] There will thus be a time when the faithful ones will receive a resurrected, glorified body. Furthermore, since the *Damascus Document* points to a future inheritance of land, perhaps even the earth (CD 2:11–12), this document likely anticipates a bodily resurrection upon entering the eschatological world.[117] This idea is in keeping with Qumran's "future hope that extended beyond death and into the future world" (cf. 1QS 4:23; 1QH 4:15; 4Q171 3:1).[118]

---

114. Knibb, *Damascus Document*, 27.

115. *Damascus Document* 8:14–15 cites Moses' words from Deut 9:5 with some alterations: "Not for your justice, or for the uprightness of your heart, are you going to possess these nations (לרשת את הגים האלה)." The most significant change is that CD 8:14–15 takes הגים as the object of לרשת, rather than ארץ as in Deut 9:5. This change could simply reflect the understanding that Israel is to possess the "nations" of Canaan. However, it could also contain a further allusion to that idea that Israel is to possess the "nations" of the earth, as in Isa 54:1–3.

116. Puech believes that a bodily resurrection may be in view ("Immortality and Life After Death," 518–20). See also Wright, *Resurrection*, 189.

117. Davies concludes that "the community, as the true remnant," awaits a time when they will "occupy the land" (*Damascus Covenant*, 202).

118. Wright, *Resurrection*, 189. Grossman argues that the *Damascus Document* presents the community as the righteous heirs "to a national covenant complete with the promise of land, community, and future survival" (*Reading for History*, 184).

Hymn Scroll (1QHª)

The *Hymn Scroll* (1QHª) is a composition of at least twenty-five hymns of praise.[119] In this document, the imagery associated with the inheritance has a strong eschatological quality, using terms such as "eternal inheritance" and "lot" which Jewish texts "commonly apply to eschatological salvation" (e.g., 1QHª 6, 11).[120] In addition to these observations, there are several passages that unambiguously speak of a future inheritance for the Qumran community.

One such passage is *Hymn* 4:14–15. Here, the hymnist says that the Lord will cause his loyal servants' descendants (זרעם) to remain before him forever. He will also raise up an eternal name for his servants, forgive their sins, and "give them as an inheritance (ולהנחילם) all the glory of Adam and plentiful days" (1QHª 4:15). The "glory of Adam," as in *Damascus Document* 3:20, likely refers to a resurrection body. Also, the hope of "plentiful days" echoes Israel's promised eternal stay in the land (Exod 5:12; Num 13:28–29; Deut 5:16). Such observations bring to light that *Hymn* 4:14–15 associates the inheritance with the eschatological themes of "resurrection" and "long life in the land" (cf. Ezek 36–37). That the inheritance is also in the same context as the themes of "eternal name" and "forgiveness of sins" provides further warrant for understanding the inheritance eschatologically.

Another important passage is *Hymn* 14:14–31, which claims that the community will dwell in the eschatological world (cf. 1QHª 15:4–10).[121] This is the place with "everlasting gates," which the sons of truth, after being "awakened," "will rule from one end to the other" (1QHª 14:29–31). Both N. T. Wright and E. P. Sanders argue that the "awakening" of the sons of truth is

---

119. Nickelsburg, *Jewish Literature*, 137. Knibb believes the *Hymn Scroll* dates from the first century AD (*Qumran Community*, 157).

120. Nickelsburg, *Jewish Literature*, 139.

121. 1QHª 14:14–17 is worth quoting at length:
They will return under your glorious commands,
your princes will be in the lot of [your holy ones.]
[Their root] will sprout like a flower [of the field] forever,
to make a shoot grow
in branches of the everlasting plantation
so that it covers all the world with its shade,
[and its tip reaches] up to the skies,
and its roots down to the abyss.
All the streams of Eden [will make] its branches [grow]
and it will be [a huge tree without limits];
The glory of the wood will be over the whole world, endless,
And [deep] as down to Sheol [its roots.]

clear evidence of the resurrection hope at Qumran.[122] In 14:29–31, "resurrection" is also tied to a "dominion with limitless borders," which is another way of describing the "kingdom" in the coming world (cf. Ps 2; 2 Sam 23). Given the evidence, it is apparent that the *Hymn Scroll* envisions that the community will dwell in the eschatological worldwide kingdom when they are resurrected from the dead.[123] Such a kingdom is likely the inheritance on which they will experience "plentiful days" (1QH^a 4:4:14–15).

War Scroll (1QM)

The *War Scroll* describes the final eschatological battle between the sons of light and sons of darkness.[124] In this struggle, the scroll uses inheritance language to portray the sons of light as the lot (גורל) of God and the sons of darkness as the lot (גורל) of Belial (e.g., 1QM 1:5; 13:1–5). The latter will be defeated and left without a remnant, while the former "shall shine to the edges of the earth" and enjoy "length of days" (1QM 1:7–8). Such "length of days" will no doubt be enjoyed on the land of their inheritance (cf. 1QH^a 4:14–15). Although the territorial inheritance is insinuated in *War Scroll* 1:7–8, it is explicit in an identical parallelism in 12:12 and in 19:4, and in the prayer in chapter 13.

The parallelism in *War Scroll* 12:12 and 19:4 is set in the context of the expected eschatological restoration of Jerusalem and the cities of Judah, following the conflict with the sons of darkness (1QM 12:12–18; 19:1–8; cf. Zech 9:9; Isa 12:6).[125]

> Fill the land with your Glory (סלא ארצכה כבוד)
> and your inheritance with blessing (ונחלתכה ברכה)

These phrases parallel "the land" (ארץ) with "your inheritance" (נחלתכה), signifying that the land is God's inheritance. The OT asserts that the land, though promised to Israel, is ultimately the heritage of God (Jer 16:18; cf. Lev 19–26). Hence, *War Scroll* 12:12 and 19:4 call on God to fill

---

122. Wright, *Resurrection*, 187; Sanders, *Judaism*, 302.

123. The expectation of a resurrection in the world to come is also found in 1QH^a 19:10–14, which claims that God will "raise the worms of the dead from the dust, to an everlasting community," so that man "can take his place . . . with the perpetual host and the [everlasting spirits], to renew him with everything that will exist."

124. Dimant claims that the *War Scroll* "is extant in one better preserved manuscript from Cave 1 and six fragments from Cave 4; their dates of writing range from the first half of the first century B.C.E. to the beginning of the first century C.E." ("Qumran Sectarian Literature," 515).

125. Wenthe, "Use of the Hebrew Scriptures," 311.

his land inheritance with glory and blessing in the coming eschaton. The broader restorative context of these passages (1QM 12:12–18; 19:1–8) even points to the day when Israel will have dominion over all the nations of the earth.[126]

The prayer in *War Scroll* 13 is intended to accompany the community's eschatological victory. Verse 7 instructs the sons of light, the priests, Levites, and elders to bless God by saying:

> You are the God of our fathers,
> we bless your name always.
> We are the people of your *[inhe]ritance* (נחלתכה).
> You established a covenant with our Fathers
> and ratified it with their offspring
> for times eternal.[127]

At first glance, this prayer seems to describe the inheritance as God's people. This prayer, however, alludes to the eternal covenant made with Abraham in Genesis 17:7–9 (Gen 12:1–13; 15:1–21), which speaks of God's promise to give the land to Abraham and his offspring as an everlasting possession, rather than affirming Israel as God's inheritance.[128] The background to *Hymn Scroll* 13:7 therefore illuminates that the inheritance is the land which, as in 12:12 and 19:4, belongs to God and on which Abraham's offspring will dwell. The community expects that God will fill this place with eschatological glory and blessing following the struggle with the sons of darkness (1QM 12:12; 19:4). Such anticipation suggests that the territorial inheritance in the *War Scroll* is oriented toward the future restoration of the land.

Psalms Pesher (4Q171 [4QpPsᵃ])

The *Psalms Pesher* primarily comments on Psalm 37. References to a futuristic inheritance of land are abundant in this document. For example, verse 2:4, citing Psalm 37:9, says that those "who hope in YHWY will inherit the land (ירשו ארץ)," and verse 2:9, citing Psalm 37:11, states that "the poor shall inherit the land (ירשו ארץ) and enjoy peace and plenty" (cf. 4Q171 2:11). Making explicit that the future inheritance has been expanded beyond Canaan, verse 3:9 claims that "those who are blessed in him shall inherit the earth (ירשו ארץ)." Similarly, verse 4:2, alluding to Psalm 37:28, asserts that

126. Davies, *1QM*, 103.

127. Emphasis mine.

128. Wenthe, "Use of the Hebrew Scriptures," 311.

the righteous "shall inherit the earth (ירשו ארץ) and live on it forever" (cf. 4Q171 4:10). The wicked, on the other hand, will have no inheritance with the righteous but will be "cut off and exterminated forever" (4Q171 4:2). The *Psalms Pesher* therefore anticipates the time when the righteous will receive the entire earth as their everlasting inheritance.[129]

Genesis Apocryphon (1QapGen)

The *Genesis Apocryphon* is a reworking of the narrative of Genesis. The surviving material of this manuscript covers events such as the life of Noah (1QapGen 9–13) and the initial portion of the Abraham story (1QapGen 19–22).[130] The references to the inheritance are almost exclusively found in the retelling of the Abraham story.[131] Like the original, this retold narrative, most evidently in chapter 21, shares the conviction that the land is the perpetual inheritance of Abraham and his offspring. Using language that closely follows Genesis 13:15–16, *Genesis Apocryphon* 21:12–13 affirms God's promise to Abraham that he "shall give all this land to your descendants and they will inherit it forever (וירתונה לכול עלמים)" (cf. 20:8).[132] This idea so permeates chapter 21 that it is the central theme of this section. Shortly thereafter, the book is abruptly cut short as Abraham is told that one of his servants will not be his heir "but someone who has left . . ." (1QapGen 22:34; cf. Gen 15:1–4). Although it does not fully recount the Abraham narrative, the *Genesis Apocryphon* views the land to be the eternal inheritance of Abraham and his descendants.

129. Nickelsburg helpfully states that "running through the commentary is the prediction of the punishment for the wicked and also reward for the righteous, often triggered by the psalmic refrain that the righteous 'will inherit the land'" (*Jewish Literature*, 130).

130. Knibb notes that the *Genesis Apocryphon* was discovered "in a poor state of preservation, and only the three innermost columns (XX–XXII) survived in reasonable condition" (*Qumran Community*, 183). The text also breaks off abruptly after retelling Gen 15:1–4 in 1QapGen 21:34. Knibb also asserts that the "manuscript dates from the end of the first century BC or the first half of the first century AD, but the work itself may have been composed a little before this" (ibid.).

131. Outside of the Abraham narrative, 1QapGen 2:19–21 interestingly speaks of the inheritance of Enoch: "Then I, Lamech, /ran/ to my father, Methuselah, and [told] him everything, [so that he would go and ask Enoch,] his father and would know everything for certain from him, since he (Enoch) is liked and well-liked [. . . and with the holy ones his inheritance is found and they show him everything."

132. Knibb, *Qumran Literature*, 197.

Summary of the Dead Sea Scrolls

Like the Apocrypha and Pseudepigrapha, the Dead Sea Scrolls mainly present the inheritance as the future land promised to God's people (e.g., 1QS 11:7–8; CD 1 7–8; 1QHª 4:14–15; 1QM 12:12; 19:4; 4Q171 2:4, 9; 1Qap-Gen 20). Several texts even provide specific evidence of an inheritance of the coming world (1QS 8:1–16; 9:1–11; CD 2:11–12; 1QHª 14–31; 4Q171 4:2).[133] Thus, the Qumran community envisions the future realization of the promised inheritance. Texts that associate the concepts of inheritance and resurrection firmly fix the fulfillment of the inheritance in the coming world (e.g., 1QHª 14:29–31).

CONCLUSION

The observations in this chapter assert that the Apocrypha, Pseudepigrapha, and Dead Sea Scrolls envision that the inheritance will be fulfilled when God's people inherit their eschatological territory. Thus, Second Temple corpuses, in line with the Psalms and Prophets, demonstrate that the inheritance is a concept that has "not yet" been fulfilled. From the OT to the Second Temple literature, God's people have been writing about the future realization of the promised inheritance, understood to be the eschatological world.

The Apostle Paul is the heir of this expectation. As one steeped in Jewish tradition, his vision of the inheritance is neither spiritual nor heavenly, for he anticipates the inheritance of a reconstituted, physical world. In his letters, Paul will highlight that Christ is the Davidic king who will one day bring this promise to fruition.

---

133. As noted, several texts also use inheritance language commonly associated with eschatological salvation, such as "lot" or "portion," to describe God's people (e.g., 1QH 6, 11; 1QM 1:5).

6

The Inheritance in Paul
Galatians

THE STUDY OF THE OT and Second Temple literature will now provide the proper background for an analysis of the inheritance in Paul.[1] I agree with Richard Hays: "If we are to arrive at a properly nuanced estimate of Paul's theological stance toward his own people and their sacred texts, we must engage him on his terms, by following his readings of the texts he heard from the word of God."[2] Having examined a large sampling of these texts, I now proceed to a study of Paul's letters. As I will argue, Paul's epistles are grounded in the worldview established in Jewish writings and thus continue the hope of an inheritance for God's people.

Of his letters, Paul's epistle to the Galatians provides the most extensive discussion of the inheritance, mainly in chapters 3–4. Thus, my analysis will focus on these chapters.[3] The inheritance is so important in Galatians 3–4 that it is the central theme of this portion of the letter.[4] When the

1. Galatians is one of the *Hauptbriefe*, which are universally accepted as authentic letters of Paul. A condensed and revised version of this chapter has been published previously. See Echevarria, "Inheritance of the Cosmic Kingdom," 2–17.

2. Hays, *Echoes*, x.

3. The inheritance in Gal 5:18–21 will be examined with other inheritance-kingdom passages (e.g., 1 Cor 6:9–11 and 15:50–58) in chap. 8, because it makes a direct contribution to that discussion.

4. Faith as opposed to works of the Law is another possible central theme for Gal 3–4. It is best, however, as this chapter will demonstrate, to see faith as the means by which believers become Abraham's descendants and beneficiaries of the promised inheritance. See Gal 3:22, 26.

inheritance is not stated specifically, it is nevertheless implied in the term "promise" (e.g., Gal 3:15–18), which harkens back to the pledge of land to Abraham and his offspring in Genesis (e.g., 12:7; 13:15; 15:18; 17:8). Reverberations of texts from the Psalms, Prophets, and Second Temple literature will demonstrate that Paul understands that the inheritance has been enlarged to include the entire world to come. Paul's eschatological view of the inheritance displays profound continuity with later Jewish tradition.

I noted in chapter one that James Hester is the only other author to have dedicated an entire volume to the inheritance in Paul's letters.[5] Similarly, Hester observes that Paul must have used the now expanded inheritance theme "to bring to mind the complex ideas which had developed around the 'inheritance' in the Old Testament and intertestamental literature."[6] I do not disagree with him on this point. I disagree with his "already-not-yet" view of the Pauline inheritance—because for Paul there is no sense in which the inheritance is fulfilled in the present; it remains a promise to be fulfilled entirely at the parousia. Since Hester mainly examines Galatians and Romans in tandem, I will critique his view of the inheritance in my analysis of Romans in the following chapter. This will permit more balanced interaction with his perspective.

This chapter will examine the inheritance in the following passages: Galatians 3:15–18; 3:19–29; 4:1–7; and 4:21–31.[7] In each of these passages, the inheritance is the future world promised to Abraham's offspring. Closely associated with the inheritance is the theme of kingdom, for Christ will reign over the coming world. Another idea linked to this concept is the Spirit's role in assuring that God's people possess the land. The OT and the Second Temple texts to which Paul alludes will make these observations apparent.

GALATIANS 3:15–18: CHRIST AS THE HEIR OF THE WORLD

Before observing the inheritance in Galatians 3:15–18, it is important to note that 3:13–14 sums up the entire argument that began in 3:2 about the Spirit.[8] Here, Paul asserts that "the blessing of Abraham" (ἡ εὐλογία τοῦ

---

5. Foreman's *Politics of Inheritance* also contributes to the study of inheritance in Paul. I do not consider his work comprehensive, because it mainly focuses on Romans.

6. Hester, *Paul's Concept of Inheritance*, 69.

7. The only passage in Gal 3–4 that this chapter will not examine is 4:8–20, for here Paul takes a brief excurses before resuming his inheritance argument in 4:21–31.

8. Hays, *Echoes*, 110.

Ἀβραάμ)[9] is fulfilled in the reception of "the promise of the Spirit" (τὴν ἐπαγγελίαν τοῦ πνεύματος). The Spirit is the blessing promised in Genesis (12:1–3; 15:1–21).[10] This is the case even though there is no explicit mentioning of the Spirit in the Abrahamic covenant promises.[11]

Paul does not make a new revelation in identifying the Spirit as the blessing of Abraham. Instead, he echoes what is already proclaimed in Isaiah 44:3:

I will pour out my Spirit on your seed (אֶצֹּק רוּחִי עַל־זַרְעֶךָ)[12]
And my blessing upon your descendants (וּבִרְכָתִי עַל־צֶאֱצָאֶיךָ)

The parallelism of these phrases identifies the "Spirit" (רוּחַ) as the "blessing" (בְּרָכָה),[13] which is what Paul affirms in Galatians 3:14. Also like Isaiah 44:3, in Galatians 3:14 Paul pairs two clauses to make his point:

ἵνα εἰς τὰ ἔθνη ἡ εὐλογία τοῦ Ἀβραὰμ γένηται ἐν Χριστῷ Ἰησοῦ
ἵνα τὴν ἐπαγγελίαν τοῦ πνεύματος λάβωμεν διὰ τῆς πίστεως.

The second ἵνα clause explains that the "blessing" (εὐλογία) of Abraham is the promised "Spirit" (πνεῦμα). This construction is similar to the way in which Isaiah 44:3 parallels two clauses to make the same assertion. Even though there is no exact citation of Isaiah 44:3 in Galatians 3:14, Paul clearly depends and interacts with the text of Isaiah. Paul, then, as Isaiah, affirms that the Spirit is the fulfillment of the promise of blessing to Abraham—a promise that extends to the nations (εἰς τὰ ἔθνη) in Christ Jesus (ἐν Χριστῷ Ἰησοῦ, Gal 3:14) and makes them Abraham's sons and heirs of the land (Gal 4:6–7).[14]

9. All Greek NT citations are from the NA 28.

10. Hays rightly explains that the "hermeneutical function of the Spirit is to generate an inspired reading that discloses the secret truth to which the story of Abraham points: God will grant the eschatological Spirit to a community of gentiles, who will thereby become recognizable as Abraham's true offspring" (*Echoes*, 111). I would add that the eschatological Spirit is also given to believing Jews, so that people from all nations might become members of Abraham's family, fulfilling the promise of universal blessing.

11. Schreiner, *Galatians*, 218.

12. Hebrew citations are from the *BHS*.

13. LXX Genesis citations are from Wevers, *Genesis*. The parallelism above is also noted by Motyer (*Isaiah*, 276). The LXX also parallels these phrases.
ἐπιθήσω τὸ πνεῦμά μου ἐπὶ τὸ σπέρμα σου
καὶ τὰς εὐλογίας μου ἐπὶ τὰ τέκνα σου.

14. Hodge argues that Paul employs Genesis passages, such as 15:3–6, to support his argument in two ways: "First, they provide a scriptural warrant for globalizing God's blessings. Each one envisions the blessings of more peoples than just Israel; God's blessings go to non-Jews as well. As we know from Galatians 3:8, Paul considers this to be

After concluding his discussion about the promised blessing, Paul shifts his attention to the inheritance in Galatians 3:15–18. The inheritance, like the blessing, is a promise of the Abrahamic covenant (Gen 12:1–3; 15:1–21). So, Paul transitions from one Abrahamic covenant promise in 3:13–14 to another in 3:15–18. He does so by employing the vocative Ἀδελφοί at the inception of 3:15 (as he does elsewhere, 1:11; 4:12, 5:13, 6:1) to indicate the beginning of a new section.[15] The use of the vocative specifies a transition from the discussion about the blessing of the Spirit in 3:13–14 to a new, but related, topic—the inheritance in 3:15–18.

At the inception of this new discussion, Paul introduces an illustration from everyday life (κατὰ ἄνθρωπον λέγω)[16] to convey that what is true even (ὅμως)[17] in the case of a human covenant (διαθήκη) is all the more true of the covenant (διαθήκη) God gave to Abraham (cf. Gal 3:17).[18] Therefore,

---

the gospel: through Christ, gentiles can receive God's blessings. Second, these passages explain how people are included: they are 'in' Abraham the way that descendants are in the seed of their ancestors. Galatians 3:7 explicitly defines the sons of Abraham" (*If Sons, Then Heirs*, 99). Dunn provides valuable insight into how zealous some Jews would have been to preserve boundary distinctions that Christ has now obliterated: "The metaphor [of being shut-out or excluded] is thus very well suited to describe the typical attitude of the Jewish zealot—that is, the burning desire to defend Israel's distinctiveness by drawing the boundary line sharply and clearly between the people of the covenant so as to exclude those not belonging to Israel; or, in particular, of the Jewish Christian zealot—to exclude all Gentiles other than proselytes from Christ, the Jewish Messiah, and from the eschatological community of his people" ("Echoes of Intra-Jewish Polemic in Galatians," 475).

15. Longenecker, *Galatians*, 126.

16. Although Paul sometimes uses the saying κατὰ ἄνθρωπον λέγω in reference to human authority (e.g., 1 Cor 9:18) or even the difference in authority between himself and Christ (e.g., 1 Cor 7:12), no such suggestion appears to be implied in Gal 3:15–18 (Burton, *Galatians*, 178). Rather, the framework of the passage supports the idea that he will now introduce an example from everyday life (Longenecker, *Galatians*, 127; Schreiner, *Galatians*, 226).

17. The particle ὅμως may also be translated as "likewise." Though this interpretation is possible, the context seems to indicate that Paul's argument in 3:15 is from the lesser to the greater. As such, the more suitable translation is "even." See discussions in BDAG, 710; Bruce, *Galatians*, 169; Schreiner, *Galatians*, 226.

18. Some scholars believe διαθήκη should be translated as "will/testament" in 3:15, rather than covenant, based on three main reasons. (1) The noun διαθήκη is commonly understood as a "will/testament" in Classical literature (e.g., Plato, *Laws* 923c–d). (2) Since Paul uses a human analogy (Ἀδελφοί, κατὰ ἄνθρωπον λέγω), διαθήκη should be understood as having a secular sense, rather than its distinctly biblical sense of covenant (Betz, *Galatians*, 154–55; Matera, *Galatians*,126; Behm and Quell, "διαθήκη," 2:128). (3) There is familiar legal terminology associated with a last "will and testament" in Gal 3:15. In particular, Paul's use of the verb ἀθετέω, which refers to "the annulling of a will" (LSJ, 31), and ἐπιδιατάσσομαι, which refers to "the adding of a codicil" (BDAG, 370). Nevertheless, those who contend that διαθήκη should be understood as "covenant"

even if a common, human covenant cannot be "annulled" (ἀθετέω) or "supplemented" (ἐπιδιατάσσομαι, Gal 3:15) once it has been "ratified" (κυρόω), how much more in the case of the Abrahamic covenant (Gal 3:17)?[19] The covenant that God made with Abraham cannot be invalidated or supplemented by any means.

Galatians 3:16 then states that "the promises were spoken to Abraham and to his seed" (τῷ δὲ Ἀβραὰμ ἐρρέθησαν αἱ ἐπαγγελίαι καὶ τῷ σπέρματι αὐτοῦ). The content of the "promises" (ἐπαγγελίαι) is apparent in the remainder of the verse. As noted, Paul discusses the promise of blessing in Galatians 3:13–14 and then transitions to another promise of the Abrahamic covenant, the inheritance, in 3:15–18. In spite of this observation, many scholars claim that the blessing in 3:13–14 is also the content of the promise in 3:15–18.[20] Not only does such an interpretation ignore the beginning of a new section in 3:15, but it also disregards the citation in 3:16, which sets the tone for the remainder of the chapter.[21]

---

have the weight of the evidence in their favor. (1) Just because Paul introduces an illustration from everyday life does not mean that διαθήκη must be understood as "will/testament." Paul makes an argument from the lesser to the greater, i.e., what is true of a lesser "covenant" (Gal 3:15) is all the more the case with a greater one (Gal 3:17; Schreiner, *Galatians*, 226; Hahn, "Covenant, Oath, and the Aqedah," 88). Legal terminology may be used with both "wills/testaments" and "covenants" (Hahn, "Covenant, Oath, and the Aqedah," 87; Schreiner, *Galatians*, 227). So, the legal terms ἀθετέω and ἐπιδιατάσσομαι do not restrict the sense of διαθήκη to a secular "will." (3) Paul, like the LXX, consistently employs διαθήκη with the sense of "covenant" (Hahn, "Covenant, Oath, and the Aqedah," 80–81; Behm and Quell, "διαθήκη," 2:107; see Rom 9:4; 11:27; 1 Cor 11:25; Gal 3:17; 4:24; Eph 4:12). (4) As opposed to a "testament," there are several examples in the OT where a "covenant" between persons was considered to be indissoluble, as in Gal 3:15 and 18 (Schreiner, *Galatians*, 227; see Gen 21:22–32; 26:26–31; 31:44–45; 1 Sam 18:3; 20:8; 22:8; 23:18; 2 Sam 3:12). (5) Since Gal 3:17 refers to the Abrahamic covenant, the context seems to indicate that διαθήκη in 3:15 should be rendered as "covenant" (ibid.). While it is possible that Paul moves from an idea of "will/testament" in 3:15 to a "covenant" in 3:17, "it is more likely that he retains the same term throughout, instead of requiring his readers to switch back and forth between 'will' and 'covenant'" (ibid.). These arguments suggest that there is more warrant for rendering διαθήκη in Gal 3:15 as "covenant" rather than "will/testament." See also the discussion in Wright, *Climax of the Covenant*, 137–67.

19. Schreiner (*Galatians*, 226) and Longenecker (*Galatians*, 126–27) note that Paul is employing an argument from the lesser to the greater.

20. Bruce, *Galatians*, 171–73; Fung, *Galatians*, 155, 165; Johnson, "Once in Custody," 211; Matera, *Galatians*, 126; Betz, *Galatians*, 156; Burton, *Galatians*, 180–211; Williams, "Promise in Galatians," 709–20.

21. Schreiner, citing Burton, claims that the "promises" in Gal 3:16 "encompass the totality of the promises made to Abraham" (*Galatians*, 228). This claim, however, is not valid, given that Paul specifically focuses on the promise of land in Gal 3:15–18, as indicated by the new section and, as will be argued, the citation from Genesis land passages.

Paul introduces the citation with the following statement: "It does not say" (οὐ λέγει).[22] The words that he then quotes are καὶ τῷ σπέρματί σου, which he takes verbatim from LXX passages in Genesis that assert the land is promised to Abraham's offspring.[23] The LXX embeds this citation throughout Genesis whenever the promise of a land inheritance is made to the descendants of Abraham (e.g., 12:7, 15:18, 13:15, 17:8, 24:7).[24] Genesis 13:15, 17:8, and 24:7 illustrate this point:

> Gen 13:15: πᾶσαν τὴν γῆν, ἣν σὺ ὁρᾷς, σοὶ δώσω αὐτὴν καὶ τῷ σπέρματί σου
>
> Gen 17:8: καὶ δώσω σοι καὶ τῷ σπέρματί σου μετὰ σὲ τὴν γῆν
>
> Gen 24:7: κύριος ὁ θεὸς τοῦ οὐρανοῦ καὶ ὁ θεὸς τῆς γῆς . . . ὤμοσέν μοι λέγων Σοὶ δώσω τὴν γῆν ταύτην καὶ τῷ σπέρματί σου

In each of these passages, the words καὶ τῷ σπέρματί σου are used when the land inheritance is sworn to Abraham's offspring. The context of these passages makes this assertion indisputable. As well, since the words καὶ τῷ σπέρματί σου strongly allude to the promise of land in Genesis, Paul's quotation is deeply rooted in this intertextual tradition. So, unless he states otherwise (and he does not), his use of the phrase καὶ τῷ σπέρματί σου follows an established OT pattern that points to the land promised to Abraham's offspring.[25]

22. Longenecker argues that God is the implied subject of the verb λέγει (*Galatians*, 131). Bruce notes that it is also possible for ἡ γραφή to be the subject of the verb (*Galatians*, 172). While these are possible options, it is best to take the cited passage as the subject of λέγει, since Paul both quotes and explains the verbatim citation from Genesis. Paul is claiming, "The cited Scripture does not say." See Acts 13:35, for another example of a cited passage as the subject of the verb λέγει.

23. Hong, *Law in Galatians*, 132; Kwon, *Eschatology in Galatians*, 105–7. Although this point is acknowledged by Bruce (*Galatians*, 171–72), Dunn (*Galatians*, 185) and Betz (*Galatians*, 157) they still equate the promise of blessing in 3:1–14 with the promise in 3:15–29. See chap. 3 for a discussion of the intertextual use of καὶ τῷ σπέρματί σου in Genesis.

24. The LXX uses τῷ σπέρματί ὑμῶν elsewhere in the Pentateuch (e.g., Exod 33:1; Deut 34:4) to indicate when the land is promised to God's people.

25. Daube notes two further points of evidence for the promise in 3:15–18 being the inheritance of land: (1) "It was in connection with the promise of land that the Rabbis resorted to an interpretation of seed "with which Paul's has much in common," and (2) it was with regard to the promise of land that the Rabbis developed chronological speculations" (*New Testament and Rabbinic Judaism*, 438–39). See also Kwon, *Eschatology in Galatians*, 106. Foreman argues against a spiritualized inheritance in Galatians (*Politics of Inheritance*, 172–95). Davies argues that Paul completely ignores the territorial promise (*Gospel and Land*, 178–99).

Earlier, I noted that W. D. Davies is one of the strongest opponents against seeing any trace of land in Paul's letters. Despite his view, Davies contends that Paul struggles with the idea of a "territory" for God's people. In his own words: "Such a Jew as Paul, we can be sure, would have *felt* the full force of the doctrine of land . . . His epistles might be expected to reveal how he came to terms with it."[26] I agree that Paul struggles with the promise of land. However, I disagree with how Davies believes that Paul "comes to terms with it." Per Davies, in Galatians "we can be fairly certain that Paul did not merely ignore the territorial aspect of the promise . . . his silence points not merely to the absence of a conscience concern with it, but to his deliberate rejection of it. His interpretation of the promise is a-territorial."[27] His justification rests on the following: "Because the logic of Paul's understanding of Abraham and his personalization of the fulfillment of the promise 'in Christ' demanded the deterritorializing of the promise."[28] Davies fails to prove how the land has lost any sense of territory for those "in Christ"—for he does not seriously interact with Paul's intertextual citation of the Genesis land promises in Galatians 3:16, explaining them away as already realized for Christians. Rather than deterritorializing the promise, in this section I will show that Paul argues that being "in Christ" makes believers fellow heirs of the territory promised to Abraham. Thus, Paul does not break with, nor transform, centuries of Jewish tradition.

That said, we may now proceed to a comparison of the Abrahamic promises of land and blessing. It is my contention that the land and the blessing should neither be confused nor merged into one singular promise, for Paul follows a different intertextual pattern in discussing each of these promises. Having already examined the inheritance, I now examine the intertextual pattern pertaining to the blessing in Genesis 22:18 and Sirach 44:21. Genesis 22:18 states, "All the nations of the earth will be blessed ἐν τῷ σπέρματί σου" (cf. Gen 26:4). Sirach 44:21 says, "Because of this, he [the Lord] assured him with an oath that the nations would be blessed ἐν τῷ σπέρματί σου."[29] In these passages, the prepositional phrase ἐν τῷ σπέρματί affirms that the promise of blessing would come to the nations "in Abraham's seed."[30]

Galatians 3:14, which also speaks of the promised blessing, says that "the blessing of Abraham" (i.e., the Spirit) comes "to the gentiles ἐν Χριστῷ

---

26. Davies, *Gospel and Land*, 166.

27. Ibid., 178–79.

28. Ibid., 179.

29. LXX Sirach citations are from Ziegler, *Sapientia Iesu Filii Sirach*.

30. The preposition ἐν carries a sense of "means" in these passages.

Ἰησοῦ." The prepositional phrase ἐν Χριστῷ Ἰησοῦ corresponds to ἐν σπέρματι in Genesis 22:18 and Sirach 44:21, in that it clarifies the one through whom the blessing comes. This notion is also witnessed below:

> Gen 22:18: καὶ ἐνευλογηθήσονται ἐν τῷ σπέρματί σου πάντα τὰ ἔθνη τῆς γῆς

> Sir 44:21: διὰ τοῦτο ἐν ὅρκῳ ἔστησεν αὐτῷ ἐνευλογηθῆναι ἔθνη ἐν σπέρματι αὐτοῦ

> Gal 3:14: ἵνα εἰς τὰ ἔθνη ἡ εὐλογία τοῦ Ἀβραὰμ γένηται ἐν Χριστῷ Ἰησοῦ

Beyond evidencing that ἐν Χριστῷ Ἰησοῦ in Galatians 3:16 corresponds to ἐν σπέρματι in Genesis 22:18 and Sirach 44:21, it appears that Paul employs the former phrase in place of the latter to specify that the one through whom the blessing of the Holy Spirit comes to the nations is "Christ Jesus."[31]

In view of these observations, the quotation of the phrase καὶ τῷ σπέρματί σου in Galatians 3:16, rather than prepositional phrases ἐν σπέρματι (Gen 22:18; Sir 44:21) or ἐν Χριστῷ Ἰησοῦ (Gal 3:15), strongly suggests that the land is in view in 3:15–18. This verbatim citation, along with the new section in 3:15, points to the fact that Paul transitions from the promise of blessing in 3:13–14 to the promise of a land inheritance in 3:15–18. As a result, the plural term "promises" (3:16) points to the various occasions in which the land was sworn to Abraham's offspring (Gen12:7; 13:15; 15:18; 26:3; 28:13–15; 35:9–12; 46:4; cf. *Pss.Sol.* 12:6).

Following his citation, Paul narrows the offspring of Abraham and the heir of the promises of land to one individual, "Christ" (Χριστός). This maneuver echoes 2 Samuel 7:12–14 and Psalm 2:6–8. Second Samuel 7:12–14 limits the "seed" (σπέρμα)[32] of David, who will reign over the land, to God's son. Since David is Abraham's descendent (e.g., Ps 89:3–4; Matt 1:1–6),[33] his royal offspring is also the "seed" of Abraham.[34] Similarly, Psalm 2:6–8 narrows the heir of the land to one individual, God's kingly son. The notions of kingship and sonship in this passage imply that, like 2 Samuel 7:12–14, God's royal son is ultimately the descendent of Abraham. The fact that both 2 Samuel 7:10–12 and Psalm 2:6–8 narrow the heir of the land to God's son,

31. Dahl claims that "the expression 'the blessing of Abraham' derives from Gen. 28:4, and 'in Christ Jesus' replaces 'in your offspring'" (*Studies in Paul*, 131).

32. LXX Samuel citations are from Rahlfs, *Septuaginta*.

33. Dunn argues that the link between the offspring of David and the offspring of Abraham is suggested in Ps 89:3–4 (*Galatians*, 184).

34. Hays argues that Paul's dependence on 2 Sam 7:12–14 permits him to interpret Abraham's seed as the Messiah (*Echoes*, 85). See also Schreiner, *Galatians*, 229. See also Hamilton, "Skull-Crushing Seed of the Woman," 30–54.

Abraham's offspring, provides valid warrant for claiming that Paul alludes to these passages.[35] This is especially evident in his employment of the parenthetical nominative phrase ὅς ἐστιν Χριστός to qualify the "seed" (σπέρμα) of Abraham as "Christ."[36]

Paul's use of the term Χριστός has an added significance. The LXX uses Χριστός to translate the Hebrew noun מָשִׁיחַ (e.g., Lev 4:3, 5, 16), meaning "Messiah."[37] The Messiah is the anticipated Davidic king who will rule over Israel in the coming age (e.g., Num 24:17–19; 2 Sam 2:5; Dan 9:25–26; Rev 20–22).[38] Confirmation that such an event will take place in the future is found in the royal Psalms (e.g., Ps 2, 20, 21, 28, 45, 72, 89, 101).[39] Several texts at Qumran even assert that God's royal son in 2 Samuel 7 and Psalm 2—the very texts that Paul is echoing in Galatians 3:16—is the anticipated Messiah (e.g., 4QDibHam [=4Q504] 3:4–7; 4Q246 2:1).[40] As well, 4 Ezra states that God's messianic son (7:28–29) "will arise from the line of David" (12:32).[41] Lastly, the Psalms of Solomon expresses the expectation that David's son will become king and restore the fortunes of Israel (17:21–46). Verse 32 of this passage states that "their king shall be Christ the Lord (χριστὸς κύριος)."[42] Against this background, Paul's use of Χριστός also alludes to the messianic

---

35. On the messianic interpretation of 2 Sam 7 and Ps 2, see Wilcox, "Promise of the 'Seed,'" 269–305; Duling, "Promises to David," 55–77. Both articles show that 2 Sam 7 and Ps 2 were interpreted messianically in Jewish texts. Hence, Paul's use of these passages in Galatians follows an already established tradition.

36. The parenthetical nominative primarily "explains" another clause or phrase. See Wallace, Greek Grammar, 54; Robertson, Grammar of the Greek New Testament, 433–35. This function is evident in Gal 3:16, in that the nominative phrase ὅς ἐστιν Χριστός explains the identity of the descendent of Abraham in the phrase καὶ τῷ σπέρματί σου. Here, it is also appropriate to note that Paul makes explicit that the land does not belong to ethnic Israel. In their examination of the covenants, Gentry and Wellum argue that the land promise of the Abrahamic covenant "does not find its fulfillment in the future in terms of a specific piece of real estate given to the ethnic nation of Israel; rather it is fulfilled in Jesus, who is the true Israel and last Adam, who by his triumphant work wins for us a new creation" (Kingdom through Covenant, 607).

37. See BDAG, 1091; Grundmann, Hesse, de Jonge, van der Woude, "χριστός," 9:493–580; Nolland, Matthew, 662–64.

38. Wright, Jesus and the Victory of God, 486–89. See 2 Sam 7; Ps 20:7; Isa 9:1–6; 11:1–9; Jer 30:9; 33:14–26, etc.

39. See Keesmaat, "Psalms in Romans and Galatians,"159–60, for the Messianic implications of Ps 89 in Gal 3:16.

40. Ibid., 485.

41. Noted in Nolland, Matthew, 663.

42. Ibid.

expectation of a king from David's lineage who will reign in the land (cf. 2 Sam 7, 23; Ps 2).[43]

What is more, the reverberation of Psalm 2:6–8 in Galatians 3:16 brings to light that the inheritance of Christ is the entire world. The reign of the Messiah will not be limited to the former borders of Canaan, for Psalm 2:8 declares that the nations are the Davidic king's "inheritance" (נַחֲלָה [MT]; κληρονομία [LXX]) and the ends of the earth are his "possession" (אֲחֻזָּה [MT]; κατάσχεσίς [LXX]). As a result, it is evident that Christ, the long awaited Davidic king, will rule over a worldwide inheritance. But, since Christ has yet to reign physically over the entire earth, the promise of an inheritance to Abraham's offspring has not been realized (neither partially nor fully).

Having made this point, it is important to return to the clause that introduces Paul's citation, οὐ λέγει. This clause is meant to clarify that the cited portion of Scripture, καὶ τῷ σπέρματί σου, does not refer to all ethnic Jews/Israelites—for, contrary to common Jewish thought, not all of Abraham's physical descendants are his "seed" (σπέρμα).[44] Paul refutes this customary Jewish understanding by stating that the cited Scripture does not say καὶ τοῖς σπέρμασιν, as if the promises of land were intended for "many" or a "multitude" (ὡς ἐπὶ πολλῶν) of offspring. Rather, he affirms that the cited passage states the promises are intended for "one single" (ὡς ἐφ᾽ ἑνός) seed, whom he identifies as Χριστός.[45]

---

43. One of the clearest passages in the NT that identifies Χριστός as the Son of God, i.e., the long-awaited Messiah, is found in Peter's proclamation of Jesus in Matt 16:16 (cf. 8:29, 14:33). Turner argues that Peter's proclamation echoes 2 Sam 7:10–12 and Ps 2:6–8 (*Matthew*, 404). Other possible echoes for Peter's confession are 1 Chr 17:13 and 89:27–29.

44. The collective, Jewish understanding of the offspring (σπέρμα) of Abraham may be seen in *Pss.Sol.* 9:15–19 and T Levi 15:4. Similarly, *Bib. Ant.* 7:4; *Jub* 16:17; 1 Macc 12:1–2. See also discussion in Hansen, *Abraham in Galatians*, 182–97. The collective sense of σπέρμα may even be evidenced in John 8:33, where the Jews say to Jesus: "We are the σπέρμα of Abraham and we have never been enslaved to anyone."

45. Wright seems to rely on the collective use of σπέρμα in 3:29 to argue that the singular σπέρμα in 3:16 is collective and refers to the idea that "in Christ all the people of God" are summed up into one family (*Climax of the Covenant*, 174). However, Das rightly notes that "the natural reading of the text is an emphatic singular in contrast to the plural (or collective) seed. . . . Wright proposes that Jesus is the Messiah who sums up all Israel in himself and thereby rescues the possibility of a collective 'seed' here. The reading seems entirely forced and depends on Wright's understanding of Jesus as Israel's Messiah in other Pauline texts. The crucial difference to Wright's theory is that he must read the text backward from Gal 3:29. On a sequential reading of the text, there is nothing to indicate a collective sense in 3:16. On the contrary, it is only in v. 29 that Christians are incorporated into the one seed" (*Paul, the Law, and the Covenant*, 73).

After having narrowed down the heir of Abraham, Galatians 3:17 concludes this passage.[46] The first part of the conclusion is that "the Law" (ὁ νόμος), which came 430 years later,[47] "does not annul the covenant previously ratified by God" (διαθήκην προκεκυρωμένην ὑπὸ τοῦ θεοῦ). The word διαθήκη undoubtedly refers to the "covenant" God made with Abraham (cf. Gen 12, 15, 17), which was "ratified before" (προκυρόω) the much later Mosaic Law (νόμος).[48] Many generations lived and died with the confidence that the terms of the Abrahamic covenant were irrevocable because the covenant had been confirmed by God. Given Paul's argument from the lesser to the greater (Gal 3:15, 17), such confidence is certainly warranted. If a human covenant cannot be altered, then it is all the truer of the covenant God made with Abraham.[49]

46. The repetition of the verb λέγω in 3:15 and 3:17 signals the inception and conclusion of the unit. Since 3:17 is a concluding statement, there are similar terms or concepts from 3:15–16 that are repeated in 3:17: διαθήκη (3:15, 17) and ἐπαγγελία (3:16, 17); κυρόω (3:15) and προκυρόω (3:17), with the temporal prefix προ- being added to the latter; and ἀθετέω (3:15) and ἀκυρόω (3:17), both of which, though different in form, carry the similar sense of "annul" or "nullify." So Longenecker, Galatians, 132–33. See also LSJ, 31–32, 59.

47. Given that Exod 12:40 notes that the period from Abraham to Moses was "430 years," the number of years of Israel's captivity in Egypt, and Gen 15:13 notes that the number of years in Egypt was "400 years," Paul's reference to the Law coming "430 years" after the Abrahamic Covenant is a bit perplexing. Longenecker argues that, though the Rabbis found the difference in time noted in Exod 12:40 and Gal 15:13 puzzling, they solved the apparent impasse "by taking the 430 years as the time between God's covenant with Abraham and Moses' reception of the Law and 400 years as the period Israel spent in Egypt" (Galatians, 133). He also states that Josephus "handles the time spans in much the same way: 400 years for Israel's sojourn in Egypt (Ant. 2. 2041; J.W. 5.382) and 430 years from Abraham's entrance into Canaan to Moses leading the people out of Egypt (Ant. 2.318)" (ibid.). Since this is the way the problem was normally solved, Longenecker concludes by asserting that Paul "is probably not relying on Exod 12:40 versus Gen 15:13, but only repeating the traditionally accepted number of years for the time span between the Abrahamic covenant and the Mosaic Law" (ibid.).

48. Though Paul does not specifically mention in 3:17 that νόμος is a reference to the Mosaic Law, the context of Gal 3 suggests that this word points to the Law established on Mt. Sinai "through angels" and "by the hand of a mediator" (3:19), i.e., the Mosaic Law (cf. 3:1–5, 15–29).

49. The chronology in Paul's thought is also noteworthy. Heitanen notes that in rabbinic circles "priority is equal to superiority" (Paul's Argument in Galatians, 123). That which comes first is therefore greater to that which comes later. Paul, in some sense, may be following this line of reasoning. As such, his chronological argument in 3:17 seems to reveal that since the covenant with Abraham came 430 years prior to the Law of Moses, the Abrahamic covenant is superior to the later Mosaic Law (Hahn, "Covenant, Oath, and Aqedah," 98). This gives further evidence that the covenant given to Abraham cannot be negated by the later, inferior Mosaic Law. Similarly, Schnelle argues: "The temporal distance of 430 years between the promise to Abraham and the

The final part of the conclusion is found in the clause εἰς τὸ καταργῆσαι τὴν ἐπαγγελίαν (3:17). The construction εἰς τὸ καταργῆσαι may carry the sense of "purpose" or "result." The framework of Galatians 3:15–17 suggests that it is best to read it as a result clause: The Mosaic Law does not make void the previously ratified Abrahamic covenant "with the result that it nullifies (καταργέω) the promised inheritance." Moreover, the power to "nullify" is a matter reserved for God.[50] He is the one who "nullifies" the things that exist (1 Cor 1:28) and "nullified" the Law of commandments in decrees (Eph 2:15). No other person or entity is capable of this activity. Since God's covenant with Abraham is irrevocable, and he is the only one who exercises the power to "nullify," the later Mosaic Law cannot invalidate the promise of a cosmic inheritance to Abraham's offspring.

Subsequently, Galatians 3:18 explains further (γάρ) the concluding remarks in 3:17. This verse affirms that the κληρονομία cannot be obtained by observing the Law's demands.[51] I noted in chapter four that κληρονομία is one of three words the LXX uses to translate inheritance related terms in the OT, the others being κληρονομέω and κληρονόμος. When the LXX uses κληρονομία, it mainly employs this term to translate the word נַחֲלָה, which refers to the "land inheritance" of Israel. The context of Galatians 3, which has thus far asserted that the territorial inheritance is in view (v. 16), strongly suggests that Paul follows the use of κληρονομία in Jewish literature. The shift to another sense for this term is unwarranted and illogical for Paul's argument. Thus, Paul's use of κληρονομία specifies that the land inheritance remains in view.

As well, the echo of Psalm 2:6–8 in Galatians 3:16 asserts that the term κληρονομία points to a worldwide inheritance. No longer is the inheritance of Abraham's offspring confined to the borders of Canaan, for this concept has been enlarged to include the entire earth. And since God has "freely given" (κεχάρισται) the cosmic inheritance "to Abraham through the promise"

---

giving of the Law shows the objective priority of the promise (3:17), which is fulfilled in the one true offspring (seed) of Abraham: Jesus Christ (3:16)" (*Apostle Paul*, 287).

50. Hübner, "καταργέω," 2:267. See also discussion in BDAG, 525–26.

51. Keesmaat insightfully points out that "within the Israelite story law is closely connected to the inheritance. . . . In the face of such an expectation, disobedience to the law has wide-ranging implications. If one did not obey the law one was threatening the coming of the new exodus; one was jeopardizing the salvation of the people of Israel. . . . Paul's emphasis on what sort of actions result in inheritance would have countered the argument that obedience to Torah results in the inheritance of land. Paul emphasizes that those who do the works of the flesh . . . are the ones who will not receive the inheritance" (*Paul and His Story*, 191–92).

(τῷ δὲ Ἀβραὰμ δι᾽ ἐπαγγελίας) (3:18),[52] it may not be earned by keeping the Law's requirements.

In sum, Paul's argument in Galatians 3:15–18 does not confuse the promise of inheritance with that of blessing. Nor does it deterritorialize the promise for those "in Christ." On the contrary, "in Christ"—Christ being the direct heir of the (now cosmically expanded) promise to Abraham—the land inheritance is clarified as a gift that may be bestowed or granted.[53] But, since Christ has yet to reign physically over the earth, the realization of the inheritance is still forthcoming.[54] The focus on the inheritance in 3:15–18 sets the tone for the remainder of chapter 3, which will continue to draw attention to this promise and show how all those who are "in Christ" are fellow-heirs of the world.

GALATIANS 3:19–29: FELLOW-HEIRS OF THE WORLD

Paul begins this section by contending that the Law remained in force until the "one for whom the promise was reserved" (ἄχρις οὗ ἔλθῃ τὸ σπέρμα ᾧ ἐπήγγελται)[55] arrived on the scene (Gal 3:19). Since Christ is the promised heir (Gal 3:16), his coming brought the Law's rule to an end. The fact that Christ originally came to the unredeemed earth suggests that he has not yet received his inheritance. Passages such as 2 Samuel 7 and Psalm 2, which will be fulfilled in Revelation 21–22, point to a time when the curse of sin will be lifted and Christ will rule physically over a redeemed earth. Such a time will not come about until, as Daniel 7:13 claims, the Son of Man comes on the clouds to receive his everlasting dominion. So, although Christ is "already" reigning at the right hand of God (Mark 16:9; Acts 7:55), he has yet to rule over an earthly inheritance.[56] This sense of the inheritance, as I will contend in the following chapter, is consistent with Paul's argument in

52. The particle δέ indicates that Paul builds the present clause upon what precedes. See discussion in Runge, *Discourse Grammar*, 28–36. Also, the context indicates that the implied noun κληρονομίαν is the direct object of the verb κεχάρισται. See BDAG, 1078.

53. For an exceptional study of gift in Paul's theology, see Barclay, *Paul & the Gift*.

54. Kwon makes the point that, in Gal 3:15–18, fulfillment is not in the mind of Paul, "since his purpose in bringing in Abraham is only to establish the temporal precedence of the hopelessly 'late' Law" (*Eschatology in Galatians*, 117–22).

55. I am following the translation of Baugh ("Galatians 3:20," 59).

56. I want to affirm that I do see an already-not-yet tension in the reign of Christ. Christ is "already" reigning, but he is "not yet" reigning physically on the earth. The inheritance is the fulfillment of the earthly reign of Christ, i.e., the "not yet" aspect of the kingdom.

Romans 4:13–25 and 8:14–25, in which he envisions the inheritance of the future eschatological world, and is also in line with passages such as 2 Peter 3:13, in which the inheritance is envisioned to be the new heavens and new earth (cf. Isa 65–66). Thus, Christ's reign over the coming world will signal the realization of the promised inheritance to Abraham's offspring.

With this in mind, in Galatians 3:21 Paul asks whether the Law (νόμος)[57] stands in opposition to the promises (κατὰ τῶν ἐπαγγελιῶν, Gal 3:21). The term ἐπαγγελία refers to the land inheritance promises mentioned in Galatians 3:15–18, for the conjunction οὖν signifies that the present discussion in 3:21 is in continuity with 3:15–20.[58] Since there is no mention of other promises in 3:21–29, ἐπαγγελία continues to point to the territorial inheritance sworn to Abraham and his offspring.

The reason why (γάρ) the Law is not contrary to the promises of land is found in the remainder of Galatians 3:21: "If a Law (νόμος) which was able to grant life (ζωοποιῆσαι) was given, then righteousness (δικαιοσύνη) would certainly be from the Law (ἐκ νόμου)."[59] James Dunn argues that the verb ζωοποιέω "almost always denotes a work exclusive to God" (Neh 9:6; Rom 4:17; 1 Cor 15:22) or "to his Spirit" (John 6:63; Rom 8:11; 1 Pet 3:18).[60] So, it seems that Paul utilizes the verb ζωοποιέω to stress the reality that the Law does not have the ability to give life—only God has this capacity.[61] And since the Law does not have this power, neither can it bestow righteousness.

The inheritance, on the other hand, does lead to life and righteousness. The OT witnesses that the recipients of the inheritance will experience life in the coming world (Isa 65–66; cf. 57:13, 58:14; cf. *Pss.Sol.* 14:10) by way of the resurrection (Isa 26:15; 27:6; Ezek 36–37). The NT affirms that the beneficiaries of the promised inheritance will possess life in the world to come (Heb 11:10, 13–16; 2 Pet 3:13; Rev 21–22). As well, the OT and NT show that the heirs of the coming world will dwell in righteousness (Isa 54:17; 60:21; Rom 4:13–25, 8; 2 Pet 3:13; cf. *1 En.* 24–27, 58–69; *4 Ezra* 7–8;

---

57. Given the strong continuity with Gal 3:15–20, νόμος in 3:20 also refers to the Mosaic Law.

58. See discussion in Runge, *Discourse Grammar*, 43–44.

59. The anarthrous noun νόμος is still a reference to the Jewish Law/Torah. Betz, *Galatians*, 174.

60. Dunn, *Galatians*, 192–93.

61. This line of argument denies the Jewish correlation between the Law and life, which is evidenced in the following examples: *t. Shabb.* 15:17: "The commands were given only that men should live through them, not that men should die through them"; and Sir 17:11: "He bestowed knowledge upon them, and allotted to them the Law of life."

2 *Bar.* 14, 51; 4Q171 4).[62] Such evidence displays that the reception of the promised inheritance leads to life and righteousness in the coming world. Keeping the Law does not lead to either of these eschatological benefits.

Having made this point, it is now appropriate to determine whether Paul has proven that the Law is not opposed to the promises. The implication of his argument is that if the Law was a source of life and righteousness, "then it would certainly be in competition with the promises, and a fundamental antithesis would exist between the two."[63] But, the point is that it is not a source of life and righteousness; thereby, it is not in contradiction to the promises. Only the beneficiaries of the promised inheritance will experience these benefits. The Law was never intended to grant the benefits that God will bestow on the recipients of the inheritance.

Furthermore, the way to become a beneficiary of the promised inheritance (ἡ ἐπαγγελία)[64] is "by faith in Jesus Christ" (ἐκ πίστεως Ἰησοῦ Χριστοῦ, Gal 3:21).[65] In support of this notion, the remainder of Galatians 3 testifies

62. This is further substantiated by the fact that the verdict of righteousness is a fundamentally eschatological event. See Gal 2:17; 5:5. Schreiner says that "justification is God's end-time pronouncement that those who trust in Christ rather than in themselves are declared to be not guilty" (*Galatians*, 391).

63. Silva, *Explorations in Exegetical Method*, 188.

64. Some scholars think that the promise here entails the blessing of the spirit and righteousness (Fung, *Galatians*, 155; see also Betz, *Galatians*, 175; Bruce, *Galatians*, 180; Longenecker, *Galatians*, 144; Dunn, *Galatians*, 194). Against this argument, the context of 3:15–29 clarifies that Paul has the promise of inheritance in mind.

65. An extensive discussion of the πίστεως Χριστοῦ debate is beyond the scope of this work. I will, however, offer a concise treatment of the subjective and objective genitive interpretations of πίστεως Ἰησοῦ Χριστοῦ in Gal 3:21. Scholars who prefer the subjective interpretation argue that this phrase refers to "the faithfulness of Jesus Christ" (Wallace, *Greek Grammar*, 116; Hays, *Faith of Jesus Christ*, 1–208), generally maintaining that the phrase is a reference to Jesus' faithfulness to give his life on the cross. Some even take this as evidence of his covenant faithfulness which rectified the unfaithfulness of Israel (Wright, *Justification*, 122–36). A reference to Christ's self-giving death—whether one decides to draw out the covenantal implications or not—seems to make theological sense and may even be seen as the equivalent to Gal 1:4: "who gave himself for our sins in order that he might deliver us from this present evil age, according to the will of God our Father" (Dunn, *Galatians*, 195). As well, subjective genitive proponents maintain that the substantival participle τοῖς πιστεύουσιν communicates the need for faith (Wright, *Justification*, 122–36). This idea may be represented in the following manner: "the promise, by means of Jesus' faithfulness, is given to those who believe," avoiding the sense of redundancy that may be noted in the objective genitive reading—"the promise, by means of faith in Jesus Christ, is given to those who believe"—which makes two references to faith in the same sentence.

Scholars who favor the objective interpretation take πίστεως Ἰησοῦ Χριστοῦ to refer to "faith in Jesus Christ" (Dunn, *Galatians*, 195; Fung, *Galatians*, 164–65; Betz, *Galatians*, 175), taking this phrase to be a reference to faith in the death and resurrection of Christ. Such a reading seems to be in line with Paul's emphasis on the significance of faith in

that believers are now "sons of God" (υἱοὶ θεοῦ) and recipients of the promise "through faith in Christ Jesus" (διὰ τῆς πίστεως ἐν Χριστῷ Ἰησοῦ, 3:26).[66] Being united with him by faith, believers also belong to Christ (ὑμεῖς Χριστοῦ) and are counted as the "seed of Abraham" (τοῦ Ἀβραὰμ σπέρμα) and "heirs in accord with the promise" (κατ᾽ ἐπαγγελίαν κληρονόμοι, Gal 3:29).[67] Thus, it is through Christ, the original successor of the promised inheritance (3:16), that people become members of Abraham's family and fellow-heirs. Importantly, Paul does not deterritorialize the promise; he simply clarifies that those "in Christ" will also receive an inheritance. Although they have yet to receive the promise, the heirs anticipate the day when they will possess the future world (e.g., 1 Cor 15:50–57; Rev 20–22).[68]

Christ as opposed to observance of the Law in 3:21–29 (Schreiner, *Galatians*, 244). In addition, those who argue for an objective genitive reading claim that the participle τοῖς πιστεύουσιν—after Paul has already noted the need for faith in Christ in the phrase πίστεως Ἰησοῦ Χριστοῦ—serves to emphasize that the promise is obtained by faith in Christ, not by the Law. Such repetition was not uncommon to Greek writers. Authors from the Homeric to the Hellenistic period used repetition as a valuable rhetorical device for the sake of emphasis (see Pickering, "Did the Greek Ear Detect,"490–99; Easterling, "Repetition in Sophocles," 14–34). Hence, Paul's reiteration of terms would have been recognized by a Greek speaker as an attempt to accentuate his point—the importance of faith in Christ.

Of the two readings, the objective genitive is the best option, for Paul, in Gal 3:21–22, desires to emphasize faith in Christ as the means by which one receives the inheritance. This is evidenced in the way he employs repetition to stress his point. Those who are inclined to reject the objective reading on account of linguistic redundancy miss the point of Paul's rhetorical style. For an overview of the πίστις Χριστοῦ debate, see Hays ("ΠΙΣΤΙΣ and Pauline Theology," 35–60); Dunn ("Once More πίστις Χριστοῦ," 61–81).

66. Schreiner, *Galatians*, 256. In the OT, the designation "sons of God" belonged to Israel. It was the title that marked them out as God's chosen and elect people. So Matera, *Galatians*, 141, 145. See Exod 4:22–3; Deut 14:1–2; Hos 11:1; Jer 9:11; Mal 1:6. Now with the arrival of Christ, Paul makes it clear that this title is the prerogative of all those who have obtained the promise through faith in Christ—both Jew and gentile. Regarding the inheritance in Gal 3:29, Hodge states: "What, exactly, the gentiles stand to inherit, Paul does not explicitly say" (*If Sons, Then Heirs*, 70). She makes this comment without interacting extensively with Gal 3:15–18. From these verses, I have already argued that the inheritance is the cosmically expanded land. Thus, we can assume that Paul intends for the term κληρονομία to continue to carry this expectation.

67. See Kwon, *Eschatology in Galatians*, 125–27. Engberg-Pedersen provides an insightful discussion on the Galatians now being sons of God at the consummation of the Christ event and the implications of locating one's identity outside of the individual self, something one shares with others, i.e., fellow-members in Christ (*Paul and the Stoics*, 149–51).

68. In view of my analysis of Gal 3:15–29, I highlight Hodge's valuable insight on kinship and ethnicity structures in the mind of Paul. She argues that "ethnicity and kinship are crucial to Paul's understanding of the relationship between the God of Israel and humans. He deploys this language when describing how people become God's in the first place. The discourse of peoplehood and birth work well as models for this

As in Galatians 3:16, the influence of Psalm 2 is evident, except that in this case it is even stronger. Psalm 2 asserts that God's son, the Davidic king, will inherit the entire earth (Ps 2:6–8).[69] It also affirms that those who refuse to honor God's kingly son will perish, while those who seek refuge "in him" (בוֹ [MT]; ἐπ᾽ αὐτῷ [LXX]) will be blessed. This verse thereby suggests that those who fail to honor the Davidic king will be destroyed and will have no prospect of living under his rule. Similarly, Galatians 3:22–29 insinuates that those who reject Christ, the long awaited Davidic king, will not inherit the world.

This idea is clarified further by comparing the language of the Psalmist and Paul. The Psalmist speaks of finding refuge "in him" (בוֹ [MT]; ἐπ᾽ αὐτῷ [LXX]), that is, the king, in Psalm 2:12. Since both the king in Psalm 2:12 and Christ Jesus in Galatians 3:26 and 28 are the same person—the long awaited Davidic ruler—the words בוֹ in the former passage and ἐν Χριστῷ Ἰησοῦ in the latter bring to light that the hope of inheriting the world is found only by trusting "in King Jesus." So, although Paul does not directly quote from Psalm 2, his words reverberate with those of this passage.

Additionally, the echo of Psalm 2 strengthens the idea that Galatians 3:15–29 presents the inheritance as the world promised to God's son. Paul anticipates that Abraham's descendants will receive a worldwide inheritance. In the apostle's mind, those who place their faith in Christ Jesus, the king to whom honor is due, are the true heirs of the promise. Those who reject his rule have no hope of inheriting the earth.

In a similar vein of thought, Caroline Johnson Hodge draws on insights from Aristotle, Seneca, Philo, and the translators of the LXX to provide a patrilineal perspective on how being "in Christ" makes gentiles heirs of the promises to Abraham. She argues: "Christ, as the genuine descendent of Abraham, serves as a crucial link between the gentiles and Abraham. Being 'in' Christ enables them to be 'in' Abraham."[70] Though the gentiles were once outsiders to the covenant promises, "Paul uses 'in' language to rework parameters of kinship for the gentiles: by becoming a part of Christ and being 'in' Christ, gentiles become 'sons of God,' 'descendants of Abraham,' and 'heirs according to the promise.'"[71] Since being "in Christ" places them in Abraham's patriarchal lineage, the promises made to their ancestor

---

relationship in part because they are ascriptive. That is, you cannot achieve membership in God's people. You cannot earn it" (*If Sons, Then Heirs*, 147). See also the larger context of her argument on pp. 137–48.

69. Craigie contends that Ps 2 points to the Davidic king's world-wide rule in Revelation (*Psalms 1–50*, 68–69; e.g., 1:5; 12:5; 19:5, etc.).

70. Hodge, *If Sons, Then Heirs*, 103.

71. Ibid., 104.

have now been conferred upon the gentiles.[72] While I agree in principal with Hodge's argument, I believe it is too limited in scope. Paul's letter to the Galatians is not directed just to gentiles, but to *both* Jews and gentiles.[73] Viewed in this light, Galatians 3:29 clarifies that Christ makes it possible for *both* groups to be in Abraham's patrilineal heritage. Paul's "in Christ" language thereby represents the universal way for mankind to be Abraham's sons and heirs of what has been promised to his offspring.

Paul's argument in Galatians 3:15–29 shows that those "in Christ" will one day inherit the world promised to Abraham. Paul does not alter the tangible hope of an inheritance from the OT and Second Temple literature—for his frequent citations and allusions to these corpuses testify that he stands in continuity with Jewish tradition. Paul will now continue his inheritance argument in Galatians 4:1–7, using another story linked to the Abrahamic promises.

GALATIANS 4:1–7: EXODUS/NEW EXODUS TO THE INHERITANCE

Most commentators of Galatians 4:1–7 claim that the Greco-Roman legal custom of guardianship is the background to verses 1–2. Hanz Deiter Betz provides the best summary of this argument:

> The illustration itself is not without difficulties. Certainly it was taken from legal practices as it was known to Paul and his readers. Paul refers to the practice in Roman law called *tutela testamentaria* ("guardianship established by testament"). According to this institution the *paterfamilias* appoints one or more guardians for his children who are entitled to inherit his property after his death. During the period of time in which the heir (ὁ κληρονόμος) is a minor (νήπιός) he is potentially the legal owner (κύριος) of the inheritance, but he is for the time being prevented from disposing of it. Although he is legally (potentially) the owner of all, he appears not to be different from a

---

72. Ibid.

73. That Paul's letter to the Galatians is directed to Jews and gentiles is a popular view in Pauline scholarship. See Betz, *Galatians*, 24–33. While Hodge rejects this notion, it is hard to see how Galatians is only directed to gentiles. In my view, Paul is bent on refuting the false gospel of the Judaizers and reminding the gentiles—who are in danger of again succumbing to the yoke of the Law—that it is only through faith in Christ that they become sons of Abraham and beneficiaries of the promises. I concur with Betz: "What the Apostle has to say, he has to say to the whole of Christianity: Jew and gentile Christians, Paulinists and anti-Paulinists" (ibid., 24).

slave (οὐδὲν διαφέρει δούλου). To be sure, this comparison must be taken *cum granu salis*. The similarity between the minor and the slave is one of appearance only.[74]

Betz himself indicates that the analogy has its difficulties and should be taken with a grain of salt. Thus, if a better reading suits the context, it should be preferred.[75]

James M. Scott contends that Galatians 4:1–2 echoes the story of the exodus.[76] The exodus story encapsulates the period when the people of Israel were enslaved in Egypt, delivered from bondage, and then journeyed forty-years through the wilderness until they entered the land. Since the exodus story culminates with Israel's entry into the land (e.g., Exod 3:7–8), such a background fits well with Paul's inheritance argument in Galatians 3:15–4:7.

Being a Jew immersed in the OT, an appeal to the exodus tradition would not have been strange to Paul. As Sylvia Keesmaat notes,

> In the scriptural writings there is a tradition which links the promise to Abraham [the inheritance] with the exodus event. Notable texts are Exod. 2.24; 3.25–26; 6:2–9; and Ps. 105.42, where God declares that he will come to save the people because he has remembered his covenant with Abraham . . . These texts contributed heavily to the intertextual matrix upon which Paul was drawing.[77]

Keesmaat's explanation shows that it is more likely that Galatians 4:1–2 echoes the exodus tradition, which culminates with the entrance into the land, than the Greco-Roman legal argument.

Another reason for acknowledging that Paul employs the story of the exodus is that it would have resonated with early Christian readers. While not directly commenting on Paul, Otto Piper's observations are worth noting:

> From Exodus the Primitive church inherited the idea that they were God's chosen people (for example, Rom. 9.25; II Cor. 6.16; Tit 2.14. . .), delivered from servitude (for example Acts 7.17, 34) and destined to inherit the earth as their kingdom (for example Matt. 5.5), but also that they were still in the wilderness

---

74. Betz, *Galatians*, 203. I first noted this citation in Morales ("Spirit and the Restoration of Israel," 160). See also Witherington, *Grace in Galatia*, 281–83.

75. I am following Morales (*Spirit and the Restoration of Israel*, 160).

76. Scott, *Adoption as Sons*, 121–86.

77. Keesmaat, *Paul and His Story*, 177.

(for example Acts 7.30, 36, 38, 42, 44; Heb. 3.7–11; Rev. 12.6, 14), migrating towards an unknown goal (for example Heb. 13.14), but unaware of the date at which they would reach it (for example Mark 13. 32–33; 1 Thess. 5.2).[78]

Indeed, Paul's readers would have viewed themselves as having been delivered from slavery under the Law and on a sojourn to the kingdom in the coming world. Otherwise said, they would have perceived themselves to be on a new exodus to the inheritance. Given this effect on Paul's readers, and the fact that the exodus story fits the inheritance argument in Galatians 3:15–4:7, Scott's exodus reading of Galatians 4:1–2 is preferable to the standard Greco-Roman legal interpretation found in the commentaries.[79]

Scott's analysis of Galatians 4:1–7 will provide the framework for examining this passage.[80] According to him, 4:1–2 follows Israel's original exodus tradition. This then sets up a parallel with the new exodus story in 4:3–7. The relationship between these verses is one of type and antitype.[81] This section will first analyze the original exodus in 4:1–2, followed by the new exodus in 4:3–7.

Galatians 4:1–2: The Original Exodus

The illustration in Galatians 4:1–2 is directly related to the preceding inheritance argument in 3:15–29.[82] The following reasons support this notion.

78. Piper, "Unchanging Promises," 15–16.

79. Like Betz, Hodge argues that Paul uses a Roman household metaphor in Gal 4:1–7 to show that gentiles have now been adopted as sons and are thus beneficiaries of an inheritance (*If Sons, Then Heirs*, 68–72). This is similar to the way a Roman male would adopt a son to become his heir. Longenecker also sees the household metaphor present in Gal 4:1–7 ("Pedagogical Nature," 53–61). While these studies are compelling, neither seems to fit the larger context of 3:15–4:7, in which heirs have been designated (3:15–29) who, as I will argue in this section, will receive what has been promised to them at the completion of the new exodus (4:1–7). Simply put, the exodus tradition provides a far better background for Paul's inheritance argument in Galatians.

Paul's use of the exodus motif is not unique to Galatians. We can see, for example, that in 1 Cor 10 Paul recalls that, after the Israelites were delivered from Egypt and crossed the Red Sea, the majority never entered the land because of disobedience. This was to serve as a warning for the Corinthians not to imitate the Israelites and suffer a similar fate. Oropeza, "Echoes of Isaiah in the Rhetoric of Paul," 87–112. As well, Wright argues that the exodus from the slavery of sin and subsequent sojourn to the promised land is the backdrop to Rom 3–8 ("New Exodus, New Inheritance," 26–35).

80. See Scott, *Adoption as Sons*, 145–93. I am following the summary of Scott in Keesmaat (*Paul and His Story*, 161–62).

81. Scott, *Adoption as Sons*, 161.

82. Kwon asserts that Gal 4:1–7 "confirms that Paul's emphasis on heirship is in

First, the development marker δέ signifies that the present argument builds upon what precedes.[83] Second, Paul begins (4:1) and culminates (4:7) this paragraph with the heir of the world (ὁ κληρονόμος) in view.[84] Such reasons demonstrate that the inheritance argument continues into 4:1–2.

Paul opens his illustration by asserting that while the heir (ὁ κληρονόμος) of a father's land is a minor (νήπιός), he is no different from a slave (4:1).[85] This is the case "even though he is the lord of all" (κύριος πάντων ὤν).[86] Dunn points out that the "idea of the (Jewish) child as 'lord of all' may well reflect and affirm the tradition already well-established which interpreted the land promised to Abraham as the whole earth."[87] Similarly, Scott argues that the phrase "lord of all" carries the notion of "universal sovereignty."[88] Pointing to passages such as Sirach 44:19–23, Scott asserts that "the Abrahamic promise was taken to mean that 'Israel will inherit from sea to sea and from the River to the ends of the earth.'"[89] That is to say, they are the "lords" of the whole world. The tradition to which Dunn and Scott refer is evidenced in other previously examined Second Temple texts, such as *Jubilees* 22 and 32 and *1 Enoch* 5:7, which are themselves in line with the worldwide inheritance promised to Israel in the Psalms and Prophets (e.g., Ps 2, 72; Isa 65–66). The exodus tradition to which Paul alludes therefore extends beyond the Hexateuch to include a matrix of texts in the Psalms, Prophets, and Second Temple literature which affirm that Israel's departure from Egypt was intended to culminate in the inheritance of the world.[90]

Given that Jewish tradition held that Israel was the heir of the world, it is best to see ὁ κληρονόμος as a reference to Israel.[91] Israel, however, had not yet received their inheritance, and thus Paul understands that their status as

---

fact not accidental. The overall flow of logic is basically the same as that in 3:25–29: the Christ event (3:25a/4:4–5), liberation (...3:25b/4:7a), status as 'seed of Abraham'/ 'sons' (3:29a/4:7a), heirship (3:29b/4:7)" (*Eschatology in Galatians*, 91).

83. See the discussion about the development marker δέ in Runge (*Discourse Grammar*, 29–36).

84. Bruce (*Galatians*, 192) and Dunn (*Galatians*, 210) also argue that the inheritance continues to be in view.

85. Schreiner similarly notes that the inheritance of the heir is his "father's estate" (*New Testament Theology*, 366).

86. The adverbial participle ὤν is functioning in a concessive manner.

87. Dunn, *Galatians*, 211.

88. Scott, *Adoption as Sons*, 131–35.

89. Ibid., 135.

90. See Halvorson-Taylor, *Enduring Exile*, who examines the pervasive tradition of continuing exile in the OT.

91. Morales, *Spirit and the Restoration of Israel*, 165.

heirs has yet to be fulfilled.[92] According to Rodrigo Morales, Israel's position as the unfulfilled heir "is the role that Jubilees and Sirach (and Paul) have in mind, since at the time of the writing of these documents Israel had not yet inherited the entire world."[93]

Although destined to receive the inheritance, there was a time when Israel was considered a νήπιός (Gal 4:1). Scott argues that such a designation "alludes here to Hosea 11.1, where, in a unique way in the Septuagint, the term refers to God's people as 'young' at the time of the Exodus when God called Israel out of Egypt as his 'son.'"[94] While Silvia Keesmaat believes that such an echo "seems quite plausible," she argues,

> Scott's assertion could have been strengthened by providing some reasons as to why it is likely that Paul would have been appealing to this particular text. Given Paul's use of Hosea elsewhere, as well as the high volume of echo between Hos. 11.1 and a passage such as Romans 8, it is both historically plausible and thematically likely that Paul is echoing Hos. 11.1 in this verse. I do not think it likely, however, that this is an intentional allusion. Paul's language here is moving within the tradition of the exodus and the text of Hosea 11 contributes to that matrix; it would be more circumspect to say, therefore, that Paul's language here echoes a text which is part of a matrix of ideas connected to the exodus event."[95]

Keesmaat is correct in arguing that Hosea 11:1 is only one of many exodus story passages that Paul has in mind, for there is an intricately related series of texts that contribute to this tradition. Among such are Exodus 2:24, 3:25–26, 6:2–9, and Psalm 105:42. While agreeing with her, I see the value in Scott's specific discussion of Hosea 11:1, for it helpfully brings to light Israel's status as a "minor" during the time they were called out of slavery in Egypt (e.g., Exod 3–4). This, as Paul asserts, was the period when Israel was a νήπιός.

Yet, as long as Israel remained under bondage, they were no better than a slave (οὐδὲν διαφέρει δούλου, Gal 4:1). This is the case even though Israel was the "lord of all." Moreover, while they were in slavery in Egypt, God's people were "under guardians and administrators" (ὑπὸ ἐπιτρόπους . . . καὶ οἰκονόμους, Gal 4:2). These two terms are official titles for Egyptian

---

92. Ibid.
93. Ibid., 165.
94. Scott, *Adoption as Sons*, 129.
95. Keesmaat, *Paul and His Story*, 161.

officials.⁹⁶ As Keesmaat argues, "Slavery in these verses refers to Egypt, to Israel's primary experience of bondage under officials in a land not her own."⁹⁷ So, although God's people were destined to inherit the world, they were under the bondage of Egypt's state officials, obligated to comply with their every demand.

Israel remained in such a state "until the appointed time of the father" (ἄχρι τῆς προθεσμίας τοῦ πατρός, Gal 4:2).⁹⁸ This phrase likely alludes to Genesis 15:13, in which God informs Abraham that his descendants will be sojourners and strangers in a foreign land where "they will be afflicted for four hundred years" (430 years in Exod 12:40–41). Scott notes that "after this follows the promise of the Exodus (Gen 15:14–16) and the land (vv. 18–21) which . . . was associated with Israel's eschatological hope of world rule."⁹⁹ The period of 400 years in Genesis 15:13 (430 years in Exod 12:40–41) could therefore point to a foreordained period of time in Israel's history, and thus "could be called a προθεσμία."¹⁰⁰ Thus, in Galatians 4:2 Paul likely uses the word προθεσμία to allude to the time that Israel was a slave in Egypt until the 400/430 years came to an end.¹⁰¹

Having considered the entire illustration in Galatians 4:1–2, it is evident that Paul is echoing the series of Jewish texts that make up the exodus story, which presents the Israelites as the rightful lords of the world who were enslaved under Egyptian rule (Gal 4:1). While in slavery, the people of Israel were subject to the authority of Egypt's officials and overseers (Gal 4:2). This lasted until the appointed time of 400/430 years was up (Gal 4:2), at which point commenced the sojourn to the (expanded) land promised to

---

96. Scott, *Adoption as Sons*, 135–40. Longenecker rightly argues that the titles "*epitropos* and *oikonomos* of 4:2 have given rise to a great deal of discussion as to their precise meaning" ("Pedagogical Nature," 56). I will not attempt an extensive survey of these terms. Without going into much detail, it is important to note that the former term has been understood as a guardian of a minor and the latter as a slave in charge of a minor. See Hodge, *If Sons, Then Heirs*, 70–71. These readings would be appropriate if the household metaphor were present in Gal 4:–7. But since I have already showed that the exodus is in view, it is best to see these terms as titles of Egyptian officials.

97. Keesmaat, *Paul and His Story*, 160–61.

98. The noun προθεσμία carries the sense of a "day appointed beforehand, a fixed or limited time" (LSJ, 1481). For those who argue the household metaphor is in view, the "appointed time" points "to an official date—for example, the date when debts are due or a period of time during which one can claim an inheritance (Hodge, *If Sons, Then Heirs*, 71). See also Dunn, *Galatians*, 211.

99. Scott, *Adoption as Sons*, 142.

100. Ibid.

101. Ibid. Contra Hafemann, "Paul and the Exile of Israel," 337–39.

Abraham. I will now compare the illustration in Galatians 4:1–2 to the new exodus in 4:3–7.

Galatians 4:3–7: The New Exodus

The words "thus also we" (οὕτως καὶ ἡμεῖς, 4:3) set up the comparison between the original exodus in Galatians 4:1–2 and the new exodus in 4:3–7.[102] Following these words, Paul asserts, "When we were minors, we were enslaved under the elements of the world" (ὅτε ἦμεν νήπιοι, ὑπὸ τὰ στοιχεῖα τοῦ κόσμου ἤμεθα δεδουλωμένοι). Like the allusion to Israel in Galatians 4:1, Paul's readers were once also "minors" (νήπιοι) and "enslaved" (δεδουλωμένοι) under a ruthless task master. In the words of Scott:

> By the οὕτως καὶ ἡμεῖς which introduces v. 3 (and with it the second half of the comparison) Paul typologically likens the slavery of Israel under the taskmasters of Egypt to the enslavement of both Jews and Gentiles under the τὰ στοιχεῖα τοῦ κόσμου. To stress this typological comparison, Paul even carries over the νήπιός of v. 1 into v. 3 (νήπιοι). As is usual in typology, there is heightening of the antitype over the type, so that both the enslaving power and the redemption are universalized here.[103]

In other words, Israel's slavery in Egypt was a type of the bondage that Jews and gentiles experienced under the "elements of the world." Such enslavement to the elements occurred during the jurisdiction of the Law (cf. Gal 3:23–29).[104]

Paul continues his comparison in Galatians 4:4 by asserting that his readers remained enslaved minors until "the fullness of the time came" (ἦλθεν τὸ πλήρωμα τοῦ χρόνου). Commentators note that the "fullness of

102. Scott points out the uses of οὕτως καὶ ἡμεῖς in typological arguments in Matt 12:40; 24:37, 39; John 3:14; Rom 5:12, 18, 19; 1 Cor 15:22 (*Adoption as Sons*, 150). Also, in this formula of comparison the pronoun ἡμεῖς refers to both Jews and Gentiles. Agreeing with Schreiner, "'We' (ἡμεῖς) could be restricted to the Jews, but since Paul speaks of the world's elements, he probably includes both Jews and Gentiles" (*Galatians*, 267). Contra Hafemann, who argues that Paul only has Jews in mind ("Paul and the Exile," 340–41).

103. Scott, *Adoption as Sons*, 157.

104. Schreiner, *Galatians*, 269. The στοιχεῖα may refer to a number of elements that ruled over humanity before the coming of Christ, such as demonic powers. For a survey of the possible interpretations, see again Schreiner (ibid., 267–69). Bundrick surveys the viable options and concludes that the "elements" are the elementary or rudimentary teachings under which Jews and gentiles were enslaved prior to freedom in Christ ("TA STOICHEIA TOU KOSMOU," 353–64). While I side with Schreiner, Bundrick's view does not change my argument in this section.

the time" is a common eschatological theme in Jewish and Christian litera-ture.[105] Among such Jewish texts is the prayer of Daniel 9 which anticipates Israel's salvation after seventy-years of judgment and refers to these years as "the number of years that . . . must pass" (Dan 9:2; cf. Hab 2:3). Among such Christian texts is Mark 1:15, in which the evangelist asserts "the time has been fulfilled and the kingdom of God has come near." Morales rightly points out that "the connection between the fulfillment of time and the kingdom is particularly noteworthy, given that later in Galatians Paul makes one of his few references to the kingdom of God (Gal 5:21), and specifically in relation to inheritance language," which is the key theme of Galatians 4:1–7.[106]

Scott also contends that "the fullness of the time" is common in Jewish and Christian literature and, after examining texts such as 2 Baruch 29:8, Tobit 14:5, and Jeremiah 36:10 (LXX), affirms that "the τὸ πλήρωμα τοῦ χρόνου refers to a date that God set beforehand."[107] This leads him to con-clude that "τὸ πλήρωμα τοῦ χρόνου stands parallel to τῆς προθεσμίας τοῦ πατρός (v. 2), the date which God had foreordained to Abraham that Israel would be delivered from bondage to Egypt."[108] It is therefore likely that Ga-latians 4:4 refers to the time when God brought to an end the period of slavery for believers, as he did for Israel in 4:2. Thus, there is a typological relationship between τὸ πλήρωμα τοῦ χρόνου (Gal 4:4) and τῆς προθεσμίας τοῦ πατρός (Gal 4:2), for "both the redemption of Israel and the redemption of believers proceed according to God's own timetable and promise."[109]

Moreover, the "fullness of the time" came to pass when "God sent forth his son, having been born from a woman, having been born under the Law" (ἐξαπέστειλεν ὁ θεὸς τὸν υἱὸν αὐτοῦ, γενόμενον ἐκ γυναικός, γενόμενον ὑπὸ νόμον, Gal 5:5). The sending of the son—the Messiah—fits well with the exodus story. Scott contends that widespread Jewish tradition, stemming from Deuteronomy 15:15–18, evidences that "the Messiah would be a sec-ond Moses who would redeem his people from oppression."[110] He supports

105. I attribute this notion and the cited verses from Dan 9:2 and Mark 1:15 to Morales (Spirit and the Restoration of Israel, 172). See also Dunn, Galatians, 213–14; Matera, Galatians, 150; Bruce, Galatians, 194.

106. Though Morales says that the inheritance "is a key theme in Gal 4:1–7" (Spirit and the Restoration of Israel, 172), I contend that the inheritance is the key theme of Gal 4:1–7. This is the case, in part, because Paul both begins (4:1) and ends (4:7) this section with this notion.

107. Scott, Adoption as Sons, 162.

108. Ibid.

109. Ibid.

110. Ibid., 164.

this, in part, by noting Moses/Christ typology in 1 Corinthians 10:1–13 and Joachim Jeremias's argument that in 1 Corinthians 10:1–2 "being baptized into Moses" was formed on analogy of "being baptized into Christ" (cf. Rom 6:3; Gal 3:27).[111] In addition to this, Christ as a second Moses is found in Gospel texts such as Matthew 2:5, which asserts that Jesus, like Moses, was called out of Egypt (cf. Mark 9:7; Hos 11:1).[112] Christ as a second Moses is supported by the NT and "coheres extremely well with contemporary Jewish expectation concerning God's new act of salvation, in which a new Moses was expected to inaugurate a new exodus event."[113] It also suits the new exodus typology of Galatians 4:3–7, in that Christ is the new Moses whom God sent to deliver his people out of bondage to the Law (cf. 3:23–29).

This point is supported in the final clause of Galatians 4:5, in which Paul asserts that God sent his son "in order that he might redeem those under the Law" (ἵνα τοὺς ὑπὸ νόμον ἐξαγοράσῃ, Gal 5:5). Like Moses, Christ redeemed his people from slavery.[114] While Moses redeemed Israel from slavery under Egypt, Christ redeemed his people from slavery under the Law (cf. Gal 3:13). Comparing Galatians 4:5 to 5:1, Scott contends, "In the words of Galatians 5:1, God delivered them from the law, the 'yoke of slavery' . . . just as he had once freed Israel from the 'yoke' of slavery in Egypt."[115] To add to Scott's observation, it is the case that freedom from Egypt was accomplished through Moses, while freedom from the Law was brought about through Christ. Christ, then, is the second Moses who delivered his people from slavery. Also like Moses, Christ freed his people in order that they may one day inherit the world.

As well, those whom Christ has redeemed from bondage under the Law are "adopted as sons" (υἱοθεσία; cf. Rom 8:15, 23; 9:4; Eph 1:5).[116] At the appointed time in salvation history, God sent Christ to redeem both Jews

111. Ibid., 166.

112. See Hengel, *Studies in the Gospel of Mark*, 56–58.

113. Keesmaat, *Paul and His Story*, 162–63.

114. Hafemann asserts that "redemption from slavery" is implied here (*Paul and the Exile*, 350).

115. Scott, *Adoption as Sons*, 163.

116. While some contend that υἱοθεσία has been adopted from the Roman world, Scott rightly argues for the OT/Jewish background for this term (ibid., 161–85). The Greco-Roman argument does not fit within Paul's echo of the exodus tradition. A further reason for seeing such a background for υἱοθεσία is "substantiated both by Rom 9:4, where the articular term occurs in a list of Israel's historical privileges (cf. Exod 4:22; Hos 11:1), and more specifically, by the broader context of Galatians 3–4 itself, which make it clear that believers are sons and heirs as they participate in baptism (Gal 3:27) in the Son of God who was sent to redeem them (Gal 4:4–5; cf. 3:13–14)" (Hawthorne, Martin, and Reed, *Dictionary of Paul and His Letters*, 17).

and gentiles to be his people. When understood in the context of the new exodus, it is clear that just as Israel, the heir to the Abrahamic promise of land, was redeemed as God's son from slavery in Egypt at the time specified by the Father (Gen 15:13; Exod 4:22; Hos 11:1), so too believers were adopted as sons from slavery under the Law "at the fullness of time and thereby became heirs to the Abrahamic promise."[117] Paul's readers, then, having been delivered from bondage, are now sons of God destined to inherit the world.[118]

After establishing that the freed sons of God will inherit the world to come, Galatians 4:6–7 will bring to light the role of the Abrahamic promises in the new exodus story. In so doing, these verses will conclude the passage.

Galatians 4:6–7: The Abrahamic Promises in the New Exodus

Galatians 4:6 states that "God has sent his Spirit into the hearts" (ἐξαπέστειλεν ὁ θεὸς τὸ πνεῦμα αὐτοῦ εἰς τὰς καρδίας) of those who are "sons" (υἱοί).[119] This verse brings the promised Spirit discussed in 3:2–14 back in view. Within the context of the exodus tradition, the primary echo here is Isaiah 48:16–17, which speaks of God sending his Spirit to rescue his people (cf. Isa 44:3).[120] Whereas for Isaiah such deliverance was still to come, Paul's

117. Ibid.

118. Keesmaat insightfully asserts: "In a discussion which identifies believers as sons of God, an appeal to the Exodus is an appeal to the paradigm which provided a definition of sonship . . . Paul's language concerning believers as the sons of God is rooted in the intertextual matrix of ideas which is informed largely by exodus traditions. It was in the exodus narrative that Israel was first called God's son; in recollection of the new exodus that such an identification was reinterpreted; in hope for a new exodus event that this sonship expected" (*Paul and His Story*, 178–79). See Exod 4:22; Deut 14, 32; Hos 2:2 (LXX); Isa 43:5–7; Jer 38:9–20; *Jub.* 1:24–25, noted by Keesmaat (ibid., 179).

119. Although Gal 4:6 places the reception of the Spirit prior to becoming sons, Longenecker rightly argues that any argument over chronology misses the point. His argument may be summed up as follows: "For Paul, it seems, sonship and receiving the Spirit are so intimately related that one can speak of them in either order (cf. the almost free intertwining categories in Rom 8:1–2 and 9–11), with only the circumstance of a particular audience, the issue being confronted, or the discussion that precedes determining the order to be used at any given time and place" (*Galatians*, 173).

Also, while implied in Gal 3:22–29, Rom 8:12–17 makes clear that the Spirit confirms one's status as God's son. Paul makes this most explicit when he claims, "You did not receive a spirit of slavery again leading to fear but you received the Spirit of υἱοθεσία by means of whom we cry, "Abba, Father!" Thus, the Spirit himself testifies with our spirit that we are sons of God (vv. 15–17).

120. Beale notes an echo of this passage in Gal 4:6 ("Old Testament Background," 10–11). See also Ezek 36:26–27. Hester argues that Paul believes the Spirit acts as a witness in the act of adoption, and thus Paul has Roman adoption law in mind (*Paul's*

readers have already been rescued by God and have received the Spirit (Gal 4:3–6). Hence, the Spirit of which Isaiah speaks presently indwells the sons of God who have been delivered from slavery and are journeying toward their inheritance.[121]

Subsequently, Galatians 4:7 asserts that the result (ὥστε) of receiving the Spirit is that the one who is a son (υἱός) is also an heir (κληρονόμος) of the inheritance promised to Abraham (cf. 3:15–18).[122] Being that the culmination of the exodus narrative is the entry into the inheritance, it is fitting for Paul to conclude the present section in 4:1–7, and the entire discussion in 3:15—4:7, with the theme of the heir who will receive what was promised to Abraham. Like the original exodus in 4:1–2, Paul's readers on a new exodus are destined to inherit the world to come. Since the inheritance of the coming world is echoed in 3:15–29, and the original exodus tradition in 4:1–2 speaks of the heir being "lord of all," the worldwide inheritance is still in view in 4:7.

In considering the entirety of Galatians 4:6–7, it seems that Paul, like Genesis (e.g., 15:1–21; cf. 12:2–3; 22:15–19), brings together the three Abrahamic covenant promises of blessing, offspring, and inheritance, in claiming that the one who has the Spirit (promise of blessing) is a son (promise of offspring),[123] which in turn makes him an heir (promise of inheritance). Identifying the presence of these promises in 4:6–7 is important, because each has a role to play in the original exodus story. The roles of the promises of offspring and inheritance are the most apparent in this tradition, given that God intended for Abraham's descendants (promise of offspring) to be delivered from slavery so that they would possess the land (promise of inheritance). The role that the promised blessing of the Spirit plays within the story, while not immediately apparent in the Hexateuch, is visible in the

---

Concept of Inheritance, 60-62). While Hester's argument is nuanced, Roman adoption is not in view, for, as argued above, the exodus tradition is the natural background of Gal 4:6–7.

121. A further implication of this point is that the reception of the Spirit assumes the status of sonship, reaffirming that the genuine sons/descendants are those who are indwelt with the promised Spirit. See Schreiner, *Galatians*, 271–72.

122. Many in the Galatian church would have been gentiles, with no rights of sonship and, consequently, no inheritance among the people of Israel. Perceiving a "slave" metaphor in Gal 4:1–7, Hodge underscores that, upon the reception of the Spirit, the "gentiles become 'sons' (Gal 4:6, 7; Rom 8:14) through adoption, which means that they would have the same rights, responsibilities, and potential to inherit as sons born into the world" (*If Sons, Then Heirs*, 69).

123. To be a "son of God" is equivalent to being "Abraham's offspring." This idea is found in Gal 3, which argues that those incorporated into Christ are both "sons of God" (v. 26) and the "offspring of Abraham" (v. 29).

later reflection of the Psalms and Prophets. These corpuses testify that the Spirit was the one whom God used to lead his people out of Egypt, through the wilderness, and into the land.[124] Isaiah 63:11–14 and Nehemiah 9 will demonstrate this point.

Isaiah 63:11–14, recounting Israel's exodus, states:

> Where is the one who brought up from the sea the shepherds of his flock? Where is the one who placed in its midst the Holy Spirit; sending to the right hand of Moses the arm of his glory; dividing the waters from before them, to make for himself an everlasting name; leading them in the depths, as a horse in the desert, they did not misstep. As cattle descend in the plain, the Spirit of the Lord gave the people rest. Thus you led your people to make for yourself a glorious name.[125]

Here, Isaiah testifies that God used the Spirit to lead his people through the wilderness and into the place of rest, the land (cf. Hag 2:4–5).[126]

Nehemiah 9 gives further insight into how the Spirit manifested himself to the people he was leading on the exodus:

> You led them by day with a pillar of cloud, and by night with a pillar of fire, to give them light in the way they were to go (v. 9) . . . for their hunger you gave them bread from heaven, and for their thirst you brought water out of a rock, and you told them to go in to possess the land that you swore to give them (v. 15) . . . in your great mercies you did not forsake them in the wilderness; the pillar of cloud that led them in the way did not leave them by day, nor the pillar of fire by night that gave them light on the way by which they should go (v. 19). You gave your good Spirit to teach them (v. 20) . . . Forty years you sustained them in the wilderness (v. 21) . . . and you gave them kingdoms and peoples, and allotted to them every corner, so that they took possession of the land (v. 22).

Nehemiah mentions the giving of the Spirit (v. 20) after recounting the pillar of cloud and fire leading Israel through the wilderness (vv. 9–19). The reference to the Spirit at this point in the passage is not coincidental. Rather, in verse 20 he mentions the Spirit in order to identify him with the pillar of

---

124. I owe my insights in this paragraph to Wilder (*Echoes of the Exodus*, 121–74).

125. This translation is based on the MT. Wilder argues that, in view of Exod 33:14, "the rest-giving action of the Spirit" implies that the Spirit accompanied God's people to the promised land (*Echoes of the Exodus*, 134).

126. In chaps. 3–4, I argue rest is associated with land. See Ps 95.

cloud and fire.[127] He is the one whom God used to lead the people of Israel through the wilderness and into the land. The cloud and fire were therefore the ways in which the Spirit visibly manifested his guidance of God's people. Such a reading of Nehemiah 9, and similarly of Isaiah 63:11–14, substantiates that the promised Spirit's role in the exodus story was to lead God's people out of slavery in Egypt, through the wilderness, and into the promised land. In other words, he was to guarantee that they would receive their inheritance (cf. Eph 1:14).

With that said, it is apparent that in Galatians 4:6–7 the discussion of the Abrahamic promises of blessing, offspring, and inheritance belongs in the new exodus story. Like the original exodus, the new exodus story evidences that the Spirit (promise of blessing) leads the sons of God (promise of offspring) out of slavery under the Law and through the wilderness of the present sinful age (Acts 7:30–44; Heb. 3:7–11; 1 Pet 2:11–12) until they inherit the coming world (promise of inheritance).

Additionally, the ongoing nature of the new exodus means that the promise of inheritance to Abraham remains unfulfilled. So, although believers are "already" indwelt with the Spirit and are the offspring of Abraham, they have "not yet" received the territory sworn to them. The inheritance is therefore the only promise of the Abrahamic covenant that remains to be realized, anticipating the day when God's people will complete the new exodus and dwell in the coming world (cf. Rom 4:12–17; 8:12–25; Rev 21–22).

The comparison between the original exodus in Galatians 4:1–2 and the new exodus in 4:3–7 is now clear. Just as Israel in the original exodus story was redeemed as God's son from slavery in Egypt and was led by the cloud toward the inheritance (Gal 4:1–2), so too believers on the new exodus have been adopted as sons from slavery under the Law and are being led by the Spirit through the present wilderness until they inherit the world to come (Gal 4:3–7). The original exodus was a type of the present exodus of which both Jews and gentiles in Christ are privileged to take part.

Such a conclusion to Galatians 4:1–7 is fitting for the larger inheritance argument in 3:15–4:7. I have shown that Paul spends the bulk of the discussion in 3:15–29 meticulously contending, by alluding to several OT and Second Temple passages, that the inheritance of the coming world will

127. Wilder asserts that although in Neh 9:20 the Spirit was given for the purpose of instruction in the Law, "the parallel between the elaboration of the law in 9:13–14 and the instruction of the Spirit in 9:20a hints at some common relation to the theophonic cloud of the exodus. Both the descent of Yahweh upon Mount Sinai (in cloud, fire, and smoke) and the appearance of the Spirit in an exodus narrative (as in Haggai 2 and Isaiah 63) represent possible allusions to the exodus cloud. Yet in each case the would-be allusion to the cloud is immediately preceded by an explicit reference to that cloud and its function in the exodus (9:12, 19)" (*Echoes of the Exodus*, 140–41).

be received by those who place their faith in Christ, the son of God and messianic king. The fact that the inheritance is rooted in Jewish tradition makes it appropriate for him to place this theme within the context of the exodus (4:1–2) and new exodus stories (4:3–7), the former recalling Israel's deliverance from slavery and journey towards the inheritance, which then serves as a type of the new and better exodus that will culminate when Paul's readers inherit the earth. Paul's masterful employment of these stories drives home for his readers that the Spirit is leading them through the wilderness of the present evil age until they at last possess the world.

GALATIANS 4:21–31: THE SARAH AND HAGAR STORY

After a brief interlude in which he encourages his readers to live free from the Law, in Galatians 4:21–31 Paul uses the Sarah and Hagar story from Genesis 21 to place an exclamation point on his inheritance argument.[128] Tom Schreiner observes that this "text is marked by polarities and opposites," especially in the contrast between "the two sons of Abraham (Isaac and Ishmael), born from the free woman (Sarah) and the slave woman (Hagar) . . . (4:22). The latter's son was born according to the flesh and the former's son" through the promise (δι᾽ ἐπαγγελίας, Gal 4:23).[129] Paul highlights the differences between Sarah and Hagar and their offspring to identify the true heir of the land (Gal 4:30).[130]

Karen Jobes notes that Galatians 4:21–31 "is rife with interesting problems and has rightly received much scholarly scrutiny."[131] Chief among these is Paul's claim that the Hagar and Sarah story from Genesis 21 should

128. Betz sees Gal 4:21–31 as the conclusion of the section that begins in Gal 3:1 (*Galatians*, 239). Using a term from classical rhetoric, Betz calls 4:21–31 the *probatio* of Paul's argument (ibid., 239–40). According to Quintilian, the *probatio* was the strongest part of an argument that should be placed either at the beginning or end of a discourse (ibid., 239). Thus, Jobes is correct in underscoring that Paul's use of Sarah and Hagar is the "*coup de grace* against his opponents in Galatia" ("Jerusalem, Our Mother," 299). Boyarin contends that Gal 4:21–31 is "the climax of the entire argument and preaching of the letter, in which all of its themes are brought together and shown to cohere" (*Radical Jew*, 32). See Howard, *Crisis in Galatia*, for a study of Paul's opponents.

129. Schreiner, *Galatians*, 295. Relying on Gaston's "Israel's Enemies in Pauline Theology," 400–23, Boyarin points out that Paul is employing "the Pythagorean practice of establishing parallel columns of corresponding dichotomies" (*Radical Jew*, 33).

130. Although Gal 4:23 asserts that Isaac is the child of promise, Kwon argues that sonship is not the issue in 4:21–31; instead, it is which son is the true heir of the land promised to Abraham (*Eschatology in Galatians*, 94). Therefore, the question that Paul is addressing "is not 'Who is Abraham's true son?' but 'Which son is the rightful heir?'" (ibid.).

131. Jobes, "Jerusalem, Our Mother," 300.

be understood "allegorically" (Gal 4:24). While some argue that here Paul uses a strictly allegorical or typological hermeneutic, I will contend that it is best to call Paul's use of the Sarah and Hagar story "typological allegory."

I will first examine Paul's employment of the Sarah and Hagar story in 4:21–27. Then, I will point out the identification of the true heirs of the world in 4:28–31.

Galatians 4:21–27: Sarah and Hagar as Typological Allegory

Paul begins this section by asserting that Isaac was born "through the promise" (δι' ἐπαγγελίας, Gal 4:23). This statement alludes to Genesis 17:19–22 and 18:10–14, passages which promise that Sarah will give birth to a son called Isaac, and in turn resonate with Genesis 13:14–17 and 15:1–19, which testify that Abraham's offspring will inherit the land. Paul's use of this tradition suggests that through Isaac's birth the promise of numerous, landowning offspring is being fulfilled.

The birth of Isaac takes place in the story of Sarah and Hagar, which, Paul claims, "is an allegory" (ἐστιν ἀλληγορούμενα, Gal 4:24). Some contend that Paul employs the kind of non-historical allegory espoused by Philo, "where one thing stands for another, and the biblical text is sundered from the historical context from which it was birthed."[132] Others claim that Paul employs typology, since the Sarah and Hagar story is rooted in the OT narrative and fits a salvation-historical reading.[133] In spite of these polarizing interpretations, neither the typological nor allegorical reading may be ruled out, for both elements appear to be present. It is thereby best to label this passage a "typological allegory."[134] As Schreiner explains,

132. Schreiner, *Galatians*, 292. Boyarin sees Paul's hermeneutic in Gal 4:21–31 as close to Philo's (*Radical Jew*, 34).

133. See, for example, Silva, "Galatians," 807–08, and Bruce, *Galatians*, 217. See also Caneday, "Covenant Lineage Prefigured," 50–77, who argues against interpreting Gal 4:21–31 as strictly allegorical or typological. Caneday provides an insightful illustration of Paul's use of Gen 21: "The notion that Paul assigns allegorical or typological significance to the personages in the Abraham narrative is akin to the side room commentary concerning the stained glass window panels of King's College chapel, Cambridge University" (ibid., 69). He then quotes: "[W]hen Christianity was a new religion, it linked itself to the sacred Jewish past. It made the Jewish scriptures its own, calling them 'The Old Testament.' It treated this 'Old Testament' as prophecy of its own 'New Testament.' 'The Old Testament' was a story of 'types'—prophecies and stories awaiting their full (Christian) actualization" (ibid.).

134. Schreiner, *Galatians*, 300. Betz sees Gal 4:21–31 as a mixture of typology and allegory (*Galatians*, 239).

> Probably the best solution is to see a combination of typology and allegory. Paul argues typologically with reference to Isaac and Ishmael, especially in 4:21–23 and 4:28–30. Hence, his reading of the text fits with his salvation-historical understanding of the Scriptures as a whole. There are clearly, however, allegorical elements in the argument, particularly in 4:24–27. The fundamental reason for seeing the text as having an allegorical component is the identification of Hagar with the Sinai covenant. Such a move does not comport with typology, where there is historical connection between type and its fulfillment. It is difficult to see how Hagar functions as a historical type of the Sinai covenant.[135]

Simply put, Schreiner argues that Galatians 4:21–23 and 4:28–30 are typological, whereas 4:24–27 are allegorical. While this perspective is helpful, I argue that the allegorical elements are confined to 4:24–26, because in 4:27 Paul cites Isaiah 54:1, a verse that foretells the innumerable offspring of the desolate woman will inherit the entire earth and is grounded in the historical Abrahamic covenant promise in Genesis (15:1–21). The historically rooted nature of the inheritance prevents Galatians 4:27 from being interpreted allegorically.

Following this claim, Paul states that in this passage there are two covenants, one from "Mount Sinai" (Σινᾶ ὄρος, Gal 4:25) and one that corresponds to the "Jerusalem above" (ἄνω Ἱερουσαλήμ, Gal 4:26). The latter, being allegorically associated with Hagar, represents those who are in slavery under the Law, and the former is related to the heavenly Jerusalem. Often these "two covenants" are identified as the covenant at Sinai and the new covenant in Christ.[136] While the words Σινᾶ ὄρος (4:25) display that the Sinai covenant is in view, the new covenant has no such support.[137] A more warranted option is the Abrahamic covenant, which, like Galatians

135. Schreiner, *Galatians*, 300. Similarly, Cosgrove, "Law Has Given Sarah No Children," 219–35. While arguing that Paul uses a mixture of typology and allegory, Betz admits that these methods of interpretation are related (*Galatians*, 239).

136. See, for example, Betz, *Galatians*, 243; Longenecker, *Galatians*, 211. Willits, "Isa 54, 1 and Gal 4, 24b–27," 198–99. DiMattei argues that Paul's use of Gen 21:10 ("Cast out the slave woman") suggests that the Sinai covenant/Law must be in view ("Paul's Allegory," 121).

137. Hays, *Echoes*, 114. Schreiner believes that the new covenant is probably in view because the "citation of Isa 54:1 in Gal 4:27 signals the eschatological fulfillment of the covenant enacted with Abraham" (*Galatians*, 300–301). While Isa 54 points to the fulfillment of the Abrahamic covenant, the promises of offspring and inheritance have not been fulfilled, for Abraham's descendants are still being gathered and the renewed world has yet to be revealed. Thus, one should not claim that the new covenant is in view, for the covenant with Abraham has not been entirely fulfilled.

4:24–27, stresses that Abraham's offspring will inherit the land (cf. Gen 12, 15). Thus, in this passage, it is likely that the Sinai and Abrahamic covenants are in view.

Paul then claims that the "Jerusalem above" (ἄνω Ἰερουσαλήμ) is the "mother" (μήτηρ) of the Galatian readers (Gal 4:26). The "Jerusalem above" is equivalent to *4 Ezra*'s description of the "New Jerusalem," which exists in heaven, awaiting the time when it will come down on the "future land" (e.g., 7:27; 10:27, 42, 44, 54, 13:36). It also corresponds to Revelation's portrayal of "the holy city, the New Jerusalem," which will descend on the "new heavens and new earth" (cf. Isa 65–66). Like these texts, it is probable that Paul envisions the New Jerusalem to be the city that will exist on the new heavens and new earth, the inheritance (Isa 54, 65–66). Since this city is the Galatians' mother, Paul assures his readers that their home is in the city that will be revealed in the coming world.[138]

Paul supports (γάρ) the notion that his readers are citizens of the New Jerusalem by quoting Isaiah 54:1:

> Rejoice, O sterile woman!
> Break forth (ῥῆξον) and cry out, O woman who suffers no birth pains!
> For the children of the desolate woman are many—
> more than the one who has a husband (Gal 4:27).[139]

Though Galatians 4:27 cites the prophecy that assures Sarah of numerous descendants, it is difficult to determine how this sole citation supports that Galatian Christians are citizens of the New Jerusalem. It is more probable that the quotation of Isaiah 54:1 initiates a ripple of echoes that extend, at the very least, to the whole of chapter 54.[140]

The first of these ripples is found in Isaiah 54:2–3, which uses the story of Sarah to foretell that God's people will be so numerous that they will possess the nations of the earth. That is to say, they will inherit the world. Such a prophecy assures Isaiah's exilic community that the promise of a territorial inheritance to Abraham's offspring will be fulfilled. Subsequently, the remainder of Isaiah 54 describes the gloriously restored nature of the inheritance (vv. 4–16) and assures the exilic community that this is indeed "the inheritance of the Lord's servants" (v. 17).

There is doubt, however, as to whether the context of the quotation in Galatians 4:27 is limited to Isaiah 54. Richard Hays argues that the context

---

138. DiMattei notes that the inheritance in this section should be identified with the heavenly Jerusalem above associated with the Abrahamic covenant promises ("Paul's Allegory," 22).

139. I am following the structure of the NA 28.

140. See Willits, "Isa 54, 1 and Gal 4, 24b–27," 192.

begins in Isaiah 54 and extends back to 51.[141] This broad scriptural frame-work, he asserts, is necessary in order "to grasp the sense of the quotation."[142] I agree with Hay's observation, given that Isaiah 52:1–10 and 51:1–3[143] echo the thought of both Galatians 4:27 and Isaiah 54:1. In particular, Isaiah 52:1–10 speaks of the future redemption of Jerusalem, the holy city, whose salvation is a cause for her to "break forth" (ῥηξάτω)[144] in singing (v. 9). Here, the call to "break forth" is the same as that in Galatians 4:27 and Isa-iah 54:1. Similarly, Isaiah 51:1–3 pictures Sarah as the mother of Jerusalem and assures Israel of the future deliverance from exile by reminding them that their parents, Abraham and Sarah, were greatly multiplied by God (cf. 51:17–20).[145] In this future liberation, the Lord will restore Zion to an Eden-like paradise, which will result in "joy and gladness" being found in her, thanksgiving and the "voice of song" (φωνὴν αἰνέσεως). The "voice of song," like the call to "break forth" in singing in Isaiah 52, is the same voice sum-moned in Galatians 4:27 and Isaiah 54:1.[146] Such evidence supports that the context for Paul's citation indeed begins in Isaiah 54 and extends back to 51.

By implication, the scriptural support for the Galatians being citizens of the New Jerusalem extends from Isaiah 54 to 51. Paul employs this back-ground to remind his readers that they will dwell in the glorious city (Gal 4:26; cf. Rev 21:1–2) that will exist on the new heavens and new earth (i.e., the inheritance) described by Isaiah. Life in this New Jerusalem will not be desolate, but will be a return to an edenic paradise. This picture is intended to persuade the Galatians that the anticipation of life in the New Jerusalem is far better than being enslaved under the Law with Hagar's descendants (Gal 4:24–25).

---

141. Hays, *Echoes*, 118–21.

142. Ibid., 119.

143. I list these chapters in descending order, since the echo in Gal 4:27 extends back from Isaiah 54 to Isaiah 51. I will continue to do so in this section.

144. LXX Isaiah citations are from Ziegler, *Isaias*.

145. Hays, *Echoes*, 119.

146. Ibid., 119–20. Hays interestingly argues that "Isaiah's description in 54:1 of Jerusalem as a 'barren one' creates an internal echo hinting at the correspondence be-tween the city in its exilic desolation and the condition of Sarah before Isaac's birth, a correspondence that also implies the promise of subsequent blessing. Consequently, Paul's link between Sarah and redeemed Jerusalem surely presupposes Isa. 51:2, even though the text is not quoted in Galatians 4. It is Isaiah's metaphorical linkage of Abra-ham and Sarah with an eschatologically restored Jerusalem that warrants Paul's use of Isa. 54:1" (ibid., 120).

Galatians 4:28–31: The True Heirs

Paul assures his readers that they, like Isaac, are children of the promise (ἐπαγγελίας τέκνα, Gal 4:28). Since Isaiah 54 to 51 is still fresh in the minds of Paul's readers (Gal 4:27), they undoubtedly imagine that, as Abraham's promised children, they will inherit the renewed world on which the eschatological Jerusalem will exist. Although Paul does not explicitly state this point, the words ἐπαγγελίας τέκνα would have brought to mind that the world to come belongs to Abraham's offspring.

Moreover, as the promised children of Abraham, the Galatians are to resist the persecutory efforts of those who desire for them to submit to the Law (Gal 4:29; cf. 3:5).[147] Doing so will not lead to an inheritance. Paul illustrates this point from Genesis 21:10 (LXX): "Cast out the slave woman and her son, for the son of the slave woman will not be an heir (κληρονομήσει) with the son of the free woman (μετὰ τοῦ υἱοῦ τῆς ἐλευθέρας, Gal 4:30)." The slave woman is the mother of those who desire to live under the Law (Gal 4:24–26). As her son, Ishmael will not receive the inheritance. The fact that Paul's citation of Genesis 21:10 (LXX) replaces the final two words μου Ισαακ with τῆς ἐλευθέρας underscores his concern for identifying Isaac, not Ishmael, as the child "of the free woman" who will inherit the world promised to Abraham.[148] Submitting to the Law will result in having no portion in the land, like Ishmael. The Galatians must therefore pay attention to this passage, for it informs them that only those who are the children of the free woman will be heirs of the world.

In closing the passage, Paul reassures his readers that they are children of the free woman (τῆς ἐλευθέρας, Gal 4:31) who will inherit the coming world. Such an ending highlights the central thought in this text, that the true heirs of the earth are Isaac and his fellow children of promise.

CONCLUSION

Of his letters, Paul's epistle to the Galatians provides the most extensive discussion of the inheritance promise. I have shown that Paul's argument in chapters 3–4 reveals that his hope for an inheritance is shaped by Jewish

147. Schreiner, *Galatians*, 305.

148. Silva, "Galatians," 809. Often commentators acknowledge that the "son of the freewoman" is the rightful heir, without defining the content of the inheritance. Throughout Galatians 3–4 the inheritance concept is grounded in the cosmic, territorial promise to Abraham. This point also applies to 4:30, for the citation of Genesis 21:10 displays that Isaac is the beneficiary of the territory sworn to Abraham (Gen 12:7; 13:15; 15:18; 17:8), whereas Ishmael must be cast out, having no portion with Isaac.

literature. Thus, he does not transform a concept that the OT and Second Temple literature interpret to be the eschatological world. These corpuses are the rich wells of scriptural tradition from which he draws, reminding the Galatians that those "in Christ" are the heirs of world. This view stands in stark contrast to scholars like Davies, who argue that the apostle displays discontinuity with Jewish eschatological expectations, for he deterritorializes or spiritualizes the tangible nature of the promise.

In the individual sections of Galatians 3–4, I have argued that in 3:15–18 Paul shows that Christ is the promised offspring of Abraham who will inherit the world, the place over which he will rule (cf. 2 Sam 7; Ps 2). Subsequently, in 3:19–29 he asserts that those who place their faith "in Christ Jesus," the Davidic king (cf. Ps 2), will be his fellow-heirs. Then, in 4:1–7 the apostle employs exodus imagery to assure his readers that they have been delivered from bondage to sin and are being led by the Spirit through the present, sinful wilderness until they inherit the world to come. In other words, they are on a new exodus to the eschatological inheritance. Lastly, in 4:21–31 Paul draws on the Sarah and Hagar story to affirm strongly that the inheritance is the future world promised to Abraham's descendants.

Looking at these texts as a cohesive argument, we see that there are three themes associated with the inheritance in Galatians. First, the inheritance is the eschatological world (Gal 3:15—4:7; 4:21–31). Second, there will be a kingdom in the world to come, for Christ will rule over his inheritance (Gal 3:15–18). Third, the Spirit guarantees that God's people will possess the territory promised to them (Gal 4:1–7).

Galatians is Paul's most systematic treatment of the inheritance, for he never again discusses the above themes in a unified argument. An examination of the remaining inheritance related texts in Paul will show incredible continuity with Galatians. Chapter six will explicitly confirm that in Paul's letters the inheritance is the renewed world (Rom 4:13–25; 8:12–25). Chapter seven will then show that the cosmic inheritance is where God will establish his final kingdom (1 Cor 6:9–11; 15:50–58; Gal 5:18–21; Eph 5:3–7; Col 1:9–14; 3:18–25), and will also bring to light that Paul views the Spirit to be the guarantee of the inheritance. That is to say, Paul believes that the Spirit will see to it that believers receive what they do "not yet" possess (Eph 1:10–14; Titus 3:4–6).

7

The Inheritance in Paul

Romans

PAUL'S LETTER TO THE Romans is in continuity with the cosmic nature of the inheritance in Galatians. In the previous chapter, I showed that in Galatians Paul alludes to texts such as Psalm 2 to establish that God's people will inherit the world. I will now show that in Romans Paul is much more explicit in defining the inheritance, calling it the κόσμος (4:13). Although this term speaks to the tangible, futuristic nature of the inheritance, some scholars argue that for Paul this theme is "already" being fulfilled in the present, while still holding that it has "not yet" been fully realized.

I have noted on several occasions that James Hester is the only other author to have written an entire monograph dedicated to the inheritance in Paul's letters. Thus, I consider him to be the chief proponent of the "already-not-yet" inheritance perspective. I have reserved more extensive interaction with his argument until this chapter, since he generally discusses the inheritance in Galatians and Romans in tandem. In sections of larger volumes, scholars such as G. K. Beale and Edward Adams provide brief arguments in favor of an "already-not-yet" view of the inheritance. Their short discussions will require less interaction.

The present chapter will address the inheritance concept in Romans 4:13–25 and 8:14–25. I will argue that Paul presents a cohesive argument of the inheritance in these passages by contending that the inheritance is the κόσμος in 4:13–25 and then describing this concept eschatologically in 8:14–25. Together these passages provide some of the clearest evidence of the Pauline understanding of the inheritance.

ROMANS 4:13-25: THE INHERITANCE AS THE ΚΟΣΜΟΣ

The examination of the inheritance in this passage will be an essential first step toward confirming the cosmic, eschatological nature of this concept in Romans.[1] Here, Paul underscores that God has sworn the eschatological world to Abraham's innumerable, diverse offspring (4:13–18), a promise from which Abraham never wavered (4:19–25).

Romans 4:13–18: The World Promised to Abraham's Offspring

Already in Romans 4:13, Paul offers specific insight into the content of the inheritance.[2] This is significant because, as Hester rightly notes, in his other letters Paul rarely bothers to define the inheritance "because there is no dispute about its contents."[3] Paul and his readers have been shaped by the worldview of the OT and Second Temple literature, corpuses that repeatedly assert that the inheritance is the eschatological world. Thus, for the Pauline communities (e.g., the Galatians) the inheritance theme carries the freight of this expectation. In Romans 4:13, however, Paul is very explicit in defining the inheritance, bringing into full view what he normally only insinuates elsewhere.

Paul unpacks the inheritance in the following statement: "The promise to Abraham and to his descendants (ἡ ἐπαγγελία τῷ Ἀβραὰμ ἢ[4] τῷ σπέρματι αὐτοῦ) that he would be the heir of the world (τὸ κληρονόμον αὐτὸν εἶναι κόσμου) was not through the Law, but through the righteousness that comes from faith."[5] The promise (ἐπαγγελία) to Abraham and his offspring is encapsulated in the phrase "that he would be the heir of the world" (τὸ κληρονόμον αὐτὸν εἶναι κόσμου), in which the content of the inheritance is the κόσμος. Most commentators agree that this cosmic view of the promise is grounded in Second Temple literature, within which "the promise of land

---

1. Romans is one of the *Hauptbriefe*. Thus, the consensus is that Romans is authentically Pauline.

2. Foreman, *Politics of Inheritance*, 59.

3. Hester, *Paul's Concept of Inheritance*, 69. Also noted by Foreman, *Politics of Inheritance*, 59.

4. The particle ἢ "comes close to the force of a copulative conjunction, especially in negative clauses" (BDF, 231). See Acts 1:7; John 8:14. This is also the case in Rom 4:13, for ἢ indicates that Abraham "and" his offspring are the beneficiaries of the promise of a cosmic inheritance.

5. All Greek NT citations are from the NA 28.

evolved to cosmic proportions."[6] Among such passages are Sirach 44:21, *Jubilees* 22:14, *1 Enoch* 5:7, and *2 Baruch* 14:13, all of which assert that Abraham's descendants will inherit the eschatological world.[7] The Second Temple view of the inheritance is itself rooted in latter OT passages such as Isaiah 65–66, which envision that God's people will inherit the future world (Ps 2, 72; Isa 54; Ezek 36–37).[8] So, from the latter OT to Second Temple literature the promise of a land inheritance to Abraham and his offspring (e.g., Gen 12, 15) is enlarged beyond Canaan to encompass the entire coming world.[9] Almost certainly, Paul's interpretation of the inheritance as the κόσμος is rooted in this tradition.[10]

Paul's choice of κόσμος over γῆ is also significant. He could have chosen γῆ, since it is often associated with the promised land in the LXX (cf. Gen 15:17). However, according to Edward Adams, his selection of κόσμος has a broad focus that "eliminates any suggestion of a reference to Palestine."[11] This term in Romans 4:13 thus undoubtedly "refers to . . . the 'world' which

6. Adams, *Constructing the World*, 167. See Schreiner, *Romans*, 227; Moo, *Romans*, 274; Middendorf, *Romans 1–8*, 353; Dunn, *Romans 1–8*, 213; Seifrid, "Romans," 625. Wilckens, *Römer*, 1:269.

7. See chap. 5 for my examination of such Second Temple passages. Besides these, Adams quotes the relevant rabbinic saying of R. Nehemiah (*Mek. Exod.* 14:31): "Thus wilt thou find of Abraham that he has taken possession of this and the future world as a reward of faith, as it is written, He believed in Yahweh and he reckoned it to him for righteousness" (*Constructing the World*, 168).

8. See chap. 4 for my observations on the inheritance in the Psalms and Prophets.

9. Dahl argues that Paul's interpretation of the inheritance as the world in Rom 4:13 is rooted in Jewish eschatological tradition (*Studies in Paul*, 129–30). Yet, he argues that Paul departs from his predecessors in that "Paul does not hope for political power in an earthly kingdom" (ibid., 130). I am unclear as to what Dahl means by "political power in an earthly kingdom," since he does not unpack this statement, only claiming that for Paul "the promise guarantees participation in universal sovereignty." While he does not advocate for political power in an oppressive sense, I will argue in the following chapter that Paul does anticipate there being a kingdom in an earthly inheritance, of which he will be a coheir (Gal 5:19–21; 1 Cor 15:50–55). This kingdom does involve participation in the rule and reign of Christ.

10. Wright says that in Rom 4:13 "Paul has built hints of other points to be developed as his argument progresses. . . . He reads the geographical promises of Genesis 15 in terms of God's intention that God's 'seed' would inherit, not one territory, but the whole cosmos. Paul here is close to one strand of Second Temple Jewish thought that developed the idea of Gen 12:3; 18:18; and 22:18 . . . through the prophetic promises of Isa 11:10–14; 42:1, 6; 49:6; 54:3; 65:16 . . . and the psalmic visions of Ps 72:8–11 (the Messiah's worldwide dominion; cf. Exod 23:31; 1 Kgs 4:21, 24) to the post-biblical thought of Sir 44:21 . . . and *Jub.* 19:21" ("Romans," 10:495). Wright also says that "Paul's development of the 'inheritance' theme, so important in Genesis 15 and elsewhere in the Pentateuch, here takes a decisive turn that looks ahead to 8:12–30" (ibid., 10:496).

11. Adams, *Constructing the World*, 170.

is to be the eschatological inheritance of God's elect, that is to say, the new or restored creation."[12]

Despite this argument, some contend that in Romans 4:13 Paul conflates the inheritance with the other Abrahamic promises. Douglas Moo, for example, acknowledges that in the latter OT (e.g., Isa 55:3–5) and Second Temple literature (e.g., Sir. 44:21; *Jub.* 22:14, 32:19) "the promise of land had come to embrace the entire world."[13] Yet, he concludes that the inheritance in Romans 4:13 "generally refers to all God promised his people," that is, land, descendants, and blessing.[14] Caroline Johnson Hodge contends that in Romans 4:13 Paul "conflates several of God's promises (multiple descendants, land of Canaan, blessing of the *ethnē* in Abraham's seed) into one aggrandized promise that the peoples of the God of Israel would inherit the earth."[15] Both of these scholars overlook that Jewish literature distinguishes the promise of inheritance from the promises of offspring and blessing (e.g., Gen 12, 15, 17; Sir 44:19–21).[16] Paul himself argues that the one who has the Spirit (promise of blessing) is a son (promise of offspring) and thereby an heir of the land (promise of inheritance, Gal 4:6–7). He makes this affirmation without combining the promises into a single promise, nor confusing them in any way. Nothing that I have examined to this point—the OT, Second Temple literature, and Paul's letter to the Galatians—establishes credible precedence for encapsulating all the promises to Abraham under a

---

12. Ibid., 169.

13. Moo, *Romans*, 274.

14. Ibid.

15. Hodge, *If Sons, Then Heirs*, 88. Hodge appeals mainly to Second Temple literature to argue that the promises have been conflated into one, singular promise of the world. While citing several passages in endnotes, she uses Sir 44:19–21 as an example (ibid., 188). This is one of the Second Temple texts I examined in chapter four. Rather than conflating promises, I showed that Sirach 44:20 confirms the vastly expanded nature of the inheritance by asserting that God promised to Abraham's seed (τὸ σπέρμα αὐτοῦ) "that he would give them an inheritance (κατακληρονομῆσαι αὐτούς) from sea to sea and from the river to the end of the earth." Nowhere does the author conflate or confuse promises. Instead, he shows that Abraham's descendants (promise of seed) will receive the world (promise of inheritance). While her study is very helpful, this is one point with which I disagree.

Stowers's *A Rereading of Romans* provides a fresh perspective on Romans. Helpfully, he contends that in Rom 4:13 Paul alludes to Gen 13:15 and 17:8, understanding the land in these texts "as a type for the whole world because he speaks of the *kosmos* in 4:13" (ibid., 246). Yet, he too, like Moo and Johnson, argues that Paul conflates the Abrahamic promises (ibid., 244–46). As I argue above, a careful examination of the way Paul and Jewish literature interact with the Abrahamic promises shows that they closely associate, but do not combine, the promises of land, seed, and blessing. See my argument in chaps. 3–5.

16. See my discussion in chapters 3–5.

singular promissory theme. Moo and Johnson's interpretation of the inheritance in Romans 4:13 is therefore inconsistent with the individual (though related) nature of the Abrahamic promises. As well, it muddles the idea that the word κόσμος necessitates a precisely territorial, enlarged understanding of the inheritance.

Although I disagree with Moo and Johnson's interpretation of Romans 4:13, neither of them deny that, in some sense, Paul has the inheritance of the world in view. We have this much in common. Halvor Moxnes, however, refutes the cosmic view of the inheritance in Romans 4:13. He interprets the phrase "heir of the world" as "the charismatic community, viewed from an eschatological perspective," because Paul focuses on the term κληρονόμος rather than κόσμος.[17] As such, he "does not go into details about the future hope . . . It is the structure and identity of the community of 'heirs to the world' with which he is concerned."[18] The community, according to Moxnes, is composed of Jews and gentiles, a thought that is supported by the immediate context in verses 11–12 and 16–18.[19] Moxnes is right to argue for a Jew-Gentile community emphasis in 4:11–18, since Paul claims that Abraham is the "father of many nations" (πατέρα πολλῶν ἐθνῶν) in verse 17. Nonetheless, he is incorrect in claiming that 4:13 does not elaborate on the content of the hope promised to Abraham's descendants, for this verse does so in asserting that Abraham's offspring are the heirs of the coming world, a declaration that would have directed the hope of Paul's Jewish and Gentile readers on their future inheritance. This pronouncement is in line with the Psalms, Prophets, and Second Temple literature, which assure God's people of an eschatological inheritance (e.g., Isa 54, 65–66; Sir. 44:21). Paul, then, in Romans 4:13, like latter Jewish tradition, assures his Jewish and Gentile readers of the hope of the coming world. So, for Moxnes to say that Paul stresses the communal aspect to the detriment of the future hope is to misunderstand the content of the inheritance in this text. Since Paul defines the promise to be the coming world, it is right to understand it as such.

The rest of Romans 4:13–18 identifies the genuine heirs of the eschatological world. Here, Paul argues that the hope of a future inheritance is not "through the Law" (διὰ νόμου, 4:13)[20] but "through the righteousness

---

17. Moxnes, *Theology in Conflict*, 249. For his entire argument, see pp. 247–49.

18. Ibid., 249.

19. See Adams, *Constructing the World*, 169.

20. I agree with Schreiner: "It is quite likely that the Mosaic Law is in view. First, the γάρ joining verses 9–12 and 13–16 establishes a close connection between circumcision and the law, and obviously the former relates to the Mosaic Law. Second, νόμος generally relates to the Mosaic Law in Romans, and thus we expect a reference to the Mosaic Law when the term appears" (*Romans*, 232).

that comes from faith" (διὰ δικαιοσύνης πίστεως, cf. Gal 3:21–29). If "those from the Law are the heirs" (οἱ ἐκ νόμου κληρονόμοι), then "faith would be emptied and the promise of inheritance (ἐπαγγελία) would be made void" (Rom 4:14; cf. Gal 3:15–18). But, the inheritance is not received through the Mosaic Law, only through faith. As such, those who rely on the Law will not inherit the eschatological world.

The reason why the promised inheritance is received by faith is so that (ἵνα) it might be given as a χάρις (Rom 4:16). The term χάρις normally carries the sense of "grace."[21] However, in Romans 4:16 it more accurately denotes the sense of "gift" (i.e., something given freely), as it does in Galatians 3:18. The OT affirms that God is the owner of the land inheritance. The clearest example of this point is in the Holiness Code of Leviticus 19–26, within which God emphatically declares, "The land is mine" (Lev 25:23).[22] The inheritance is linked to an owner who is not compelled to bestow his territory on those who attempt to earn it.[23] For this reason, Paul insists that God grants the promised inheritance as a "gift" (χάρις) to those who exhibit the same faith as Abraham (cf. Rom 4:18–21). As Mark Foreman argues, "It is likely that when Paul refers to the promise which 'depends on faith' and rests 'on grace,' one of his intentions is to remind his audience that the future inheritance is not something which is earned or deserved but . . . is always a grant or gift of God."[24]

Since the inheritance is a gift, it follows that it is a "promise guaranteed for all the seed" (βεβαίαν τὴν ἐπαγγελίαν παντὶ τῷ σπέρματι, Rom 4:16).[25] Like Galatians 3:16, Paul employs τῷ σπέρματι to refer to Abraham's "seed." Here, though, he does not intend to narrow the seed to one individual

---

21. BDAG, 1079.

22. See my discussion in chapter 3.

23. Hodge rightly notes that Paul's "point is that no one, Jew or gentile, can achieve righteousness before God (by Law-keeping or any other practice); righteousness is rather a product of God's mercy" (*If Sons, Then Heirs*, 189).

24. Foreman, *Politics of Inheritance*, 94. Barclay sees some overlap, though with a shift in emphasis, on the theme of gift/grace in Galatians and Romans: "In respect to both Torah and Israel, Romans develops the theology of Galatians, adding dialectical counterpoints that alter the impact of the whole. . . . These changes reflect not the weakening but the expansion of Paul's central perfection of grace—its incongruity with the worth of its recipients. By placing this incongruous grace within a wider frame, Paul demonstrates its centrality to the promises to Israel, and thus to the history of the Abrahamic family. The communities created by the Christ-gift are the fulfillment of the scriptural promise whose effects have always taken a paradoxical form, now manifested as Jews and gentiles are equally suspended from the unconditional mercy of God" (*Paul & the Gift*, 454–55).

25. Dunn notes that βεβαίος "would probably be familiar in a technical sense to denote legally guaranteed security" (*Romans 1–8*, 216).

(Christ). Instead, he employs the modifier παντὶ in relation to τῷ σπέρματι to confirm that the promised inheritance is assured "to all the offspring" of Abraham.

Paul further specifies the identity of the offspring in the remainder of Romans 4:16 as not those "from the Law only" (ἐκ τοῦ νόμου μόνον) but also those "from the faith of Abraham" (ἐκ πίστεως Ἀβραάμ). At first glance, this phrase seems to contradict the previous assertion that the inheritance is only received from faith (Rom 4:13). Tom Schreiner provides a clear explanation of this seemingly problematic statement:

> This phrase is rather strange because it seems to say that the inheritance is available either by the law or by faith. This would imply that Jews, who did not believe that Jesus was the Messiah, would receive the inheritance via the law . . . But this would contradict the clear intention of the previous verse. For instance, verses 11–12 say that Jews who are circumcised but lack faith are not true children of Abraham, and verses 13–15 contend that the promised inheritance cannot be gained through the law. Thus Paul is likely using the phrase ἐκ τοῦ νόμου in a different sense than the phrase ἐκ νόμου in verse 14. Here the intent is to say that the inheritance is available to both Jewish Christians and Gentiles who share the faith of Abraham.[26]

Indeed, as Schreiner argues, Paul's comments in Romans 4:16 do not contradict his previous assertion about the way the inheritance is received. Rather, they clarify that the heirs of the eschatological world consist of believing Jews and gentiles, a thought that further unpacks what Paul means in the phrase παντὶ τῷ σπέρματι.[27]

Abraham, then, is certainly the father of all believers (πατὴρ πάντων, Rom 4:16). Paul, in Romans 4:17, supports this point by citing Genesis 17:15 (LXX): "I have made you a father of many nations" (πατέρα πολλῶν ἐθνῶν τέθεικά σε)—a citation that elaborates on the promise of innumerable descendants who will possess the land in Genesis 15:5 (cf. 15:1–21).[28] This quotation affirms that the Jew-Gentile descendants of Abraham (cf. Rom

---

26. Schreiner, *Romans*, 232–33. Similarly, Moo, *Romans*, 278–79; Cranfield, *Romans*, 1:242–43.

27. Davies argues that territory is not in view in Rom 4:13–16 (*Gospel and Land*, 175–76). Davies, however, does not interact with Romans 4:13, in which Paul claims Abraham is an "heir of the world." It seems that Davies casually imposes a landless view of Paul's letters for which he has thus far argued. In so doing, he fails to address Paul's most explicit explanation of the content of inheritance. This is a major weakness of his argument.

28. Seifrid, "Romans," 626.

4:16) are fulfilling the promise of multitudinous offspring from every nation who will receive the inheritance.

Subsequently, in Romans 4:18 Paul declares that Abraham had confidence in the promise that he would be the "father of many nations" (πατέρα πολλῶν ἐθνῶν). This verse asserts that Abraham's assurance was in accord with "what was written" (τὸ εἰρημένον) in Genesis 15:5: "Thus will your offspring be" (οὕτως ἔσται τὸ σπέρμα σου). Reading πατέρα πολλῶν ἐθνῶν from Genesis 17:5 in light of οὕτως ἔσται τὸ σπέρμα σου from Genesis 15:5 makes it apparent that the promise of innumerable descendants from every nation is rooted in the covenant God made with Abraham. This leaves no doubt that the offspring promised to Abraham will include believers from all nations who will one day inherit the world.

The fact that the promise rests on faith eliminates any prior merit or ethnic privilege. Jews have no more of a claim to an inheritance than gentiles, for only those who exhibit the faith of Abraham become his children and heirs of what has been promised to him (cf. Gal 3).[29] John M. G. Barclay is correct in arguing:

> . . . the *mode* of Abraham's relationship to God (faith), and the *means* by which his seed has come into being (creation *ex nihilo*) are also objects of central attention [in Romans]. What integrates these concerns is the fact that the Abrahamic family, from the beginning, has been created by the grace and the calling of God, who has never paid regard to human capacity or worth.[30]

In the mind of Paul, Jews and gentiles who exhibit Abraham's faith have equal claim on the coming world. This kind of extravagant equity is made possible by the God who shows no partiality, calling those who once where "nothing" and making them heirs of the promises (Rom 4:17).

That which Paul has said to this point in Romans 4:13–18 demonstrates that he views the inheritance to be the eschatological world, standing in continuity with the Psalms, Prophets, and Second Temple literature. He unpacks clearly that to which he alludes, and assumes his audience will understand, in Galatians—that the inheritance has been cosmically enlarged. In so doing, he shows that people from every nation (Rom 4:16–18) who

29. Schnelle makes an insightful observation: "Precisely the figure of Abraham shows that God acts contingently and that it is not possible for any group to claim God's action exclusively for itself. Everything rests in God's own hands, whose promises may be trusted now, as they were then, despite all appearances to the contrary" (*Apostle Paul*, 326).

30. Barclay, *Paul & the Gift*, 481.

have the faith of Abraham will inherit the world (Rom 4:13–16). Rightly did God call Abraham the father of many nations (Gen 15:5, 17:5).[31]

Romans 4:19–25: Abraham's Faith in the Promise

Verses 19–21 of this passage recount the faith of Abraham despite the bareness of Sarah's womb. In the original story in Genesis 17:15–17, God promises Abraham that his wife will bear a child, to which Abraham responds: "Can a child be born to a man who is a hundred years old? Can Sarah, who is ninety years old, bear a child?"[32] Abraham's response seems to reflect doubt in God's promise. Paul, however, portrays him as being more confident in what God had sworn to him: "Not weakening in faith, he regarded his own body as already being dead . . . and the deadness of Sarah's womb" (Rom 4:19). He "did not doubt the promise (τὴν ἐπαγγελίαν) of God in unbelief but was strengthened in faith, giving glory to God" (Rom 4:20). Paul goes on to say that Abraham was convinced that God "was also able to do what he had promised" (Rom 4:21).

Commentators often contend that this passage mainly develops the argument of faith over works.[33] This interpretation does not consider that Romans 4:13–18 and 4:19–21 are interrelated, the former focusing on the "inheritance of the world" and the latter on Abraham's confidence in "God's promise of innumerable offspring." Together, they link the notions of "land" (Rom 4:13–18) and "offspring" (Rom 4:19–21) witnessed throughout the OT (e.g., Gen 24:1–9; 26:1–3; 28:1–5; 35:9–12). Genesis 17, the passage to which Romans 4:19–21 alludes, makes this specific connection. The fact that the land promise has been cosmically enlarged means that Romans 4:19–21 also echoes Isaiah 54 (cf. Gal 4:27), which reinterprets Genesis 17 and foretells that Abraham's descendants will become so numerous that they will inherit the coming world.[34] The presence of this reinterpretation suggests that the link between Romans 4:13–18 and 4:19–21(where the "inheritance of the world" is closely tied to the "offspring of Abraham") "would not have been entirely unexpected for his audience and that Paul might

---

31. Martin provides a good discussion of the inheritance in the Pauline Epistles (*Bound for the Promised Land*, 131–40). Here, he helpfully shows the typological trajectory of the inheritance promise from the OT to Paul's letters, underscoring that the land has expanded to encompass the world.

32. Also cited in Foreman, *Politics of Inheritance*, 86.

33. See Jewett, *Romans*, 336–43; Cranfield, *Romans*, 1:247–52.

34. Foreman, *Politics of Inheritance*, 85–92. See chap. 4 for my discussion of Isa 54.

have intentionally evoked this earlier tradition."[35] Thus, Romans 4:19–21, read along with 4:13–18, asserts that Abraham believed God would make his people so numerous that they would one day inherit the eschatological world. Such a claim suggests that Paul recounts the story of Abraham's faith mainly to develop the inheritance argument in Romans 4, rather than to advance the notion of faith over works.

Furthermore, because of his faith in the promise, Abraham "was declared righteous" (ἐλογίσθη αὐτῷ εἰς δικαιοσύνην, Rom 4:22). Romans 4:23–25 contends that this pronouncement is not solely for Abraham, but also "for whom it is about to be reckoned (οἷς μέλλει λογίζεσθαι), that is, those who believe upon the one who raised Jesus our Lord from the dead, who was handed over for our transgressions and was raised for our righteousness."[36] As Abraham believed in the God "who makes alive the things that were dead" (Rom 4:17), so also "Christians believe in the God who raised Jesus from the dead."[37] The result is that they, like Abraham, will be declared righteous.

The notion of righteousness in Romans 4:24 has a deliberate futuristic sense. Paul could have used the aorist tense verb ἐλογίσθη to highlight the righteousness that has already been pronounced on believers (as he does with respect to Abraham in Rom 4:22). In its place, though, he employs the construction οἷς μέλλει λογίζεσθαι, which has neither a past nor present connotation, but points to the verdict that "is about to be reckoned" at the future judgment (cf. 2:16; 3:6; 8:33–34).[38] The futuristic view of righteousness in 4:24 coheres with 4:13–25, which looks forward to a cosmic eschatological inheritance for Abraham's offspring. Paul's association of "eschatological inheritance" and "future righteousness" also runs through texts in the OT and Second Temple literature (Isa 54:1–17; 1 En. 24–27, 58–69; 4 Ezra 7–8; 2 Bar. 14, 51; 4Q171:4). Among such is Isaiah 54:1–17, which evidences that God will bestow the status of righteousness on his people when they receive their inheritance. Being steeped in Jewish tradition, Paul, in Romans 4:13–25, likely sees his readers as those who will be righteous when they

---

35. Ibid., 87.

36. Dunn insightfully notes, "Rom 4:25 is evidence . . . that Isa 53 provided the first-generation Christians with an important scriptural means of understanding the death of Jesus, and the fact that the reference is a formulaic allusion rather than a carefully argued scriptural proof . . . strongly suggests that the use of Isa 53 was widespread in earliest Christian apologetic and exercised a major influence on earliest Christian thought" (Romans, 241).

37. Schreiner, Romans, 242.

38. Dunn, Galatians, 240.

inherit the world. Not only does this assert future righteousness in this passage, but also the eschatological nature of the inheritance.

With that said, it is apparent that in Romans 4:13–25 Paul appeals to texts such as Genesis 15 and 17 and Isaiah 54 to argue that Abraham's innumerable diverse offspring will not merely inherit "one piece of territory but the whole cosmos."[39] This is the passage in Paul that most clearly demonstrates that Canaan is a type of the greater inheritance that awaits God's people. What is more, here Paul links the notions of "inheritance of the world" and "future righteousness," underscoring that God's people will be righteous when they receive the inheritance.

The theme of inheriting the world in Romans 4:12–25 now anticipates the argument in Romans 8:14–25, in which Paul further describes the inheritance of Abraham's descendants as the redeemed creation.[40] In so doing, it will be unmistakable that God's people will dwell in a place far better than the land of Canaan.

ROMANS 8:14–25: THE INHERITANCE AS THE RECREATED WORLD

After discussing the eschatological inheritance in Romans 4, and not discussing it in chapters 5–7, Paul resumes this theme again in chapter 8. N. T. Wright explains that there is logical flow in the intervening context of chapters 5–7, one that evokes the imagery of the new exodus. In his own words,

> The narrative sequence is as follows: those who were enslaved in the "Egypt of sin," an enslavement the law only exacerbated, have been set free by the "Red Sea" event of baptism, since in baptism they are joined to the Messiah, whose death and resurrection are accounted as theirs. They are now given as their guide, not indeed the law, which, although given by God, is unable to more than condemn them for their sin, but the Spirit, so that the Mosaic covenant is replaced, as Jeremiah and Ezekiel said it would be, with the covenant written on the hearts of God's people by God's own Spirit.[41]

The story of the new exodus in Romans 5–7 is therefore the glue that holds chapters 4–8 together. Since Paul discusses the inheritance of the eschatological world in 4:13–25, and now again in 8:14–25, it seems that the

39. Wright, "New Exodus, New Inheritance," 31.

40. Ibid., 31–35. Wright, "Paul and Caesar," 189.

41. Wright, "New Exodus, New Inheritance," 29.

intervening chapters serve to remind his readers that they will inherit the world after completing the Spirit-led new exodus.[42]

With this in mind, in 8:14–25 Paul summarizes the highpoints of the new exodus to reassert that the Spirit is leading God's sons through the present wilderness (8:14–17) until they inherit the recreated cosmos (8:18–25).

Romans 8:14–17: The New Exodus to the Inheritance

The opening phrase of Romans 8:14, "as many as are led by the Spirit" (ὅσοι πνεύματι θεοῦ ἄγονται), resonates with the Spirit's leading of Israel in the exodus. Paul's use of ἄγω is significant for asserting this echo. Silvia Keesmaat argues that the LXX employs ἄγω, often prefixed with ἐξ, and its synonym ὁδηγέω to recount how God lead his people in the exodus.[43] Three examples from the Psalms will illustrate this point:

> Psalm 77: "He led them (ὡδήγησεν) in the cloud by day and the entire night with a fiery flame (v. 14) . . . He led (ἀνήγαγεν) them as a shepherd in the wilderness."[44]

> Psalm 104: "And he led them out (ἐξήγαγεν) with silver and gold (v. 37) . . . for he remembered his holy promise to his servant Abraham and led out (ἐξήγαγεν) his people with great joy and his chosen ones with festivity."

> Psalm 142:10: "Your good Spirit will lead (ὁδηγήσει) me on level ground (ἐν γῇ εὐθείᾳ)."

Each of these passages demonstrates God leading (ἄγω) his people on the exodus journey. In particular, the emphasis in Psalm 142:10 on "ἐν γῇ εὐθείᾳ (on level ground) calls to mind those passages which outline a new exodus for the people of God—one in which there will be a straight and level path through the wilderness."[45] Paul's use of ἄγω likely indicates that he draws on Spirit-leading imagery from such texts. As such, the phrase ὅσοι πνεύματι θεοῦ ἄγονται in Romans 8:14 would likely have prompted Paul's readers to

42. Jewett argues that Paul has arranged Romans according to the arrangement of classical rhetoric (*Romans*, 29–30). Within this structure, he sees Rom 5–8 as the second rhetorical "proof" of Paul's argument. While he was likely familiar with the norms of classical literature, Paul the Jew most likely employed an OT image such as the exodus to link Rom 5–8. As he uses this theme in Gal 4:1–7, he now does so again in Romans to make a similar argument.

43. Keesmaat, *Paul and His Story*, 55–60. The following examples are drawn from Keesmaat (ibid., 58).

44. LXX Psalms citations are from Rahlfs, *Psalmi cum Odis*.

45. Keesmaat, *Paul and His Story*, 59. See Isa 40, 49.

envision that he is applying the new exodus tradition to them, in that they are the ones now being led by the Spirit through the wilderness until they inherit the world.

Paul goes on to claim that that those being led by the Spirit are "the sons of God" (υἱοὶ θεοῦ, Rom 8:14). Throughout the OT, Israel is considered to be God's son (e.g., Exod 4:22; Hos 11:1). There are several LXX passages that use the verbs ἄγω and ὁδηγέω to recall God leading his son during the exodus. Deuteronomy 32 describes how God "led" (ἤγεν, v. 12) the Israelites, recognized as his "sons" (υἱοί, vv. 19–20), through the wilderness. Closer to the language of Paul is Isaiah 63, which refers to Israel as God's children (τέκνα, vv. 8–9), whom the Spirit led (ὡδήγησεν, v. 14) in the exodus. These passages show that God guided his children, by means of his Spirit (Isa 63; Neh 9), on the exodus journey. Such texts, given the similarity in context and language, form part of the intertextual background of Romans 8:14.

Another important passage is Jeremiah 38 (LXX [31 MT]).[46] In this new exodus/new covenant chapter, God says, "I lead (ἄγω) them from the north, and I will gather (συνάξω) them from the end of the earth . . . and they will come back here. With tears they went out, and with comfort I will lead them up (ἀνάξω), causing them to dwell in streams of water" (vv. 8–9).[47] God will do so because he has become a "father" (πατέρα) "to Israel" (τῷ Ἰσραηλ, v. 9). This text also notes that the place to which Israel will be gathered is the renewed land (v. 17) from which it will not be uprooted (v. 40). Jeremiah 38 (LXX) thereby demonstrates that God will guide his children on the new exodus until they enter the reconstituted land. Paul appears to apply this tradition to his readers, describing them as God's children being guided on the new exodus journey (Rom 8:14–17) to the permanent reconstituted abode (8:18–25), thereby fulfilling Jeremiah's prophesied sojourn to the inheritance.

Since those being led by the Spirit are God's sons, Paul argues that they have not received "a spirit of slavery again leading into fear" (πνεῦμα δουλείας πάλιν εἰς φόβον, Rom 8:15). During the original exodus, there are various accounts of Israel being fearful in the face of danger and as a result desiring to return to slavery in Egypt. One of these is Exodus 14 (LXX),

---

46. Ibid., 64.

47. Thompson argues that "the *flowing streams* may be a contrastive allusion to the water from the rock of Exod. 17:1–7; Num. 20:1–13, where there was an intermittent flow. Now there will be water in flowing streams. . . . The imagery of this verse is strongly reminiscent of Deutero-Isaiah, where the return from captivity in Babylon is depicted. But the event transcends the Exodus from Egypt in every way (Isa. 43:16–29; cf. Jer. 16:14–15" (*Jeremiah*, 570). LXX Jeremiah citations are from Ziegler, *Ieremias, Baruch, Threni, Epistula Ieremiae*.

which records God's deliverance of Israel through the Red Sea, in spite of his children being afraid (φοβέω) of the Egyptians marching behind (v. 10) and questioning whether it would have been better to return to Egypt as slaves (δουλεύω) than to die in the wilderness (vv. 11–12).[48] Deuteronomy 1 and Numbers 14 also reveal Israel's fear leading to a longing to return to bondage in Egypt. Such texts "parallel the dynamic which Paul is outlining in Rom. 8.15," thus forming the "conceptual background" for this text.[49] Unlike the Israelites, Paul's readers are not to allow their present difficulties to make them so fearful that they desire to return to slavery. Whereas Israel was once enslaved to Egypt, Paul's readers were at one point enslaved to the Law (cf. Gal 4:3–7). This is the slave master to whom they should not return. The Spirit, however, has set God's people free from bondage to the Law (Rom 8:2) and is leading them on a new exodus to the coming world (Rom 8:14–25; cf. Gal 4:1–7). Returning to slavery would result in forfeiting the journey to the inheritance.

Rather than receiving a "spirit of slavery" (πνεῦμα δουλείας), Paul's readers have received the "Spirit of sonship" (πνεῦμα υἱοθεσίας, Rom 8:15). James Scott argues that "the opposition of δουλεία and υἱοθεσία in Rom. 8:15 . . . presupposes the same exodus typology as in Gal. 4:1–7, where redemption from slavery accompanies divine adoption (v.5), so that believers are no longer slaves but sons."[50] Scott is correct in arguing that Paul uses the same typological reading of the exodus story in Romans 8 as he does in Galatians 4. To add to Scott's comments, the Spirit is the one who redeems God's children from the Law and directs them on a new exodus (Gal 4:6; Rom 4:14–17) the same way he redeemed the Israelites from slavery in Egypt and guided them on the original exodus (cf. Deut 32; Ps 142; Isa 63; Neh 9). Unlike the original exodus, the present exodus will not culminate in a reentry into Canaan. Instead, it will climax in the Spirit leading God's sons to the coming world (e.g., Ps 2; Isa 54, 65, 66; Rom 4:13). Those who are driven back into slavery on account of fear have no such hope.

What is more, in leading God's people, the Spirit bears witnesses that they are "children of God" (τέκνα θεοῦ, Rom 8:16). Paul again draws on new exodus texts to make this claim. One such text is Isaiah 43–44, in which God's guidance of his people to the restored land bears witness that they are his progeny.[51] Another is Sirach 36:10–14, in which the author foretells that God will bear witness (μαρτύριον) to his people who will be gathered

---

48. LXX Exodus citations are from Wevers, *Exodus*.

49. Keesmaat, *Paul and His Story*, 69.

50. Scott, *Adoption as Sons*, 265.

51. Keesmaat, *Paul and His Story*, 78–80.

together (συνάγω) and given an inheritance (κατακληρονομέω).[52] Such new exodus passages affirm "the Spirit witnesses that believers are God's children precisely in the act of leading them" to the restored inheritance.[53] That which Isaiah and Sirach foretold is therefore being fulfilled as the Spirit confirms to believers that they are God's children as he leads them on a new exodus.

Furthermore, as God's "children" (τέκνα), Paul's readers are also "heirs" (κληρονόμοι, Rom 8:17). The term κληρονόμοι takes up the theme of the promised eschatological world from Romans 4:13.[54] Although Abraham is not mentioned in 8:17, as he is in 4:13, there is no warrant for claiming that Paul now changes the content of what believers will inherit. This is supported by the fact that Galatians 4:4–7, which "closely follows the logic of Romans 8:17," uses κληρονόμος to point to the Abrahamic heir who will possess the eschatological world.[55] Since this is the case in the closely associated passage of Galatians 4:4–7, then it is also likely the case in Romans 8:17.[56] The following discussion in 8:18–25 also confirms that the inheritance of God's children is the future renewed earth. The evidence, then, strongly suggests that the term κληρονόμοι in 8:17 picks up the idea of the inheritance of the coming world mentioned in 4:13.[57]

Paul now provides further insight into his readers' status as heirs. Specifically, he says that they are "heirs of God" (κληρονόμοι θεοῦ, Rom 8:17). Some, such as C. E. B. Cranfield, argue that θεοῦ should be the objective genitive of κληρονόμοι, meaning that the heirs will inherit God.[58] This understanding of κληρονόμοι θεοῦ is highly unlikely, given that 8:14–25

52. LXX Sirach citations are from Ziegler, *Sapientia Iesu Filii Sirach.*

53. Keesmaat, *Paul and His Story,* 81.

54. Contra Cranfield who argues that Rom 8:17 should not be explained in light of Rom 4 (*Romans,* 1:405–7).

55. Scott, *Adoption as Sons,* 249. See Scott's side-by-side parallel of Rom 8:14–17 and Gal 4:4–7.

56. Italics mine. Beale argues that "the link between 4:13–14 and 8:17 is evident in that these are the only passages in Romans where this [plural] Greek word for 'heirs' occurs" (*New Testament Biblical Theology,* 761).

57. Considering what has been noted thus far in Rom 8:14–17, it is evident that, like Gal 4:6–7, this passage brings together the three Abrahamic covenant promises of blessing, offspring, and inheritance (cf. Gen 12, 15, 17). It does so by contending that the Spirit (blessing; Rom 8:14–16) testifies to Paul's readers that they are God's children (offspring; 8:16) and in turn heirs (inheritance; 8:17). Paul weaves these promises into the framework of the new exodus story in Rom 8:14–17, as in Gal 4:6–7, to bring to mind that the Spirit is leading God's sons through the present sinful wilderness until they inherit the coming world. Paul's readers will continue to be led by the Spirit until they possess what has been promised to them.

58. Cranfield, *Romans,* 1:407. See also Dunn, *Romans 1–8,* 455; Schreiner, *Romans,* 427.

suggest that the new exodus story will culminate in the inheritance of the recreated world, and that the term κληρονόμος in 8:17 points back to the inheritance of the world in 4:13.[59] Therefore, the present context, as well as the resonance of the cosmic inheritance in 4:13, makes it improbable that God is now the content of the inheritance. Thus, it is best to read θεοῦ as the subjective genitive of κληρονόμοι, meaning that "God is the bestower of the inheritance rather than the inheritance himself."[60]

Besides this, Paul's readers are also "fellow-heirs with Christ" (συγκληρονόμοι Χριστοῦ, Rom 8:17).[61] This statement encapsulates what has already been affirmed in Galatians 3:15–29—that believers are coheirs of the coming world with Christ. This prospect is contingent (εἴπερ) upon whether they "suffer with him in order that they might also be glorified with him" (Rom 8:17). Simply put, believers must continue to suffer the anxieties and persecutions of the present world (cf. Phil 1:29; 3:10; 2 Cor 1:5), if they are to dwell in glory along with Christ.

Hester argues that believers' status as sons of God, which necessitates present suffering, is evidence that the inheritance is "already" being fulfilled.[62] He claims that, having the Spirit, believers in Christ have been delivered from slavery to the elements of the world and are now sons of God and thus fellow-heirs with Christ (Gal 3:15–4:7; Rom 8:14, 17). As such, their status as sons compels them to suffer in the present, so as to guarantee that they will receive the fullness of the inheritance, i.e., the "glory" they do "not yet" possess (Rom 8:17). In short, for Hester the "already" of the inheritance is the Christ event that brings the possibility of sonship into the present, and the "not yet" is the glorious inheritance to come.

I agree that believers await a glorious inheritance that they do "not yet" possess. This has been my main point throughout this book. My disagreement with Hester lies in his contention that in sonship the promised inheritance is "already" being realized. Hester summarizes his "already" view of the inheritance as follows:

---

59. Keesmaat, *Paul and His Story*, 83.

60. Foreman, *Politics of Inheritance*, 115. The fact that the eschatological world is the content of inheritance in Rom 8:17 also fits the argument of Romans. As Keesmaat argues: "In the context of Romans, which emphasizes the sonship of believers in contrast with slavery, and then goes on to speak of the importance of the sons in relation to the earth, it seems that the conceptual context coheres with the sons as the heirs who will receive the earth" (*Paul and His Story*, 83).

61. Wallace notes that in Rom 8:17 Χριστοῦ is a genitive of association in relation συγκληρονόμοι (*Greek Grammar*, 128–29). This is often the case when the genitive modifies a noun prefixed with συν-.

62. Hester, *Paul's Concept of Inheritance*, 90–101.

... the 'already' of Inheritance can be described as the work of Christ and the obligations of sonship. Because of the work of Christ which Paul believes to be already accomplished, Christians are presently responsible to bear the obligations of the position of sonship in which His redeeming work places them. They should be able by the power of the Spirit to live as a son of God, and to bear the suffering that the Son and sons bear.[63]

Hester rightly proposes that the work of Christ makes it possible for believers to be Spirt-indwelt sons of God, who must persevere so as to receive the "glory" that lies ahead. However, being a "son" does not suggest that believers experience a present sense of the inheritance. As I have shown earlier, the Abrahamic covenant distinguishes between the promise of sonship/descendants and that of inheritance (Gen 12, 15, 17).[64] Paul also follows this precedent when he differentiates between these promises (Gal 4:6–7).[65] That these promises are normally grouped together does not suggest that they should be confused or blended together. The Abrahamic covenant contains multiple promises (land, seed, and blessing), and thus authors like Paul are likely to discuss these related, though distinguishable, promises in similar contexts without blending their contents. Earlier in this chapter, I showed that in Romans 4:13 Moo and Johnson make the error of conflating the promises under the singular promissory theme of inheritance. Though more detailed in his argument, Hester makes a similar error. One cannot assume that being a "son" suggests that the "inheritance" is "already" being realized. The Abrahamic covenant keeps theses promises separate, guaranteeing that the "land inheritance" will be given to the "sons" of Abraham (Gen 12, 15, 17). Hester fails to see this distinction in the promises to Abraham, which Paul himself follows in Galatians 4:6–7. Thereby, his view of the inheritance is flawed, for there is no sense in which the territorial inheritance has "already" been fulfilled. What one can claim is that God is presently fulfilling the promise of offspring, for believers in Christ are called "Abraham's sons" (Gal 3:29). These are the "sons" who will inherit the "glory" they do "not yet" possess.

Paul will clarify what he means by "glory" in 8:18–25. Here, he will make evident that this term points to the future redeemed world, that is, the inheritance, which believers have yet to possess. Until its appearance, believers, in the face of many sufferings, must continue the Spirit-led new

---

63. Ibid., 96.
64. See my argument in chapter 3.
65. See my argument in chapter 6.

exodus, knowing that they will one day complete the journey and dwell in the glorious future world described in 8:18–25.[66]

Romans 8:18–25: The New Exodus to the Recreated World

In Romans 8:18, Paul uses γάρ to signify that what follows will further explain the glory he speaks of in 8:17.[67] The children of God will experience this state upon completing the new exodus. While this journey may include sufferings and difficulties, such things pale in comparison to the "glory about to be revealed" (Rom 8:18; cf. 1 Pet 5:1).

Paul's use of κτίσις, which he first mentions in Romans 8:19, is significant for determining the future that awaits God's sons. James Dunn notes that "what all is included in κτίσις has been the subject of debate for centuries."[68] Of the possible interpretations, three merit serious attention: (1) κτίσις is the unbelieving human world;[69] (2) κτίσις refers to both non-believers and the inanimate creation;[70] and (3) κτίσις is inanimate creation.[71] Edward Adams argues that the first two options are improbable:

> It is highly doubtful that Paul would say that unredeemed humanity was subjected to futility and enslaved to decay 'not of its own will,' that is, through no fault of its own [Rom 8:20] . . . For this reason it is difficult to accommodate any reference to non-Christians in these verses. The suggested meanings of "unbelievers" and "unbelievers and the non-human creation" would seem equally implausible.[72]

The third option, however, is well supported by the context, for Paul compares the presently cursed creation with the redeemed creation to come (Rom 8:18–25). This view of κτίσις fits "with the established sense of the term (Wis 2:6; 5:17; 16:24; 19:6)"[73] and suggests that it points to the inanimate creation.[74]

---

66. Beale argues that Paul will now discuss of what believers are heirs in Rom 8:18–23 (*New Testament Biblical Theology*, 761).

67. Schreiner, *Romans*, 434.

68. Dunn, *Romans 1–8*, 469.

69. Schlatter, *Gottes Gerechtigkeit*, 270.

70. Käsemann, *Romans*, 233.

71. Dunn, *Romans 1–8*, 469; Schreiner, *Romans*, 434; Adams, *Constructing the World*, 176–78.

72. Adams, *Constructing the World*, 177.

73. Ibid., 178.

74. Henceforth, the κτίσις, i.e., the inanimate creation, will solely be called the

With this in mind, Paul contends that the creation (κτίσις), which was subject to futility, eagerly awaits "the revelation of the sons of God" (τὴν ἀποκάλυψιν τῶν υἱῶν τοῦ θεοῦ, Rom 8:19–20), at which time it will be freed "from the slavery of corruption" (ἀπὸ τῆς δουλείας τῆς φθορᾶς, Rom 8:21). Here, Paul insinuates that the curse of Genesis 3 will be reversed, and the world will be renewed into an Eden-like state when God's children are "revealed" (ἀποκάλυψις), that is to say, when they are resurrected.[75] This idea is grounded in OT passages such as Ezekiel 36–37, where the themes of "resurrection" and a "renewed land" are intimately related. The close link between these concepts is based on the belief that God's people will be "resurrected" to dwell in the "recreated world" (cf. Isa 65–66). This idea is carried into Second Temple passages such as 1 Enoch 51, which promise that the resurrected righteous ones will dwell upon the redeemed earth (cf. 1 En. 45). Such OT and Second Temple texts are fulfilled in Revelation 20–22, which prophecies of the time when God's children will be resurrected to inherit the reconstituted world (cf. 1 Cor 15:20–28). Paul's words in Romans 8:18–21 are in step with this expectation, for they point to the time when the entire creation, such as the stars, moon, sea, and stars, will no longer be subject to corruption and decay but will be restored once God's children are raised from the grave. When this event occurs, the people of God will at last dwell in the worldwide inheritance promised to Abraham.

Edward Adams arrives at a similar conclusion. In doing so, he rightly argues for the link between the κόσμος in 4:13 and the redeemed κτίσις in Romans 8:21:

> Christians ... are destined for "glory"—a glory that is to be shared with the liberated κτίσις of 8:21 ... the association of ideas in 8:17–23 strongly suggests that the inherited κόσμος of 4:13 is to be equated with the emancipated κτίσις of 8:21. If this interpretation is sufficiently accurate, 8:18–23 may, on one

---

"creation."

75. See Wright, "Romans," 596; Beale, *New Testament Biblical Theology*, 171. Middleton makes an insightful observation about Rom 8:19–23: "It is important here to understand the logic by which Paul includes the nonhuman creation in God's specific plan. In Paul's picture the human race implicitly takes the place of Pharaoh; we have subjected creation to futility or frustration, much as the Egyptians oppressed the Israelites. According to the first chapters of Genesis, humanity was granted stewardship over their earthly environment. But then came the fall, which distorted but did not abrogate our stewardship. . . . Human corruption has affected that which has been entrusted into our care, with result that the nonhuman creation is now 'subjected to futility.' There are echoes here of Genesis 3:17" (*New Heavens*, 160). The creation will experience redemption when "the oppressors (the human race)" are "liberated from their own sin," experiencing resurrection (ibid.).

level, be understood as an explication of the construction τὸ κληρονόμον αὐτὸν εἶναι κόσμου.[76]

Adams's observation illuminates the important link between the cosmic inheritance (κόσμος) in 4:13 and the redeemed creation (κτίσις) in 8:21, showing that the latter further explains the nature of the glorious inheritance. Paul strives to explain that it will be "a suitable inheritance for the people of God."[77]

In the interim, "the creation groans and experiences birth pains" (ἡ κτίσις συστενάζει καὶ συνωδίνει, Rom 8:22). Keesmaat argues that the "language of groaning with the travail of birth echoes those passages in the Old Testament where the travail of birth is associated with the coming day of the Lord's judgment or salvation."[78] Passages such as Isaiah 13:8, 26:17, and 66:7–8 point to the age of future deliverance, the last of these specifying that it will occur in the recreated world (cf. Jer 22:23; Hos 13:13; 1QH 3:6–19; 11:7–18). The present creation, suffering the pains of birth, looks forward to this time, for then it will be liberated from the curse of sin and gloriously transformed into the redeemed world on which God's children will dwell.

Like the creation, believers also groan (στενάζω), as they "eagerly await sonship (υἱοθεσίαν), the redemption of the body" (Rom 8:23). The sonship of which Paul speaks is eschatological, "for it involves the redemption of the body . . . so that it is raised from the dead and no longer a corruptible body but one that is incorruptible and immortal (1 Cor. 15:42–44, 53–54)."[79] So, although believers are presently sons (Rom 8:15–17), they long for the fulfillment of their sonship at the resurrection. Ultimately, however, they do not long for the resurrection itself, but for the recreated world which they will inhabit. Hence, it may be said that believers are eager to be raised from the dead so that they may reside in their inheritance.[80]

In anticipation of this time, believers have "the first fruits of the Spirit" (τὴν ἀπαρχὴν τοῦ πνεύματος, Rom 8:23). That is to say, in the Spirit they experience "a part of God's future redeeming power brought forward into the

---

76. Adams, *Constructing the World*, 170.

77. Hester, *Paul's Concept of Inheritance*, 82.

78. Keesmaat, "Intertextual Transformation of Tradition," 46.

79. Schreiner, *Romans*, 439.

80. Wright argues that "those who are raised from the dead also enjoy 'glory' in the sense of new responsibilities within the creation. This leads the eyes towards the 'inheritance,' the theme we met in Galatians 3 and 4 and Ephesians 1 and which now forms the main theme of verses 18–25. This part of Paul's larger picture of the world to come, the promised new age, focuses not so much on what sort of bodies those 'in Christ' will have in the resurrection, but on the sphere over which they will exercise their rule" (*Resurrection*, 258).

present."[81] The Spirit is the redeeming power that "is the *present* guarantee of the *future* inheritance and of the body which will be appropriate for that world" (cf. Rom 8:11, 17).[82] This idea is in line with Ephesians 1:14, in which Paul declares that the Spirit is the "guarantee" of the future inheritance (cf. Eph 1:14).[83] Believers may be confident of resurrected life in the eschatological world because the Spirit is the assurance of what they will one day possess.

Although Adams argues that the inheritance is the cosmos, he proposes that the presence of the Spirit in Romans 8:23–25 represents a present fulfillment of the inheritance theme. According to Adams, there is an already-not-yet tension in this passage, because the Spirit within Christians is a "foretaste" (8:23), or a portion, of what they will one day enjoy in full.[84] In chapter six, I contended that in Galatians 3:14 Paul identifies the Abrahamic promise of blessing as the Spirit, following the precedent in Isaiah 44:3. Then, in Galatians 3:15–29 he transitions to a distinct, but related, Abrahamic promise, the inheritance. Thus, Paul follows the distinction of these promises in the OT. Adams seems to overlook this evidence. In so doing, he too conflates the Abrahamic promises which Paul clearly distinguishes. In view of this error, I would like to restate what Paul has already argued: Believers in Christ have the Spirit (promise of blessing) and are thereby "sons" (promise of offspring) who are being led to the recreated cosmos (promise of inheritance, Gal 4:6–7; Rom 8:14–25). Differentiating between the promises is essential for grasping Paul's argument.

In the closing verses in Romans 8, Paul contends that the hope for which believers long is the coming world. He does so by claiming that they have been saved "in hope" (τῇ ἐλπίδι, Rom 8:24). The word ἐλπίς anticipates the future salvation that is not yet visible. Paul then elaborates on this future hope: it is that which is unseen, for no one hopes in what can be seen (Rom 8:24). What he emphasizes, then, is the "not yet" aspect of salvation, which is life in the recreated world. Since Christians do not currently possess this aspect of their salvation, they "eagerly anticipate it with endurance" (8:25). This last statement assures believers that what awaits them renders the present difficulties inconsequential.[85] As such, they are to continue to endure the sufferings of the present age, knowing that they will one day be resurrected to dwell in their redeemed inheritance.

81. Wright, "Romans," 597.

82. Ibid.

83. Wright, *Resurrection*, 256. See Schreiner, *Romans*, 438.

84. Adams, *Constructing the World*, 174.

85. Schreiner, *Romans*, 440.

According to G. K. Beale, the theme of resurrection in Romans 8 suggests that believers are "already" experiencing part their inheritance. Since the Spirit brings the end-time renovation event of resurrection into the present (in a spiritual sense, Rom 8:10), even before their bodily resurrection (Rom 8:11, 18–23), believers in Christ "begin to experience part of their new-creational inheritance through their resurrection existence."[86] Certainly, in Romans 8:10 Paul underscores that the presence of the Spirit suggests that believers experience new life in the present by means of a "spiritual" resurrection. Even still, I argue that being raised spiritually does not mean that Christians "already" experience a portion of their new creation inheritance. In chapter three and earlier in this chapter, I showed that Ezekiel 36–37 promises that believers will inherit a renewed world (i.e., a new Eden), when the Spirit raises them physically from the grave. *Enoch* 51 is an example of a Second Temple text that follows this line of thought. Such texts from Jewish literature shaped Paul's view of resurrection, which is closely tied to the hope of an inheritance. Neither Paul nor Jewish authors ever contend that spiritual resurrection represents a partial fulfillment of the inheritance, for they anticipate the fulfillment of the promise when believers' renewed bodies are resurrected to live on a fully restored earth. As such, Beale misunderstands the inheritance theme in Romans 8. From the texts that we have observed in Romans, the sons of God and fellow-heirs with Christ have "not yet" experienced an end-time renewal of their bodies that will make them fit for an inheritance.

The entirety of Romans 8:18–25 thus describes the nature of the inheritance that awaits God's children—the future redeemed world on which they will be resurrected to dwell (cf., Ezek 36–37). Believers are to continue their Spirit-led journey through the present unredeemed age (8:14–17) until they enter the world to come (8:18–25). They should endure this sojourn, despite present difficulties, knowing that the Spirit guarantees that they will receive what has been promised to them (8:14, 23). What is more, that which they have been promised, and will indeed inherit, will be unmistakably more glorious than the land of Canaan.

CONCLUSION

Paul's inheritance discussion in Romans 4:13–25 and 8:14–25 is in continuity with what he has already said in Galatians 3–4. That is, he envisions the inheritance to be the renewed world. In Romans, however, Paul is more explicit in defining the content of this promise, calling it the κόσμος—i.e.,

---

86. Beale, *New Testament Biblical Theology*, 762.

the renewed world on which God's sons will dwell when they are raised from the grave. Since the bodily resurrection has "not yet" occurred, God's children still anticipate possessing the world.

If we read Paul's argument in this light, it is evident that Hester is mistaken to argue that believers' status as "sons" means that the inheritance is "already" being realized (Gal 3:15–4:7; Rom 8:14–25). As I have shown throughout this book, the promises to Abraham, though related, are distinct (Gal 12, 15 17; cf. Gal 4:6–7). Thus, the promise of "sonship" should not be confused with that of "inheritance." Moo and Hodge make a similar error in conflating the Abrahamic promises into one promissory theme (Rom 4:13).

Beale also presents a skewed view of the inheritance, arguing that the Spirit's work to give new spiritual life to believers represents an "already" sense of the new creation inheritance (Rom 8:14–25). Contrary to Beale, I have shown that Paul follows Jewish texts such as Ezekiel 36–37 and *Enoch* 51 to underscore that Christians will inherit the new cosmos when they experience bodily resurrection. Similarly, Adams claims that the inheritance is "already" being realized in the present, contending that the Spirit presents a foretaste of the new cosmos that they will inherit (Rom 8:14–25). I have contended that the Spirit should not be confused with the inheritance, for the Spirit is the fulfillment of the Abrahamic promise of blessing that assures God's sons of receiving what has been promised to them. Being a distinct promise to Abraham, the Spirit does not, in any way, represent even a partial fulfillment of the promise of inheritance. In view of the confusion regarding the Abrahamic promises, it is important to restate the following: The Spirit (promise of blessing) leads God's children (promise of offspring) on a new exodus until at last they dwell in the renewed cosmos (promise of inheritance).

In the next chapter, I will examine the inheritance theme in relevant passages in 1 Corinthians and the disputed Pauline letters of Ephesians, Colossians, and Titus. Here, I will show that Paul's view of the inheritance also includes theme of kingdom. In these passages, Paul makes an explicit inheritance-kingdom connection that he already alludes to in Galatians 3:15–18. Since Paul also makes this connection in Galatians 5:19–21, I will also discuss this passage in the following chapter.

Hester likewise sees an inheritance-kingdom connection in Paul's letters. But since his work focuses on the *Hauptbriefe*, I will only be able to interact with his comments on these letters. An analysis of Pauline texts that Hester does not address will solidify the cosmic nature of the inheritance and reaffirm that the Spirit guarantees that God's people will receive the inheritance they do "not yet" possess.

8

The Inheritance in Paul
Undisputed Letters and Beyond

IN THE PREVIOUS CHAPTER, I showed that Romans affirms the cosmic nature of the inheritance. In the present chapter, I will examine inheritance passages in 1 Corinthians, Ephesians, Colossians, and Titus, showing that Paul's vision of the inheritance also encompasses the theme of kingdom. I will also display that Paul trusts that the Spirit is the guarantee that believers will receive their inheritance.

I have noted that Hester's *Paul's Concept of Inheritance* does not venture beyond the *Hauptbriefe*. This is not uncommon for Pauline studies. Most scholars have difficulty attributing anything to Paul outside of his undisputed letters.[1] So, it is understandable for Hester to stay mainly within the safe, acceptable confines of Romans, Galatians, and the letters to the Corinthians. I will, however, push beyond these boundaries, including texts from the disputed Pauline letters. While some may be shocked by this, Christians have historically attributed such letters to Paul. Even those who hold to their pseudonymous or deutero-Pauline authorship admit that these letters reflect the apostle's thought. One such scholar is Mark Harding, who argues that those who wrote in Paul's name "articulated something of the force and dynamic of his personality . . . They made Paul speak afresh . . . They wrote to confirm the content of the Pauline and apostolic faith for the salvation and eternal felicity of the faithful."[2] No study of the inheritance

---

1. A minority of New Testament scholars regard all the letters in the Pauline corpus to be authentic. Harding, "Disputed Letters of Paul," 137.

2. Ibid., 168.

is therefore complete without an examination of Paul's disputed epistles, regardless of one's view of their authenticity. To ignore this corpus is to disregard testimony that leads to a fuller understanding of Paul's theology. I will attempt to avoid this pitfall.

This chapter will first examine inheritance-kingdom related passages in Paul's epistles. Then, this chapter will observe Pauline passages that mention the role of the Spirit in assuring believers of an inheritance. In all, my analysis of these (undisputed and disputed) Pauline letters will show that the Spirit guarantees that believers will inherit the kingdom in the coming world.

THE INHERITANCE AS THE ESCHATOLOGICAL WORLDWIDE KINGDOM

Several times Paul speaks of "inheriting the kingdom." For Paul, the OT promise of God's people reigning in the land would have greatly informed his inheritance-kingdom association. Seen in this light, I will now examine 1 Corinthians 6:9–11 and 15:50–55; Galatians 15:18–21; Ephesians 5:3–5; and Colossians 1:12–13 and 3:22–24, passages in which Paul connects the themes of inheritance and kingdom.

1 Corinthians 6:9–11

Paul begins this section by asking, "Do you not know that the unrighteous will not inherit the kingdom of God?" (οὐκ οἴδατε ὅτι ἄδικοι θεοῦ βασιλείαν οὐ κληρονομήσουσιν, 1 Cor 6:9).[3] His question brings together the themes of inheritance and kingdom witnessed in the OT. The link between these themes is evidenced as early as Exodus 19:5–6, where God announces his intention to make Israel a kingdom of priests and a holy nation in the land, and Deuteronomy 17:14–20, which describes God's prescriptions for the monarchy in the land. Although this hope seems to be fulfilled in the narrative of Samuel to Chronicles, God's people are eventually taken into exile, suggesting that the promised kingdom is still forthcoming. Later OT authors, such as the Psalmist and Ezekiel, confirm this idea as they look forward to the realization of the territorial kingdom (Ps 2, 72, 96; Ezek 37; cf. 2 Sam 7, 23; Dan 7). Paul's comments in 1 Corinthians 6:9–10 are in step

3. 1 Cor is one of the undisputed letters of Paul. Thus, no extensive discussion is warranted. So sure is Paul's authorship of 1 Cor that most commentaries provide no extensive treatment of the letter's authenticity. See, for example, Garland, *1 Corinthians*; Thiselton, *First Corinthians*.

with this expectation. The future tense phrase κληρονομήσουσιν βασιλείαν asserts that he too anticipates the forthcoming fulfillment of the kingdom. Moreover, since he, in line with later Jewish literature (e.g., Isa 65–66; Sir 44), views the inheritance to be the eschatological world (e.g., Rom 4:13–25; 8:12–25), it is evident that the borders of the kingdom have been enlarged to accommodate for this expansion (cf. Rev 21–22). Paul's question in 1 Corinthians 6:9 thus foresees a universal monarchy in the eschatological world.

What is more, Paul's question clarifies that the unrighteous (ἄδικοι) will not inherit the kingdom. He then lists ten vices that are associated with such people (sexual immorality, idolatry, adultery, homosexuality, thievery, greediness, drunkenness, slander, and swindlery, 1 Cor 6:9–10) and asserts that those who practice such things "will not inherit the kingdom of God" (οὐχ βασιλείαν θεοῦ κληρονομήσουσιν, 1 Cor 6:10). Interestingly, Exodus 19:6 links keeping the prescriptions of the Mosaic covenant with becoming a kingdom in the land.[4] In addition, Deuteronomy 1–6 repeatedly confirms that God's people will inherit the land if they keep the Ten Commandments (cf. Deut 30).[5] While Paul's list of vices do not overlap verbatim with the Ten Commandments of the Mosaic covenant, they do confirm what the OT stresses to those who desire to inherit the land: They must live in obedience to God.[6] The failure to do so means they will not dwell in the place where God's people will be a kingdom of priests.

By implication, then, only the righteous will inherit God's cosmic kingdom. The OT and Second Temple literature support the idea that the inheritance is reserved for the righteous (Isa 65–66; 1 En. 48, 58; 4 Ezra 7; 4Q171 4). Paul is also in line with this expectation in claiming that the "unrighteous will not inherit the kingdom," for the insinuation of this statement is that solely the righteous are fit for an inheritance.

In short, 1 Corinthians 6:9–10 provides further clarity into Paul's view of the inheritance, establishing that God's people will inherit a future worldwide monarchy. The unrighteous, whom Paul describes with a list of ten vices, will receive no such inheritance. While other passages affirm the cosmic nature of the inheritance, in 1 Corinthians 15:50 Paul will now make it explicit that he expects that his readers will inherit an eschatological

---

4. Ciampa and Rosner, "1 Corinthians," 712.

5. Ibid.

6. Another Pauline passage that supports keeping the Law/obeying God with receiving an inheritance is Eph 6:1–2. Here, Paul, directly alluding to Exod 20:12 and Deut 5:16, links "honoring your father and mother" with living a "long life in the land." Though not the focus of this book, Paul's Law-inheritance connection certainly warrants further attention.

kingdom that has been expanded beyond the borders of the original promised land.

1 Corinthians 15:50–55

The theme of resurrection permeates all of 1 Corinthians 15: verses 15:1–11 confirm the resurrection of Christ; verses 15:12–49 assert that Christians will be resurrected in the manner of Christ; and verses 15:50–55 proclaim that the present, perishable bodies of believers will be raised imperishable. Such resurrection saturated language gives this chapter a decidedly eschatological tone.

In the latter part of this context (1 Cor 15:50), Paul speaks of the inheritance of the kingdom: "Flesh and blood are not able to inherit the kingdom of God, nor can the perishable inherit the imperishable." I note the Greek parallel structure below:

σὰρξ καὶ αἷμα βασιλείαν θεοῦ κληρονομῆσαι οὐ δύναται
οὐδὲ ἡ φθορὰ τὴν ἀφθαρσίαν κληρονομεῖ.

Some take this to be a synthetic parallelism, in which each line refers to a different classification of believers.[7] Joachim Jeremias contends, "The first line refers to those who are alive at the parousia, the second line to those who died before the parousia."[8] Gordon Fee rightly argues that "the real difficulty with this proposition lies in ... identifying the abstract noun ἡ φθορά with the already dead. That forces Paul's language into such a narrow sense that it simply cannot be sustained."[9]

Others take Paul's statement to be a synonymous parallelism, in which the second line restates what is said in the first.[10] The implication of this is twofold. First, "flesh and blood" (σὰρξ καὶ αἷμα) and "the perishable" (ἡ φθορά) are equivalent, referring to the present, temporary bodies of believers.[11] Second, "kingdom" (βασιλεία) and "imperishable" (ἀφθαρσία) are also equivalent, pointing to an eternal, unfading kingdom. This coheres with the

7. Jeremias, "Flesh and Blood," 152. Barrett follows Jeremias's argument (*First Corinthians*, 379).

8. Jeremias, "Flesh and Blood," 152.

9. Fee, *First Corinthians*, 798.

10. Foreman, *Politics of Inheritance*, 215–17. Fee, *First Corinthians*, 798. Lockwood, *1 Corinthians*, 599. Wright argues that this construction is like a Hebraic parallelism (*Resurrection*, 359).

11. Fee rightly argues that "flesh and blood" refer "simply to the body in its present form, composed of flesh and blood, to be sure, but subject to weakness, decay, and death, and as such ill-suited for life in the future" (*First Corinthians*, 799).

expectation of a permanent kingdom for God's people (Dan 7; 1 Pet 1:3–4; Rev 21). Together, both lines of the parallelism point to the time when the resurrected saints will inherit an everlasting dominion. This reading fits the context of 1 Corinthians 15, for it demonstrates that only the resurrected body is fit for life in the future kingdom of God.

The fact that Paul links the "inheritance of the kingdom" to the "resurrection" is significant. Such an association suggests that believers will inherit the kingdom when their bodies are raised from the grave (cf. Ezek 36–37).[12] Besides this, it also proposes that the kingdom will exist on the coming world, the place on which God's people will be raised to dwell (cf. Rom 4:13–25; 8:14–25; Rev 20–22).

The examination of 1 Corinthians 6:9–10 and 15:50 establishes that Paul envisions the inheritance of the future worldwide kingdom. This is the territorial monarchy that was foretold in the OT (e.g. Exod 18:6; Dan 7; 2 Sam 7) and will come to fruition in the eschaton (Rev 20–22). The temporary kingdom in Canaan (Samuel–Chronicles) serves as a type of the kingdom in the future world. This typological connection supports the idea that the promise of inheritance has "not yet" been fulfilled, for the saints have yet to be resurrected to dwell in the cosmic monarchy.

Galatians 5:18–21

Having exhorted his readers to live in freedom from the Law (Gal 5:13–17), Paul pens the following in Galatians 5:18: "But if you are led by the Spirit, you are not under the Law" (εἰ δὲ πνεύματι ἄγεσθε, οὐκ ἐστὲ ὑπὸ νόμον).[13] As in Romans 8:14, the verb ἄγω evokes the image of the Spirit leading God's people on a new exodus (cf. Isa 57; Ps 142; etc.). G. K. Beale argues that Isaiah 63:11–15, which also uses ἄγω in connection with πνεῦμα, may have been one of the texts from which Paul was drawing, to communicate to his readers that they are fulfilling the promise of a Spirit-led new exodus.[14]

---

12. Foreman contends, "The fact that one must experience transformation in order to be part of the kingdom is a clear indication that he expects the inheritance to include the restoration of creation. This suggests that Paul expects God not to destroy but to restore, renew and transform the recreated order. Far from God's abandoning creation or physical bodies, there are indications that for Paul the inheritance involved the redemption of creation" (*Politics of Inheritance*, 216).

13. In chapter 6, I affirmed that Galatians is one of the *Hauptbriefe*.

14. Beale, "Old Testament Background" 12–14. Schreiner cites Beale's article and notes that "Paul may well draw here on Isa 63:11–15, which refers to God's end time leading of his people by his Spirit" (*Galatians*, 345). See also Wilder, *Echoes of the Exodus*, 79–174. I have argued more extensively for Paul's echo of this imagery in my

Those on this journey are no longer enslaved to the Law (cf. Gal 4:4–5). Instead, they are being led by the Spirit through the wilderness of the present sinful age, longing to inherit the kingdom of God (cf. Gal 4:4–7; Rom 8:14–17).[15]

While in this new wilderness, the Galatians must not succumb to the works of the flesh, which Paul specifies with a list of vices (sexual immorality, impurity, sensuality, idolatry, sorcery, enmity, strife, jealousy, anger, rivalries, dissensions, factions, Gal 5:19–20). If they do such things, "they will not inherit the kingdom of God" (βασιλείαν θεοῦ οὐ κληρονομήσουσιν, Gal 5:21). In this text, like 1 Corinthians 6:9–10, Paul alludes to Exodus 19 and Deuteronomy 1–6 to argue that those who practice certain wicked deeds will not inherit the future kingdom. Such people walk according to the flesh (Gal 4:16; 5:18), demonstrating that they are not part of God's Spirit-led people. Those guided by the Spirit do not commit such acts, confirming that they are the genuine children of God journeying to their kingdom inheritance.

Paul's use of the future tense phrase κληρονομήσουσιν βασιλείαν (Gal 5:21) shows that the inheritance of the kingdom is forthcoming (cf. 1 Cor 6:9–10; Eph 5:5). Considering this passage along with 1 Corinthians 15:50 makes evident that the kingdom will exist in the coming world. Paul, then, is not speaking of a heavenly abstract realm, for his kingdom-inheritance connection confirms the expectation of a future worldwide monarchy. Only those led by the Spirit on the new exodus have the hope of such a magnificent inheritance.

Ephesians 5:3–5

In Ephesians 5:3–5, Paul employs another vice-list (sexual immorality, uncleanliness, and covertness, which is idolatry)[16] to describe the kinds of people "who do not have an inheritance in the kingdom" (οὐκ ἔχει κληρονομίαν

---

discussion of Rom 8:14, in chapter 7.

15. Wilson notes, "For Paul the Galatians occupy a particular narrative location: they are somewhere in between an Exodus-like redemption and the inheritance of the 'kingdom of God' (5:21). They are, that is, in the wilderness" ("Wilderness Apostasy," 570). See the entire article, pp. 150–71, for a better understanding of his insightful perspective.

16. Arnold argues that in Eph 5:5 "Paul repeats the triad of vices that he mentioned in 5:3a but here in a personal form . . . and not in their abstract form. This probably serves to indicate that Paul is now commenting on the identity of the individuals and not referring to believers who lapse into sinful behavior" (*Ephesians*, 324).

ἐν τῇ βασιλείᾳ).[17] Whereas in earlier passages he uses the future tense form of κληρονομέω to speak of the inheritance of the kingdom (1 Cor 6:9–10; Gal 5:19–21), in Ephesians 5:5 he uses the present tense verb ἔχει in conjunction with noun κληρονομία. This leads some commentators to conclude that Paul is arguing for a present realization of the inheritance.[18] This reading overlooks that the inheritance concept has a distinctly futuristic and territorial association in the OT (e.g., Exod 6:8; Num 33:53), Second Temple literature (e.g., Sir 44:20; 1 En. 5:7), and elsewhere in the NT (1 Cor 6:9–10; Rom 4:13, 8:18–25; Gal 5:21; 1 Pet 1:3–4; Rev 21:7–8). This broad testimony makes it unlikely for the inheritance to be fulfilled in the present, for believers will only dwell in the land when they are raised from the grave (Rom 8:14–25). If Paul were arguing for a present fulfillment of the inheritance, he would be contradicting the wide inheritance testimony in Jewish literature and what he has said about this concept in Galatians, Romans, and 1 Corinthians. Thus, it is highly unlikely that the apostle makes such an argument in Ephesians 5:5.

It is more probable that the phrase οὐκ ἔχει κληρονομίαν ἐν τῇ βασιλείᾳ carries a "future-referring present" connotation,[19] suggesting that the evildoers mentioned in Paul's vice list will not have an inheritance in the future kingdom. This reading fits with Paul's view of the inheritance that has been witnessed to this point and does not contradict the previous testimony of the OT and Second Temple literature.

What is more, the future kingdom inheritance that awaits believers is "of Christ and of God" (Eph 5:5). Paul has already asserted that the kingdom is "of God" (1 Cor 6:9–10; Gal 5:21). Now he says that the kingdom is also "of Christ." This phrase alludes to the time when the Messiah will reign over the coming world (2 Sam 7; Dan 7; Ps 2; Rev 21–22). At that point, the kingdom will be both "of Christ and of God" (Rev 11:15). Evidently, this is the time to which Paul refers.[20]

---

17. This is not the place for an extensive discussion of the authenticity of Ephesians. There are many excellent treatments on this topic. Besides, I have already contended that Pauline authorship of Ephesians is not necessary to include this letter in a study of the inheritance. For an argument in favor of Paul's authorship of Ephesians, see Hoehner (*Ephesians*, 1–59).

18. See, for example, Arnold, *Ephesians*, 323–24; Hoehner, *Ephesians*, 661–62; Thielman, *Ephesians*, 333.

19. Porter cites Eph 5:5 as "future referring present" (*Verbal Aspect*, 232). Porter, following Stahl (*Kritisch-historische Syntax*, 94), observes that "prophets make noteworthy use of the future-referring present. Because of the prophetic nature of the NT, perhaps this accounts for what some posit as an expansion of the use of the present in future contexts in the NT" (ibid., 232).

20. Lincoln rightly argues that "the notion of two successive forms of God's rule

What Paul asserts about the inheritance of the kingdom in Ephesians 5:5 is consistent with his presentation of this theme in 1 Corinthians 6:9–10; 15:50; and Galatians 5:19–21. These passages show that he views the inheritance to be the future worldwide kingdom of Christ and God. Believers will dwell in the coming kingdom when, as affirmed in 1 Corinthians 15:50, they receive their imperishable bodies.

Colossians 1:12–13

Colossians 1:12 reads, "giving thanks to the Father who qualified you for a portion of the inheritance of the saints in the light" (εὐχαριστοῦντες τῷ πατρὶ τῷ ἱκανώσαντι ὑμᾶς εἰς τὴν μερίδα τοῦ κλήρου τῶν ἁγίων ἐν τῷ φωτί).[21] Interpreters often conclude that this passage is evidence of Paul's spiritualized interpretation of the land inheritance. H. C. G. Moule provides one of the clearest examples of a spiritualized reading of this text, contending that here the inheritance refers to "the light of the spiritual knowledge, purity and joy; the mystical Canaan of the redeemed."[22]

Although this interpretation has a wide acceptance, it disregards that the phrase εἰς τὴν μερίδα τοῦ κλήρου τῶν ἁγίων "for anyone familiar with the Jewish Scriptures . . . would evoke the characteristic talk of the promised land."[23] In particular, the terms μερίς and κλήρος have a permanent place in the story of the apportioning of the land of Israel in the Septuagint (Deut 10:9; 12:12; 14:27; 32:9; Josh 19:9; Isa 57:6).[24] The following texts will serve as examples:

> Because of this, Levi does not have a portion (μερίς) or lot (κλήρος) [of the land] with his brothers (Deut 10:9).[25]

> The inheritance (ἡ κληρονομία) of the tribes of the sons of Judah is from the lot (ἀπὸ τοῦ κλήρου) of Judah, for it happened that the lot (ἡ μερίς) of the sons of Judah is greater than theirs; and

---

should not be read into Eph 5:5" (*Ephesians*, 325). Contra Arnold, *Ephesians*, 325.

21. Like Ephesians, a discussion of the authorship of Colossians is unwarranted. The similarities between both letters, however, point to Paul's likely authorship. See Bruce, *Colossians, Philemon, and Ephesians*, 28–33.

22. Moule, *Colossians and Philemon*, 74. Moule's comments are also noted by Foreman (*Politics of Inheritance*, 220).

23. Dunn, *Colossians and Philemon*, 76.

24. Lohse, *Colossians and Philemon*, 35.

25. LXX Deuteronomy citations are from Wevers, *Deuteronomium*,

the sons of Simeon received an inheritance (ἐκληρονόμησαν) in the midst of their lot (τοῦ κλήρου, Josh 19:9).[26]

Paul's use of μερίς and κλῆρος, as in the LXX, points to the apportioning of the territorial inheritance. In asserting that the land inheritance is present in this passage, Wright observes that for Paul "the promise of land is widened into the promise of a whole new creation (Rom 4:13; 8:17–25)."[27] Wright's comments are in keeping with the development of the inheritance concept. Furthermore, they also suggest that God will allot to believers a portion of the eschatological worldwide inheritance in the same way he allotted the land of Canaan to the tribes of Israel.[28]

The modifying phrase "in the light" (ἐν τῷ φωτί, Col 1:12) further clarifies the type of inheritance that will be apportioned to believers. Ralph Martin argues that with this phrase "Paul wishes to make clear that while Israel was allotted Canaan as God's promised land to His elect people, the inheritance of the new Israel is no territorial possession but a spiritual dimension, the realm of light."[29] This expression, however, should not be spiritualized. Two Qumran texts that parallel Colossians 1:12 will substantiate this thought:[30]

> To those whom God has chosen . . . he has given them an inheritance *in the lot of the holy ones* (1QS 11:7–8).[31]

> For your glory you have purified man from sin, so that he can make himself holy for you . . . to become united with the sons of your truth and in *in the lot of your holy ones*, to raise the worms of the dead from the dust, to an everlasting community . . . so that he can take his place in your presence with the perpetual

26. LXX Joshua citations are from Rahlfs, *Septuaginta.*

27. Wright, *Colossians and Philemon*, 61. Contra Bird, who argues that the "New Testament inheritance . . . has a decidedly non-geographic meaning" (*Colossians and Philemon*, 43).

28. Schweitzer contends, "What is said about the 'inheritance' which falls to a person is rooted in the Old Testament account of God graciously allotting the land of Canaan to Israel. However, this idea has long since been transferred, in an eschatological way, to the hereditary portion, which at some point in the future is supposed to be allotted to the believer (Dan 12:3; Eth. Enoch 37:4; 39:8; 48:7; 58:5)" (*Colossians*, 50).

29. Martin, *Colossians*, 38.

30. Dunn, *Colossians*, 77; Forman, *Politics of Inheritance*, 222; Beale, "Colossians," 850.

31. I am following the translation of García Martínez and Tigchelaar (*Dead Sea Scrolls*, 97). Italics mine.

host and the [everlasting] spirits, to renew him with everything
that will exist (1QH 11:10–13).[32]

Both Qumran passages and Colossians 1:12 contrast "the kingdom of
light" and the "kingdom of darkness."[33] This contrast does not need to be
spiritualized,[34] for there is clear resurrection and recreation language in
Hymn Scroll 11:10–13. What is more, the promise of a future worldwide
kingdom for the Davidic son of God (2 Sam 7; Ps 2:7; Dan 7) underlies the
notion of the "kingdom of his beloved son" (βασιλείαν τοῦ υἱοῦ τῆς ἀγάπης
αὐτοῦ) in Colossians 1:13.[35] The fact that this text is rooted in the Davidic
promise tradition suggests that what is meant by "in the light" (ἐν τῷ φωτί)
is not a spiritualized kingdom but the world over which Christ will reign.[36]
This is the cosmic kingdom that will be apportioned to believers, the one
they will inherit along with Christ (Gal 3:15–29; Rom 8:14–25).[37]

These observations underscore that Colossians 1:12 presents no
evidence of a spiritualized view of the inheritance. This is apparent in that
Colossians 1:12–13 echoes LXX texts that discuss the apportioning of the
land of Israel (Deut 10:9; 12:12; 14:27; 32:9; Josh 19:9; Is 57:6) and Davidic
promise texts that anticipate the Son of God reining over the coming world
(Ps 2; 2 Sam 7). The evidence therefore demonstrates that Paul's vision of the
inheritance is still the eschatological worldwide kingdom on which God's
people will dwell.[38] Understanding the physical and future worldly nature of
inheritance makes the function of 1:12–13 apparent. Paul wants his readers
to recall that "the world is in the process of being physically transformed
and that they must now live in accordance with this new world, the new
kingdom of 'light.'"[39]

32. García Martínez, *Dead Sea Scrolls Translated*, 353. Italics mine.

33. Foreman, *Politics of Inheritance*, 222.

34. Ibid., 222–23.

35. See Schweitzer, *Colossians*, 52.

36. Ibid.; Foreman, *Politics of Inheritance*, 223. Wright insightfully observes, "The
language of 1:13 is, in fact, firmly grounded in the world of Jewish expectations and
in the fulfillment of those hopes in the Messiah, Jesus" (*Colossians and Philemon*, 62).

37. The futuristic Davidic promise background to Col 1:12–13 necessitates that the
aorist tense verb clause μετέστησεν εἰς τὴν βασιλείαν τοῦ υἱοῦ τῆς ἀγάπης αὐτοῦ be read
proleptically. Wallace notes that "an author sometimes uses the aorist for the future to
stress the certainty of the event" (*Greek Grammar*, 56). Such a description clarifies that
Paul is likely confirming that Christians will one day be transferred into the universal
kingdom of Christ.

38. MacDonald observes that "the reference to 'sharing in the inheritance of the
saints in the light' is language of belonging, boldly announcing that believers ultimately
belong to a transformed world" (*Colossians and Ephesians*, 56).

39. Foreman, *Politics of Inheritance*, 223.

Colossians 3:22–24

In Colossians 3:22–23, Paul urges slaves to obey their earthly masters in everything, doing so for the Lord. Then, in 3:24 he reminds slaves that their motivation for obedience is grounded in that "from the Lord you will receive the reward of the inheritance" (ἀπὸ κυρίου ἀπολήμψεσθε τὴν ἀνταπόδοσιν τῆς κληρονομίας). As in 1:12, interpreters commonly spiritualize the inheritance in 3:24. David Hay's interpretation is indicative of this reading. For him, the idea that Christ will give the inheritance to slaves equates to "an after-death heavenly compensation making up for the fact that Roman law did not permit slaves to inherit anything."[40] Although Paul's words would have given future hope to first-century slaves, this hope is not consigned to a spiritual heavenly realm.[41]

Instead, in Colossians 3:24 the term κληρονομία alludes to the promise of a territorial inheritance. Dunn also agrees with this observation. He argues that in 3:24 this word "picks up on the inheritance promised to Abraham . . . primarily the land of Canaan (Gen 15:7–8; Deut 1:39; 2:12; etc.)."[42] Paul has previously displayed that the original land promise has been expanded to include the entire eschatological world (Rom 4:13–25; 8:14–25). Furthermore, earlier in Colossians 1:12, as elsewhere in Paul (1 Cor 6:9–10; 15:50; Gal 5:19–21; Eph 5:5), he demonstrates that theme of inheritance also encompasses the future kingdom. This points to the fact that Paul envisions the inheritance to be the eschatological worldwide kingdom. Since this claim is supported earlier in Colossians and elsewhere in his letters, it is most likely the case that the reference to the inheritance in 3:24 communicates to slaves that they may expect to receive the kingdom in the coming world as a reward for their obedience.

The eschatological nature of the slaves' inheritance is affirmed by the future tense phrase ἀπολήμψεσθε τὴν ἀνταπόδοσιν τῆς κληρονομίας. The fact that the noun ἀνταπόδοσις commonly carries the sense of a future recompense at the eschaton strengthens this idea (e.g., Ps 19:11; 69:22; 91:8; 94:2; Isa 34:8; 61:2; 63:4).[43] Thus, Paul assures slaves of the eschatological reward of the future worldwide kingdom.[44] This, of course, would have been

40. Hay, *Colossians*, 146.

41. Foreman, *Politics of Inheritance*, 223.

42. Dunn, *Colossians*, 257.

43. Ibid., 256. Böttger insightfully notes that "recompense" in the OT is often used in reference to the future bestowal of land. In the NT, this term "emphasizes what is given in return . . . in reference to the divine recompense (Lk. 14:12; Rom. 11:9) at the final judgment (Col. 3:24)" ("Recompense," 3:134–36).

44. Wright contends that the reference to the inheritance in Col 3:24 "is clearly . . .

very attractive to first-century slaves who had no prospect of a tangible inheritance. Dunn rightly observes: "The paradox of slaves becoming heirs of God's kingdom would not be lost on the Colossians. Under Roman law slaves could not inherit anything; so it was only by being integrated into this distinctively Jewish heritage that their legal disability as slaves could be surmounted."[45] Such a prospect would certainly have motivated slaves to obey their masters. Although their circumstances were difficult, and they had no legal property of their own, they will one day inherit a kingdom that stretches from one side of the world to the other. Here, they will not fear any oppressive slave owner, for they will belong to and dwell alongside the king to whom they have been obedient, Jesus Christ (Rev 21–22). This hope is extended to all believers, to whom Paul also promises the inheritance of a future territorial kingdom (1 Cor 6:19–20; 15:50; Gal 5:21; Eph 5:5; Col 1:12).

In all, the examination of inheritance-kingdom passages (1 Cor 6:9–10; 15:50; Gal 5:18–21; Eph 5:3–5; Col 1:12–13; 3:22–24) displays that Paul views the inheritance to be the eschatological worldwide kingdom. These passages bring to light that the future world discussed in Romans 4:13–25 and 8:14–25 is where God will establish his reign. The future cosmic kingdom will be Israel's long-awaited monarchy. Though the monarchy in Canaan fell short of this expectation, God's people have the hope that they will inherit the kingdom when they are resurrected from the grave (1 Cor 15:50; cf. Rom 8:18–25; Rev 20–22). Having affirmed this thought, I will now examine the Spirit's role in assuring that believers receive their inheritance.

THE INHERITANCE GUARANTEED BY THE SPIRIT

The inheritance that believers await is a sure promise from God. Earlier Pauline passages (Rom 8:14–25; Gal 4:5–7; 5:19–21) suggest that the Holy Spirit himself is the surety of the inheritance. This section's examination of Ephesians 1:10–14 and Titus 3:4–6 will now confirm what such passages insinuate.

---

life in the age to come" (*Colossians and Philemon*, 150).

45. Dunn, *Colossians*, 257.

Ephesians 1:10–14

Ephesians 1:10–11 asserts that those in Christ[46] "have been made heirs" (ἐκληρώθημεν).[47] The word κληρόω is lexically related to the land allotted to God's people in Jewish literature (e.g., Num 26:55–56; 1Q7 11:7–8) and the NT (Acts 26:18; Col 1:12). Of the NT references, the most relevant is Colossians 1:12, in which Paul uses the cognate noun κλῆρος to argue that believers will receive a "lot" or "portion" of the eschatological world. Such observations affirm that in Ephesians 1:10–11 the content of what the heirs will inherit is the future world.

Being in Christ also means that believers have been sealed "by the Spirit of promise, who is a down payment of our inheritance" (πνεύματι τῆς ἐπαγγελίας τῷ ἁγίῳ, ὅ ἐστιν ἀρραβὼν τῆς κληρονομίας ἡμῶν, 1:13–14; cf. Isa 44:3; Luke 24:29; Gal 3:14).[48] Some argue that here the Spirit represents the present realization of the inheritance and not just the guarantee of its coming.[49] Such a view contradicts the eschatological context of Ephesians 1:10–14, which does not focus on what Christians currently possess but on what is to come. This is apparent in that 1:10 speaks of the future "heading up" (ἀνακεφαλαιόω)[50] of all things in the heavens and on the earth, that is,

46. The phrase ἐν ᾧ in 1:11 points back to ἐν τῷ Χριστῷ in 1:10, demonstrating that the one "in whom" the Ephesians have an inheritance is "Christ."

47. Hoehner argues that ἐκληρώθημεν should be rendered "we were inherited," suggesting that believers are God's inheritance (*Ephesians*, 225–26). He contends for this reading because "it has OT precedent where Israel is called God's possession (Deut 4:20; 7:6; 14:2) or heritage (Deut 9:26, 29; 32:9; cf. 1QS 2:2)" (ibid., 227). Thielman has a more persuasive argument: "Although the verb κληρόω does not mean 'inherit,' it shares a root with the nouns κληρονόμος (heir) and κληρονομία (inheritance), and with the verbs κληρονομέω (inherit) and κατακληρονομέω (inherit). These terms appear throughout the Greek Scriptures in reference to God's people as his 'heirs' (Rom. 8:17; cf. James 2:5), to the land as Israel's 'inheritance' or as something they will 'inherit' (Num. 33:54; Deut. 4:1; Acts 13:19; cf. Zech. 8:12), and to God's people as God's 'inheritance' (Deut. 32:9) or as something he will 'inherit' (Zech 2:16 [2:12 MT]). Sometimes, the verbal idea that Israel 'will inherit' (κατακληρονομήσετε) the land is linked with the notion that God will give the land to Israel 'by lot' (κλήρῳ; Num. 33:53–54; 34:13). . . . In the Ephesians benediction itself, Paul will say in verse 14 that the Spirit is the down payment of our inheritance (κληρονομίας ἡμῶν), a phrase that . . . refers to the eschatological inheritance of God's kingdom, over which Jesus, the Messiah, rules as God's vice regent (5:5). In verse 18 Paul will speak of God's 'inheritance in the saints' (τῆς κληρονομίας αὐτοῦ ἐν τοῖς ἁγίοις). It seems probable, therefore, that when Paul uses the term ἐκληρώθημεν here in verse 11, he intends for it to not simply be an 'allotment' or 'portion' . . . but specifically to an 'inheritance.' As such, ἐκληρώθημεν carries the sense that believers 'have been made heirs'" (*Ephesians*, 73).

48. The phrase ἐν ᾧ in 1:13 also points back to ἐν τῷ Χριστῷ in 1:10.

49. Beale, *New Testament Biblical Theology*, 763; Hoehner, *Ephesians*, 241–43.

50. Merklein argues that the verb ἀνακεφαλαιόω points towards "the eschatological

when everything will be subjected to Christ (cf. 1:19–23; Phil 2:10); and 1:14 anticipates the future "redemption of the possession" (ἀπολύτρωσιν τῆς περιποιήσεως). Such a framework for 1:10–14 is overwhelmingly eschatological, necessitating a futuristic reading of the phrases τῷ πνεύματι τῆς ἐπαγγελίας τῷ ἁγίῳ, ὅ ἐστιν ἀρραβὼν τῆς κληρονομίας ἡμῶν.

The word ἀρραβών is another element that does not allow for a present realization of the inheritance. This term carries the sense of a "pledge" or "down payment," guaranteeing the future payment of what is owed.[51] For example, in 2 Corinthians 1:22 Paul asserts that "the Corinthians have received the *pledge* of the Spirit, a 'down payment' . . . to guarantee the consummation of salvation, which is yet to come" (cf. 2 Cor 5:5).[52] Similarly, in Ephesians 1:14 the word is used in relation to the Spirit being the guarantee of the future inheritance. As Frank Thielman argues, "God has given believers the Holy Spirit . . . as a sign that he will fulfill his commitment to his people in the future and give them an inheritance."[53] Consequently, there is no sense in which the inheritance in Ephesians 1:14 is fulfilled in the present, for the Spirit's function as the ἀρραβών does not direct Paul's readers to what they currently enjoy, but to what he assures that they will receive in the eschaton.

The Spirit will serve in this capacity "until the redemption of the possession" (εἰς[54] ἀπολύτρωσιν τῆς περιποιήσεως, Eph 1:14). Some commentators argue that περιποίησις is a reference to God's people as his "possession," since this expression is used in Malachi 3:17 (LXX) and 1 Peter 2:9 to describe the people of God.[55] This idea, however, does not cohere with Paul's argument in Ephesians 1:10–14, which focuses on the future inheritance, not the coming redemption of God's people. The noun περιποίησις more accurately denotes the "possession" of property,[56] functioning synonymously with κληρονομία in the previous clause. The OT supports this reading in identifying the "land inheritance" as the "possession" of Abraham's offspring (Lev 25:25; Ezek 11:5; Ps 2:8; cf. *Jub.* 14). Psalm 2:8 (LXX) presents the

---

goal for the sake of which the entire creation was brought into being so that it encompasses the universe in its spatio-temporal dimensions" ("ἀνακεφαλαιόω," 1:83).

51. LSJ, 246; BDAG, 134; Kerr, "ΑΡΡΑΒΩΝ," 92–97.

52. Sand, "ἀρραβών," 1:158.

53. Thielman, *Ephesians*, 82.

54. The eschatological context of Eph 1:11–14 suggests that the preposition εἰς carries temporal sense.

55. See Thielman, *Ephesians*, 83; Hoehner, *Ephesians*, 1:14.

56. Spica notes: "in the three occurrences in the papyri, two mean property: *P.Tebt.* 317, 26, κατὰ τό τῆς περιποιήσεως δίκαιον (second century AD); SB 10537, 34: καὶ ἀποδείξαντες περιποίησιν ἐμοῦ (third century)" ("περιποίησις," 3:102).

clearest evidence of this connection in paralleling the terms "inheritance" (κληρονομία) and "possession" (κατάσχεσίς), suggesting that the latter is equivalent to the former. Though in Ephesians 1:14 Paul uses περιποιήσις instead of κατάσχεσίς, he, as the Psalmist, employs a word that carries the sense of property ownership and employs it synonymously with κληρονομία, signifying that the inheritance is the eschatological possession of God's people.

In view of this argument, the phrase εἰς ἀπολύτρωσιν τῆς περιποιήσεως underscores that the Spirit guarantees the inheritance to believers until the redemption of the world, that is, their future possession. The redemption of the inheritance/possession, as in Romans 8:18–25, will take place in the eschaton. At that time, the creation will be freed from the curse of sin (Gen 3), and God's children will finally possess their inheritance (cf. 1 Thess 5:9; 2 Thess 2:14). Since believers have received the "Holy Spirit of promise" (Eph 1:13), they may be confident that they will take possession of the restored creation. Such an observation validates that the Spirit is the surety of the inheritance.

Titus 3:4–6

In Titus 3:4–5, Paul commends that God's kindness and philanthropy led to the deliverance of his people "through the washing of regeneration and the renewal of the Holy Spirit" (διὰ λουτροῦ παλιγγενεσίας καὶ ἀνακαινώσεως πνεύματος ἁγίου, cf. 1 Cor 6:11).[57] These verses recall that the Spirit has delivered believers from slavery to sin through the waters of baptism (e.g., 1 Cor 6:11; Eph 5:26; Rom 8:14–17; cf. 1 Pet 3:19–21) in a similar manner to the way he liberated Israel from bondage in Egypt through the Red Sea (e.g., Exod 13–14; Isa 63:11–14; Ezek 36:25–27). Believers, like Israel, arose from the waters renewed, having experienced the saving power of God (e.g., Exod 15:1–21).

Using another water metaphor, Paul goes on to say that God has freely "poured out" (ἐξέχεεν) the Holy Spirit upon believers "through Christ Jesus" (διὰ Ἰησοῦ Χριστοῦ, Titus 3:6). The verb ἐκχέω alludes to the promise of the Spirit's outpouring upon God's people in the last days (Joel 2:28, 3:1–22;

---

57. I admit that the Pauline authorship of Titus, as with 1 and 2 Tim, is highly debated. At the very least, as I have already argued, one must concede that Titus is an accurate reflection of Paul's theology. Whatever hand others may have had in finalizing the letter, I agree with Towner, that Paul is the author of the Pastorals "however much or little others contributed to their messages and composition" (*Letters to Timothy and Titus*, 88).

Acts 2:17–18, 33; cf. Isa 44:3; Ezek 36:26; 39:29).[58] The goal of this is "so that, having been made righteous by his grace" (ἵνα δικαιωθέντες τῇ ἐκείνου χάριτι), they "might become heirs" (κληρονόμοι γενηθῶμεν, Titus 3:7). Since the participle δικαιωθέντες modifies the subjunctive verb γενηθῶμεν, it is apparent that the aim of the Spirit being poured out on believers is to make them heirs. This does not mean that righteousness has no significance for heirship, for Romans 4:13 establishes that being an heir of the promise to Abraham depends on the righteousness that comes from faith. With this said, the clause δικαιωθέντες τῇ ἐκείνου χάριτι κληρονόμοι γενηθῶμεν affirms that becoming an heir is a direct result of receiving the promised Spirit (cf. Gal 4:6–7). Simply put, receiving the Spirit guarantees the status of heir.

Such heirship is "in accord with the hope of eternal life" (κατ' ἐλπίδα ζωῆς αἰωνίου). The notion of "eternal life" may seem to suggest that God's people will inherit an abstract heavenly realm. This idea is unwarranted because Second Temple literature evidences that "inheriting eternal life" is equivalent to "inheriting life in the world to come" (e.g., *1 En.* 38:1–4, 40:9). This observation coheres well with the understanding that Paul views the inheritance to be the coming world, and may even be the very notion he was following in claiming that God's people are "heirs in accord with eternal life."

Titus 3:4–7 thereby shows that the same Spirit who delivered believers through the Red Sea event of baptism has also made them heirs of life in the world to come. Though they have yet to dwell in the eschatological world, the fact that the Spirit has been "poured out" upon them guarantees they will inherit such a place.

In summarizing this section, the examination of Ephesians 1:10–14 and Titus 3:4–6 displays explicitly what is suggested in earlier Pauline passages: that the Spirit is the guarantee of the inheritance. To put it another way, the Spirit assures that nothing can deter believers from receiving what has been promised to them.

CONCLUSION

My examination of the relevant texts in this chapter show that Paul's vision of the cosmic inheritance (Rom 4:13–17; 8:14–25) includes the idea of kingdom (1 Cor 6:9–10; 15:50; Gal 5:18–21; Ephesians 5:3–5; Col 1:12–13 and 3:22–24). These themes are so intertwined that speaking of "inheriting the kingdom" is a shorthand way of saying "dwelling in the cosmic monarchy." This future kingdom will fulfill the OT expectation of a monarchy

---

58. Marshall, *Pastoral Epistles*, 322; Lea and Griffin, Jr., *1, 2 Timothy and Titus*, 324.

in the land (e.g., 2 Sam 7; 1 Chron 17; Ezek 36–37; Dan 7; cf. Rev 21–22), because it will be the place where the people of God are gathered together and will enjoy the full reign of God.[59] This, then, is how the notions of land and kingdom converge under the concept of inheritance, a concept that the Spirit guarantees (Eph 1:10–14; Titus 3:4–6) will be realized when God's people are raised to life.

As in Galatians and Romans, in 1 Corinthians, Ephesians, Colossians, and Titus, Paul does not spiritualize the inheritance concept. Nor does he insinuate that the inheritance is realized in the present. Instead, there is sufficient evidence to argue that he looks forward to the tangible fulfilment of this promise in the eschaton. Hence, the inheritance remains a tangible promise that has "not yet" been fulfilled.

Since Hester only examines the *Hauptbriefe*, his work on the inheritance is incomplete. I have argued that the disputed letters of Paul are essential for a robust understanding of the inheritance theme. Even those who hold to a pseudepigraphal or duetero-Pauline view of Paul's disputed epistles must acknowledge that they are reliable testimonies to the apostle's thought. While Hester has done a great service in addressing a gap in Pauline studies, his examination fails to capture the entirety of *Paul's concept of inheritance*. My study has not excluded any relevant inheritance texts attributed to Paul. Thus, I contend that I have provided a more complete study, showing that Paul expects that believers will inherit a cosmic kingdom when the Spirit raises them from the grave. We see this more clearly when we examine all the letters that testify to his thought.

---

59. Hester, *Paul's Concept of Inheritance*, 80.

9

Conclusion

IN THIS BOOK, I have has sought to determine Paul's view of the inheritance. James Hester's *Paul's Concept of Inheritance* is the only other work that has attempted a comprehensive examination of this theme in the Pauline epistles. Hester contends that the inheritance is primarily focused on the future fulfillment of the land promise, while also arguing that the indwelling of the Spirit represents a present realization of this notion. Thus, for him the inheritance is an "already-not-yet" concept, with the main emphasis on the "not yet." I have contended that this argument is flawed, for the inheritance is a tangible concept that will be fulfilled when believers are resurrected to dwell in the new creation. As well, Hester's work does not venture beyond the *Hauptbriefe*. While not uncommon in Pauline studies, Paul's disputed letters are credible witnesses to the apostle's thought, and thus we cannot ignore their contents.

Beyond Hester, I have also interacted with those, such as W. D. Davies, who argue that for Paul the inheritance is "already" fulfilled in the present. For these proponents, the realization of this promise rests on believers either being in Christ or indwelt by the Spirit. I agree with Davies that those in Christ are free from the Law. I disagree, however, that those in Christ are also free from the land. Christians are not stripped from what is tangible and material; instead, they will inherit the physical realm after it has been freed from the curse and made fit to be their eternal dwelling. Davies fails to see this point in his "landless" view of Paul.

Others, such as Yon-Gyong Kwon, contend that the inheritance in Paul is a promise that has "not yet" been fulfilled, for God's people are not

181

dwelling in the eschatological world. My argument falls into this latter group, because I affirm that in Paul the inheritance promised to Abraham and his descendants has been expanded to include the entire renewed world where God will establish his permanent kingdom. Still, I must point out that these authors focus on a single epistle or several epistles, but not all the Pauline letters that address the inheritance theme.

Central to making my argument is that Paul's understanding of the inheritance arises out of the OT and Second Temple literature. These corpuses shaped his theological framework, within which the inheritance is a central theme. Thus, I will now review the development of this notion throughout said Jewish literature. Then, I will summarize how Paul's view of the inheritance follows an established Jewish understanding of this notion. Following this survey, I will conclude by noting the contribution of this study for recapturing the biblical hope of a new creation.

INHERITANCE IN THE OLD TESTAMENT

The inheritance theme develops throughout the OT narrative. In the Hexateuch and historical books, the inheritance is identified as the land of Canaan. Later, in the Psalms and Prophets the inheritance is expanded to encompass the new heavens and earth, i.e., the new cosmos. I will now summarize my findings on the development of this theme in the OT.

Hexateuch and Historical Books

Within the narrative of the Hexateuch and historical books, Genesis to Joshua recounts Israel's sojourn to the inheritance. Before describing the journey, Genesis grounds the inheritance concept in the land promised to Abraham and his offspring (e.g., 12:1–9, 15–21; 17:8). While this concept is closely associated with the promises of blessing and descendants, only the inheritance is identified as the land, thereby distinguishing it from other Abrahamic promises (e.g., Gen 12:1–9; 15:1–21). Exodus to Deuteronomy then narrates God's people journeying to the land. Subsequently, the book of Joshua depicts the incomplete occupation of the territory promised to Abraham's offspring, for there remain enemies who reside within its borders (cf. Josh 13:1–7). Israel, then, is not at rest, which suggests there must be a better inheritance that awaits the people of God.

Samuel to Chronicles recounts the monarchial period. Initially, the people anticipate that Saul will be the king to deliver them from the remaining enemies in the land. Unfortunately, Saul was not the one who would accomplish this work, so the hope of a king who would bring God's people rest in their inheritance is placed on David. Although he does not achieve this task, God promises David that his royal offspring (2 Sam 7:12–13) will plant Israel in the land (2 Sam 7:11) and bring lasting rest (2 Sam 7:10). Whereas the inception of Solomon's reign suggests that he will bring this promise to fruition (1 Kgs 6–8), the remainder of his rule evidences that he turns his heart to foreign gods (1 Kgs 11:1–8). This leads to partitioning the kingdom after his death (1 Kgs 11:30–40) and Israel's eventual exile. Solomon was not the king who would establish God's people in their everlasting inheritance. Nevertheless, there remains the hope of a Davidic king who will bring Israel lasting rest in the land (2 Sam 7:10–12; 23:1–7). Long after Israel has been taken into exile, the Chronicler reminds them that God will fulfill his promise (1 Chr 17:1–15). Although Canaan was not the true inheritance of God's people, they have the assurance that a Davidic monarch will one day bring them into the land and establish an everlasting kingdom.

Following Chronicles, Ezra seems to insinuate that God's people have returned to the land and the promises to Abraham's offspring are being fulfilled (Ezra 1–3). I have argued that this is only a preview of the true return from exile, for God's people are still under foreign rule and are thereby slaves (Ezra 9; cf. Neh 9). We see this clearly in Ezra's prayer, in which he admits that "we are slaves" (Ezra 9:8). Slavery is not the intended posture of Abraham's sons. The children of Abraham are to be a "kingdom of priests" (Exod 19:6), not slaves to a foreign ruler. I contend, then, that the land promise has not been fulfilled. At this point in the narrative, the Israelites still await to be ushered into the land promised to their forefathers, where they will experience the righteous rule of the Messiah.

Psalms and Prophets

The Psalms and Prophets reassure God's people of a future inheritance. In the Psalms, the inheritance undergoes a clear development: the promise is no longer restricted to Canaan, but is expanded to include the entire world (Ps 2, 72). The Psalms also establish that the true heir of this promise is the Davidic king, i.e., God's son (Ps 2).

In the Prophets, the expansion of the inheritance is reiterated, affirming that the original promised land has been enlarged to include the entire world (Isa 54:1–17). This corpus also further describes the cosmic inheritance as the new heavens and new earth, making this a distinctly eschatological concept (Isa 65–66). As well, the Prophets contend that the fellow-heirs of the coming world along with God's son are those who place their trust in him (Isa 57:1–13; cf. Ps 2). Ezekiel 36–37 solidifies the eschatological nature of the inheritance by noting that the people of God will possess a reconstituted land when they are resurrected from the dead, at which time David's royal descendent will reign over them forever.

Though the conclusion of the OT evidences that the promise of land has "not yet" been realized, God's people still have the assurance that they will one day receive an inheritance that stretches beyond the borders of Canaan to encompass the entire future world. At that time, they will experience the rule of the promised Davidic king and the rest from enemies for which they have longed. When this comes about, the promise of inheritance will at last be fulfilled.

One of the ways in which we witness the continued hope of an inheritance is that Second Temple literature frequently discusses this promise in much the same way as the Psalms and Prophets. It is important to point that this hope is not "other worldly" or "spiritualized" or "disembodied." Rather, it remains grounded in a tangible land promised to Abrahams's offspring. I will now turn to a summary of the inheritance theme in Second Temple literature.

INHERITANCE IN SECOND TEMPLE LITERATURE

The hope of a future inheritance is carried into Second Temple literature (587BC–AD 70). The Apocrypha, Pseudepigrapha, and Dead Sea Scrolls anticipate that Abraham's offspring will possess the future world. One of the clearest passages in which this is found is Sirach 44:20, which confirms that God's people will receive an inheritance "from sea to sea and from the river to the end of the earth" (cf. *1 En.* 5:5–10).[1] In addition, *4 Ezra* alludes to the Davidic covenant in suggesting that there will be a messianic kingdom in the future world (*4 Ezra* 7). The *Hymn Scroll* even confirms that God's people will be resurrected to dwell in the coming world, firmly fixing the fulfillment of the inheritance in the eschaton (1QH[a] 14:29–31; cf. Ezek 36–37; *1 En.* 51:1–5).

Undoubtedly, Second Temple literature does not nullify the promise of an inheritance. Though Israel is in exile, this corpus holds to the expectation that Abraham's descendants will inhabit the coming world. At that time, they will experience the reign of David's descendent.

The entirety of Jewish literature, then, from the OT to Second Temple literature, confirms the hope of an inheritance. So strong is this expectation that it runs through these corpuses like a central thread. Being a Jew, Paul

1. The LXX Sirach citation is from Ziegler, *Sapientia Iesu Filii Sirach*.

would have been acquainted with this dominant theme. Interpreting the inheritance in his letters therefore necessitates rightly understanding this concept in the OT and Second Temple literature, for these corpuses shaped his hope of a cosmic possession for God's people, one to which they will be resurrected to dwell (Ezek 36–37; 1QHᵃ 14:29–31) and over which Messiah will reign (2 Sam 7; Ezek 36–37; *4 Ezra* 7). Having established Jewish literature as the matrix of Paul's thought, I will now overview his interpretation of the inheritance in his letters.

THE INHERITANCE IN THE PAULINE EPISTLES

Paul discusses the inheritance in six of his letters. Other than Romans 4:13, he rarely defines the content of this theme. That is why a grasp of the inheritance in the OT and Second Temple literature is essential, for it gives us access to the body of literature that would have shaped his view of the inheritance. What follows is a summary of my findings on the inheritance in Galatians, Romans, and the remaining undisputed and disputed letters of Paul.

Galatians

Paul's inheritance argument in Galatians comes on the heels of his discussion of the promised blessing in 3:2–14. Paul relies on OT texts such as Isaiah 44:3 to identify the Spirit as the fulfillment of the Abrahamic promise of blessing. Leaving this promise behind, he presses on to his discussion of the inheritance in Galatians 3:15.

At the inception of his inheritance argument, Paul cites the exact words καὶ τῷ σπέρματί σου (Gal 3:16) from LXX passages in Genesis that assert that the land is promised to Abraham's offspring (12:7; 15:18; 13:15, 17:8; 24:7).[2] The intertextual background of this citation suggests that the territorial understanding of the inheritance is in view. Galatians 3:16 also alludes to 2 Samuel 7 and Psalm 2, underscoring that the territorial inheritance to which Paul refers is the coming world—a thought supported by the echo that extends back from Isaiah 54 to 51, in Galatians 4:21–31. The resonance of 2 Samuel 7 and Psalm 2 also confirms that Christ is the promised king who will rule over the cosmic inheritance. Thus, it appears that Paul anticipates there will be a kingdom in the future world. Those who place their faith in Christ, the promised Davidic king, will also receive such

---

2 All Greek New Testament citations are from the NA 28.

an inheritance (Gal 3:19–29; cf. Ps 2). Believers, though, will not possess their worldwide heritage until they complete the Spirit-led new exodus (Gal 4:1–7).

Much of Paul's inheritance argument in Galatians is affirmed in his discussion of this theme in Romans. Simply put, the content of the promise remains the same. The only difference is that in Romans he is more explicit about the cosmic nature of the inheritance.

Romans

Of the passages in Romans, 4:13–25 and 8:14–25 affirm that Paul views the inheritance to be the eschatological world. The most explicit evidence of this is found in Romans 4:13, in which Paul compactly states that God promised to Abraham that "he would be the heir of the world" (τὸ κληρονόμον αὐτὸν εἶναι κόσμου). Believers have the hope that they will be raised to dwell in the glorious future world (8:14–25) when they complete the Spirit-led new exodus (8:14–25; cf. Gal 4:1–7). Since the eschatological world to which the Spirit is leading his people is incomparably greater than the land of Canaan, the latter serves as a type of the future worldwide heritage of Abraham and his offspring.

The remaining Pauline epistles solidify the vision of the inheritance in Galatians and Romans. Few Pauline scholars, however, venture beyond the *Hauptbriefe*. As I have argued, though such methodology may be in accord with modern, scholarly consensus, it leaves us with an impoverished grasp of Paul's view of the inheritance.

DISPUTED AND UNDISPUTED EPISTLES

Pauline letters beyond Galatians and Romans (1 Cor 6:9–10; 15:50; Gal 5:18–21; Eph 5:3–5; Col 1:12–13; 3:22–24) show clearly that the future world is where God will establish his eternal kingdom. This will be the monarchy for which Israel has longed, fulfilling the OT expectation of a kingdom in the inheritance (e.g., 2 Sam 7; 1 Chr 17; Ezek 36–37; Dan 7). The implication of this is that the monarchy in Canaan is a type of the future cosmic kingdom, the one which God's people will inhabit forever and where they will live under the righteous rule of the Messiah (cf. Gal 3:15–18; Rev 21–22). The monarchy in the original promised land was never meant to be the place where God would reign permanently over Israel. Rather, it was intended to foreshadow the eschatological kingdom that will stretch from one side of the world to the other. As the cloud and pillar of fire led Israel on the original exodus, the Spirit leads God's people on a new exodus, guaranteeing that they will receive what has been promised to them (Eph 1:10–14; Titus 3:4–6).

In all, my analysis of the inheritance related passages in Paul's letters reveals that (1) the inheritance is the world (2) on which there will be a kingdom (3) secured by the Spirit. Believers in Christ are the beneficiaries of such an inheritance. Though they do "not yet" dwell in their inheritance, the Spirit assures them that they will be raised from the grave to possess what God swore to the patriarchs, therefore fulfilling—at long last—the promise for which the people of God have been yearning since the Genesis narrative. At that time, the rightful ruler of the land, the Messiah, will crush their enemies and give his people eternal rest (Rev 20–22).

Seen in this light, Paul is not looking forward to heaven or spiritual life separated from matter. Nor is he looking forward to a bodiless state. Such an eschatology would have been contrary to Jewish expectations. Drawing from the deep wells of Jewish tradition, Paul's eschatological vision encompasses the redemption of the cosmos. This is "eternal life" for which believers have longed throughout the narrative of the Bible. Paul sees clearly that this tangible hope will be fulfilled in Christ.

CONTRIBUTION

In this book, I have shown that Paul expects an eternal existence on a reconstituted earth. Though believers do "not yet" dwell in the new creation, the apostle anticipates that the Spirit will raise them from the grave to receive the promised inheritance. This Pauline view of eternal life stands in stark contrast to popular eschatology, which places the believer's hope on a spiritualized, disembodied existence. Christians often call this state "heaven."

I must reiterate that Paul's eschatology was shaped by the longing expectation of a land promised to God's people in the OT and Second Temple literature. That Paul spiritualizes the promises is therefore incorrect. That he alters the eschatological vision in Jewish literature is also incorrect. What I do conceded is that he clarifies that the promises to Abraham's offspring will be fulfilled in Christ. Throughout salvation history, believers, like Paul, have not looked forward to a spiritualized eternity. They have anticipated a long life on the (new) earth.

It is this vision of a new creation that Christians must recapture. Works such as Oren Martin's *Bound for the Promised Land* and J. Richard Middleton's *A New Heavens and a New Earth* have made great strides in showing that this is the biblical hope promised to God's followers. Beyond providing a corrective to Hester's work, I hope that my study contributes in drawing attention to the glorious place for which the apostle Paul longed: the new cosmos where believers will reign forever with Christ.

Appendix A

Lexical Understanding of the Inheritance in the OT

THE VERB נָחַל AND the noun נַחֲלָה are the main Hebrew words associated with the inheritance concept in the OT. In the qal, piel, and hiphil stems, the verb נָחַל refers to "the giving (e.g., Num 34:17; Deut 1:38, 3:28; Josh 19:49), apportioning (e.g., Josh 19:51; Num 34:29) or leaving of an inheritance" (1 Chr 28:8) to someone.[1] In the Hofal and Hitpael stems, this verb means "to become the inheritor (Job 7:3) or to maintain possession"[2] of the land (Num 33:54; 34:13). In each of the stem uses of נָחַל, what is mainly given or received as an inheritance is the land of promise.[3] A near synonym of נָחַל is the verb יָרַשׁ,[4] which in the qal stem means "to take or gain possession of" (e.g., Isa 57:13; 69:36) or "to inherit/to be an heir" (e.g., Gen 15:3, 7; Isa 54:3) and in the piel stem means "to totally possess" (Deut 28:42).[5] Frequently, the object of יָרַשׁ is אֶרֶץ (e.g., Gen 15:7; Deut 1:8),[6] i.e., the land of Canaan. In view of these observations, the verb נָחַל is indeed closely linked with יָרַשׁ, since both terms are associated with the notion of inheritance.[7]

The noun נַחֲלָה generally carries the sense of "inheritance." This noun refers to the portions of land belonging to the clans of Israel (e.g., Num 33:54; Josh 15:20, 18:28) or the entire land as the inheritance of Israel (e.g.,

---

1. *HALOT*, 2:686.

2. Ibid.

3. Wright notes that נָחַל and its cognates generally refer "to the division of the land within the kinship structure of Israel and thus signifies the permanent family property allotted to the tribes, clans, families of Israel" ("נָחַל," 3:77).

4. Lipinski, "נָחַל," 9:320.

5. Wright, "יָרַשׁ," 3:547.

6. Harris, "Eternal Inheritance," 33.

7. Wright, "יָרַשׁ," 2:547.

Judg 20:6; Ezek 35:15).[8] Although it is Israel's inheritance, it is understood that the land is ultimately the נַחֲלָה of Yahweh (1 Sam 26:19; 2 Sam 20:19).[9] Thus, only he can give (נָתַן) the land (e.g., Gen 12:7; 13:15). Besides these uses, נַחֲלָה also carries the sense of Israel as the inheritance of Yahweh (Jer 10:16, 51:19).[10] This function of נַחֲלָה is less frequent than its use as the land inheritance of Israel and, ultimately, God.

In sum, the verb נָחַל and the noun נַחֲלָה are the primary Hebrew words associated with the inheritance notion in the OT. The verb יָרַשׁ is a close synonym of נָחַל, since it is also associated with the inheritance concept. Although both נָחַל and נַחֲלָה normally refer to the land of Canaan, נַחֲלָה occasionally refers to Israel as God's inheritance. Since this later use is infrequent, it is warranted to understand that נָחַל and נַחֲלָה mainly refer to the land inheritance.

8. Wright, "נָחַל," 3:78.

9. Ibid., 3:79.

10. Ibid.

Appendix B

Lexical Understanding of the Inheritance in the LXX

LXX TRANSLATORS COMMONLY EMPLOY κληρονομέω, κληρονομία, and κληρονόμος in rendering OT inheritance terms. The verb κληρονομέω is most often used to translate יָרֵשׁ (111 times) and less often נָחַל (27).[11] The noun κληρονομία is mainly employed to translate the word נַחֲלָה (143 times). In sixteen other instances, κληρονομία is used to translate "words of the stem יָרֵשׁ."[12] Also, the noun κλῆρος is employed in rendering the word נַחֲלָה (49 times) and even words associated with the stem יָרֵשׁ (11). On occasion, the noun κλῆρος functions synonymously with κληρονομία as the "inheritance" of Israel (e.g., Exod 6:8; Num 33:53).[13] These words usually coincide "when the form in which the Israelites took possession of Canaan, and the land itself as God's special God-given possession, are described."[14] Although κλῆρος may function synonymously with κληρονομία, the former may be used with the sense of an individual "lot" or "portion" of the larger inheritance of Israel (11 times in Josh 17–21), whereas the latter carries no such function. This is because κληρονομία mainly refers to the "entire" inheritance of Israel (e.g., 1 Kgs 8:36; 1 Chr 21:12).[15] These observations make evident that the translators of the LXX consistently employ κληρονομέω, κληρονομία, and κληρονόμος for rendering OT inheritance terms.

---

11. Foerster and Herrmann, "κληρονομέω," 3:769. The word counts in this section come from pp. 767–85 of this source, unless otherwise specified.

12. Ibid.

13. Ibid., 759

14. Ibid.

15. Eichler, "Inheritance, Lot, Portion," 2:298. LSJ, 959–60.

Bibliography

Adams, Edward. *Constructing the World: A Study in Paul's Cosmological Language.* Edinburgh: T. & T. Clark, 2000.

Alexander, T. Desmond. "Beyond Borders: The Wider Dimensions of Land." In *The Land of Promise: Biblical, Theological and Contemporary Perspectives*, edited by Philip Johnston and Peter Walker, 35–50. Downers Grove, IL: InterVarsity, 2000.

Allen, Leslie. *Ezekiel 20–48.* Word Biblical Commentary 29. Dallas: Word, 1990.

Anderson, A. A. *2 Samuel.* Word Biblical Commentary 11. Dallas: Word, 1989.

Atkinson, Kenneth. *An Intertextual Study of the Psalms of Solomon: Pseudepigrapha.* Lewiston, NY: Edwin Mellen, 2001.

Attridge, Harold. "Historiography." In *Jewish Writings of the Second Temple Period: Apocrypha, Pseudepigrapha, Qumran Sectarian Writings, Philo, Josephus*, edited by Michael E. Stone, 157–84. Philadelphia: Fortress, 1984.

Avemarie, Friedrich. "Bund als Gabe und Recht." In *Bund und Tora: Zur theologischen Begriffsgeschichte in alttestamentlicher, frühjüdischer und urchristlicher Tradition*, edited by Friedrich Avemarie and H. Lichtenberger, 163–216. Tübingen: Mohr Siebeck, 1996.

Baker, David L. *Two Testaments, One Bible: The Theological Relationship between the Old and New Testaments.* Downers Grove, IL: InterVarsity, 2010.

Baldwin, Joyce G. *1 and 2 Samuel.* Theological Old Testament Commentary. Leicester, UK: InterVarsity, 1988.

Baltzer, Klaus. *Deutero-Isaiah: A Commentary on Isaiah 40–55.* Hermeneia—A Critical and Historical Commentary on the Bible. Minneapolis: Fortress, 2001.

Balz, Horst, and Gerhard Schneider, eds. *Exegetical Dictionary of the New Testament.* 3 vols. Grand Rapids: Eerdmans, 1991.

Barclay, John M. G. *Paul & the Gift.* Grand Rapids: Eerdmans, 2015.

Barrett, C. K. *The First Epistle to the Corinthians.* Black's New Testament Commentaries. Peabody, MA: Hendrickson, 1968.

Bauckham, Richard. "Apocalypses." In *Justification and Variegated Nomism: The Complexities of Second Temple Judaism*, edited by D. A. Carson, Peter T. O'Brien, and Mark A. Seifrid, 1:135–89. Grand Rapids: Baker, 2001.

Bauer, Walter. *A Greek Lexicon of the New Testament and Other Early Christian Literature.* 3rd. ed. Revised and edited by Fredrick William Danker. Chicago: University of Chicago Press, 2000.

Baugh, S. M. "Galatians 3:20 and the Covenant of Redemption." *Westminster Theological Journal* 66 (2004) 49–70.

Beale, G. K. "Colossians." In *Commentary on the New Testament Use of the Old Testament*, edited by G. K. Beale and D. A. Carson, 841–70. Grand Rapids: Eerdmans, 2007.

———. *A New Testament Biblical Theology: The Unfolding of the Old Testament in the New.* Grand Rapids: Baker, 2011.

———. "The Old Testament Background of Paul's Reference to 'the Fruit of the Spirit' in Galatians 5:22." *Bulletin for Biblical Research* 15 (2005) 1–38.

———. *The Temple and the Church's Mission: A Biblical Theology of the Dwelling Place of God.* New Studies in Biblical Theology 17. Downers Grove, IL: InterVarsity, 2004.

Ben Zvi, Ehud, and Christoph Levin, eds. *The Concept of Exile in Ancient Israel and Its Historical Contexts.* Berlin: De Gruyter, 2010.

Bergen, Robert D. *1, 2 Samuel.* New American Commentary. Nashville: Broadman & Holman, 1996.

Betz, Hans Dieter. *Galatians.* Hermeneia—A Critical and Historical Commentary on the Bible. Philadelphia: Fortress, 1979.

Bird, Michael F. *Colossians and Philemon.* New Covenant Commentary Series. Eugene, OR: Cascade, 2009.

Black, Matthew. *The Book of Enoch or 1 Enoch: A New English Edition with Commentary and Textual Notes.* Leiden: Brill, 1985.

Blass, F., A. Debrunner, and Robert W. Funk. *A Greek Grammar of the New Testament and Other Early Christian Literature.* Translated and revised by Robert W. Funk. Chicago: University of Chicago Press, 1961.

Blenkinsopp, James. "Introduction to the Pentateuch." In *New Interpreters Bible*, 1:305–18. Nashville: Abingdon, 1994.

Bockmuehl, Markus. "1QS and Salvation at Qumran." In *Justification and Variegated Nomism: The Complexities of Second Temple Judaism*, edited by D. A. Carson, Peter T. O'Brien, and Mark A. Seifrid, 1:381–414. Tübingen: Mohr Siebeck; Grand Rapids: Baker, 2001.

Botterweck, G. Johannes, Helmer Ringgren, and Heinz-Josef Fabry, eds. *Theological Dictionary of the Old Testament.* Translated by David E. Green. 12 vols. Grand Rapids: Eerdmans, 1998–2003.

Boyarin, Daniel. *A Radical Jew: Paul and the Politics of Identity.* Berkeley: University of California, 1994.

Braulik, Georg. "Gottes Ruhe—Das Land oder der Tempel? Zu Psalm 95, 11." In *Freude and der Weisung des Herrn, Beiträge zur Theologie der Psalmen, Festgabe zum 70. Geburtstag von Heinrich Gross*, 33–44. Stuttgart: Katholisches Bibelwerk, 1986.

Breneman, Mervin. *Ezra, Nehemiah, Esther.* New American Commentary 10. Nashville: Broadman & Holman, 1993.

Brown, Colin, ed. *New International Dictionary of New Testament Theology.* 4 vols. Grand Rapids: Zondervan, 1986.

Bruce, F. F. *The Epistle to the Galatians.* The New International Greek Testament Commentary. Grand Rapids: Eerdmans, 1982. Reprint, 2002.

———. *Galatians.* New International Greek Testament Commentary. Grand Rapids: Eerdmans, 1982. Reprint, 2002.

Brueggemann, Walter. *1 & 2 Kings.* Smith and Helwys Bible Commentary. Macon: Smyth & Helwys, 2000.

———. *Isaiah 40–66*. Westminster Bible Companion. Louisville: Westminster John Knox, 1998.

———. *The Land: Place as Gift, Promise, and Challenge in Biblical Faith*. Philadelphia: Fortress, 1977.

Budd, Phillip J. *Numbers*. Word Biblical Commentary 5. Waco, TX: Word, 1984.

Bundrick, David R. "TA STOICHEIA TOU KOSMOU (GAL 4:3)." *Journal of the Evangelical Theological Society* 34 (1991) 353–64.

Burton, Ernest De Witt. *Galatians: A Critical and Exegetical Commentary*. International Critical Commentary. Reprint, Sheffield: T. & T. Clark, 2001.

Butler, Trent. *Judges*. Word Biblical Commentary 8. Dallas: Word, 2009.

Campbell, Jonathan G. *The Use of Scripture in the Damascus Document 1–8, 19–20*. Berlin: Walter de Gruyter, 1995.

Caneday, A. B. "Covenant Lineage Prefigured: 'Which Things are Interpreted Allegorically' (Galatians 4:21–31)." *Southern Baptist Journal of Theology* 14 (Fall 2010) 50–77.

Charlesworth, James H., ed. *The Old Testament Pseudepigrapha*. 2 vols. Garden City, NY: Doubleday, 1983–85.

Childs, Brevard. *Biblical Theology of the Old and New Testaments: Theological Reflection of the Christian Bible*. Minneapolis: Fortress, 1992.

Chisholm, Robert. *From Exegesis to Exposition: A Practical Guide to Using Biblical Hebrew*. Grand Rapids: Baker, 1998.

Ciampa, Roy E., and Brian S. Rosner. "1 Corinthians." In *Commentary on the Old Testament Use of the New Testament*, edited by G. K. Beale and D. A. Carson, 695–752. Grand Rapids: Baker, 2007.

Collins, John J. *Jewish Wisdom in the Hellenistic Age*. Louisville: Westminster John Knox, 1997.

Cooper, Lamar Eugene. *Ezekiel*. New American Commentary 17. Nashville: Broadman & Holman, 1994.

Cosgrove, Charles H. "The Law Has Given Sarah No Children (Gal 4:21–30)." *Novum Testamentum* 29 (1987) 219–35.

Craigie, Peter E. *Psalms 1–50*. Word Biblical Commentary 19. Dallas: Word, 2004.

Cranfield, Charles E. B. *The Epistle to the Romans*. International Critical Commentary. 2 vols. Reprint, London: T. & T. Clark, 2004.

Dahl, Nils Alstrup. *Studies in Paul: Theology for the Early Christian Mission*. Minneapolis: Augsburg, 1977.

Das, Andrew. *Paul, the Law, and the Covenant*. Grand Rapids: Baker, 2001.

Daube, David. *The New Testament and Rabbinic Judaism*. London: University of London, 1956. Reprint, Peabody, MA: Hendrickson, 1990.

Davies, Peter A. "Didactic Stories." In *Justification and Variegated Nomism: The Complexities of Second Temple Judaism*, edited by D. A. Carson, Peter T. O'Brien, and Mark A. Seifrid, 1:99–134. Grand Rapids: Baker, 2001.

Davies, Philip R. *1QM, The War Scroll from Qumran: Its Structure and History*. Rome: Biblical Institute, 1977.

———. *The Damascus Covenant: An Interpretation of the "Damascus Document*. Sheffield: JSOT, 1982.

Davies, William D. *The Gospel and the Land: Early Christian and Jewish Territorial Doctrine*. Berkeley: University of California Press, 1974. Reprint, Sheffield: Sheffield Press, 1994.

Delling, G. "Die Weise, von der Zeit zu Reden, im Lieber Antiquatatum Biblicarum." *Novum Testamentum* 13 (1971) 305–21.

Dempster, Stephen G. *Dominion and Dynasty: A Theology of the Hebrew Bible.* Downers Grove, IL: InterVarsity, 2003.

Denton, D. R. "Inheritance in Paul and in Ephesians." *Evangelical Quarterly* 53 (1982) 157–62.

deSilva, David A. *Introducing the Apocrypha: Message, Context, and Significance.* Grand Rapids: Baker, 2002.

DeVries, Simon J. *1 Kings.* Word Biblical Commentary 12. Waco, TX: Word, 1985.

Di Lella, Alexander A. "The Deuteronomistic Background of the Farewell Discourse in Tob 14:3–11." *Catholic Bible Quarterly* 41 (1979) 380–89.

Dimant, D. "Qumran Sectarian Literature." In *Jewish Writings of the Second Temple Period: Apocrypha, Pseudepigrapha, Qumran Sectarian Writings, Philo, Josephus,* edited by Michael E. Stone, 483–50. Philadelphia: Fortress, 1984.

DiMattei, Steven. "Paul's Allegory of the Two Covenants (Gal 4.21–31) in Light of First-Century Hellenistic Rhetoric and Jewish Hermeneutics." *New Testament Studies* 52 (2006) 102–22.

Dozeman, Thomas B. *Exodus.* Exegetical Critical Commentary. Grand Rapids: Eerdmans, 2009.

Draisma, Sipke, ed. *Intertextuality in Biblical Writings: Essays in Honour of Bas van Iersel.* Kampen: Kok, 1989.

Duling, Dennis C. "The Promises to David and Their Entrance Into Christianity: Nailing Down a Likely Hypothesis." *New Testament Studies* 20 (1973–74) 55–77.

Dumbrell, William. *Covenant and Creation: A Theology of the Old Testament Covenants.* Exeter: Paternoster, 1984.

Dunn, James D. G. "Echoes of Intra-Jewish Polemic in Paul's Letter to the Galatians." *Journal of Biblical Literature* 112 (1993) 459–77.

———. *The Epistle to the Galatians.* Black's New Testament Commentary. Peabody, MA: Hendrickson, 2002.

———. *The Epistles to the Colossians and to Philemon.* New International Greek Testament Commentary. Grand Rapids: Eerdmans, 1996.

———. "Once More πίστις Χριστοῦ." In *Pauline Theology: Looking Back, Pressing On,* edited by E. E. Johnson and D. M. Hay. Society of Biblical Literature, Symposium Series 4. Atlanta: Scholars, 1997.

———. *Romans 1–8.* Word Biblical Commentary 38a. Dallas: Word, 1988.

Easterling, P. E. "Repetition in Sophocles." *Hermes* 101 (1973) 14–34.

Echevarria, Miguel. "The Inheritance of the Cosmic Kingdom in Galatians 3:15—4:7." *Luther Rice Journal of Christian Studies* 1 (Spring 2016) 2–17.

Elliger, K., and W. Rudolph, eds. *Biblica Hebraica Stuttgertensia.* Stuttgart: Deutsche BibelGesellschaft, 1998.

Ellis, E. Earl. "Biblical Interpretation in the New Testament Church." In *Mikra: Text, Translation, Reading and Interpretation of the Hebrew Bible in Ancient Judaism and Early Christianity,* 691–725. Philadelphia: Fortress, 1988.

———. *Paul's Use of the Old Testament.* Grand Rapids: Eerdmans, 1957.

Engberg-Pedersen, Troels. *Paul and the Stoics.* Edinburgh: T. & T. Clark, 2000.

Enslin, Morton S. *The Book of Judith: Greek Text with an English Translation, Commentary and Critical Notes.* Edited by Solomon Zeitlin. Leiden: Brill, 1972.

Fee, Gordon. *The First Epistle to the Corinthians.* New International Commentary on the New Testament. Grand Rapids: Eerdmans, 1987.

Fishbane, Michael. *Biblical Interpretation in Ancient Israel.* Oxford: Clarendon, 1985.

Flint, Peter W., ed. *The Bible at Qumran: Text, Shape, and Interpretation.* Grand Rapids: Eerdmans, 2001.

Flusser, David. "Psalms, Hymns and Prayers." In *Jewish Writings of the Second Temple Period: Apocrypha, Pseudepigrapha, Qumran Sectarian Writings, Philo, Josephus,* edited by Michael E. Stone, 551–78. Philadelphia: Fortress, 1984.

Follingstad, Carl M. *Deictic Viewpoint in Biblical Hebrew Text: A Syntagmatic and Paradigmatic Analysis of the Particle* כי. Dallas: SIL International, 2000.

Foreman, Mark. *The Politics of Inheritance in Romans.* Society for New Testament Studies Monograph Series. Cambridge: Cambridge University Press, 2011.

Forshey, H. "The Construct Chain Nahalat YHWH/Elohim." *Bulletin of the American Schools of Oriental Research* 220 (1975) 51–53.

Fretheim, Terrence E. "The Book of Genesis." In *New Interpreters Bible,* 1:335–674. Nashville: Abingdon, 1994.

Fuller, Michael E. *The Restoration of Israel: Israel's Regathering and the Fate of the Nations in Early Jewish Literature and Luke-Acts.* Berlin: Walter de Gruyter, 2006.

Fung, Ronald. *The Epistle to the Galatians.* New International Commentary on the New Testament. Grand Rapids: Eerdmans, 1988.

García Martínez, Florentino. *The Dead Sea Scrolls Translated: The Qumran Texts in English.* Translated by Wilfred G. E. Watson. Leiden: Brill; Grand Rapids: Eerdmans, 1996.

García Martínez, Florentino, and Eibert J. C. Tigchelaar, eds. *The Dead Sea Scrolls: Study Edition.* 2 vols. Leiden: Brill, 1997.

Garland, David E. *1 Corinthians.* Baker Exegetical Commentary on the New Testament. Grand Rapids: Baker, 2003.

Gaston, Lloyd. "Israel's Enemies in Pauline Theology." *New Testament Studies* 28 (1982) 400–23.

Gentry, Peter J., and Stephen J. Wellum. *Kingdom through Covenant: A Biblical-Theological Understanding of the Covenants.* Wheaton, IL: Crossway, 2012.

Gesenius, Wilhelm. *Hebrew Grammar.* Edited by E. Kautzsch. Translated by A. E. Cowley. Oxford: Clarendon, 1983.

Goldingay, John. *Psalms 1–41.* Baker Commentary on the Old Testament Wisdom and Psalms. Grand Rapids: Baker, 2006.

Goldstein, Jonathan. *1 Maccabees: A New Translation with Introduction and Commentary.* Anchor Bible. Garden City, NY: Doubleday, 1976.

———. *II Maccabees: A New Translation with Introduction and Commentary.* New York: Doubleday, 1983.

Goppelt, Leonhard. *Typos: The Typological Interpretation of the Old Testament in the New.* Translated by Donald H. Madvig. Grand Rapids: Eerdmans, 1982.

Grossman, Maxine. *Reading for History in the Damascus Document: A Methodological Method.* Leiden: Brill, 2002.

Gundry, Stanley N. "Typology as a Means of Interpretation: Past and Present." *Journal of the Evangelical Theological Society* 12 (1969) 233–40.

Hafemann, Scott. "Paul and the Exile of Israel in Galatians 3–4." In *Exile: Old Testament, Jewish, and Christian Conceptions,* edited by James Scott, 329–71. Leiden: Brill, 1997.

Hahn, Scott. "Covenant, Oath, and the Aqedah: διαθήκη in Galatians 3:15–18." *Catholic Biblical Quarterly* 67 (2005) 79–100.

Halvorson-Taylor, Martin A. *Enduring Exile: The Metaphorization of Exile in the Hebrew Bible*. Leiden: Brill, 2011.

Hamilton, James M., Jr. *God's Glory in Salvation through Judgment: A Biblical Theology*. Wheaton, IL: Crossway, 2010.

———. *God's Indwelling Presence: The Holy Spirit in the Old and New Testaments*. Nashville: B&H, 2006.

———. "The Skull-Crushing Seed of the Woman: Inner-Biblical Interpretation of Gen 3:15." *Southern Baptist Journal of Theology* 10.2 (2006) 30–54.

———. "The Typology of David's Rise to Power: Messianic Patterns in the Book of Samuel." *Southern Baptist Journal of Theology* 16 (2012) 4–25.

Hamilton, Victor P. *The Book of Genesis*. New International Commentary on the Old Testament. Grand Rapids: Eerdmans, 1990.

———. *Exodus: An Exegetical Commentary*. Grand Rapids: Baker, 2011.

Hammer, Paul L. "A Comparison of KLERONOMIA in Paul and Ephesians." *Journal of Biblical Literature* 79 (1960) 267–72.

———. "The Understanding of the Inheritance in the New Testament." ThD thesis, The University of Heidelberg, 1958.

Hanhart, Robert, ed. *Iudith*. Septuaginta: Vetus Testamentum Graecum 8.4. Göttingen: Vandenhoech & Ruprecht, 1979.

———, ed. *Maccabaeorum Liber II*. Septuaginta: Vetus Testamentum Graecum 9.2. Göttingen: Vandenhoech & Ruprecht, 1959.

———, ed. *Tobit*. Septuaginta: Vetus Testamentum Graecum 8.5. Göttingen: Vandenhoech & Ruprecht, 1983.

Hansen, G. Walter. *Abraham in Galatians*. Journal for the Study of the New Testament. Supplement Series 29. Sheffield, UK: Sheffield Academic, 1989.

Harding, Mark. "Disputed Letters of Paul." In *The Pauline Canon*, edited by Stanley E. Porter, 129–68. Leiden: Brill, 2004.

Harris, Dana. "The Eternal Inheritance in Hebrews: The Appropriation of an Old Testament Motif by the Author of Hebrews." PhD diss., Trinity Evangelical Divinity School, 2009.

Hartley, John E. *Leviticus*. Word Biblical Commentary 4. Dallas: Word, 1992.

Hawthorne, Gerald, Ralph Martin, and Daniel Reed, eds. *Dictionary of Paul and His Letters*. Downers Grove, IL: InterVarsity, 1993.

Hay, David M. *Colossians*. Abingdon New Testament Commentaries. Nashville: Abingdon, 2000.

Hays, Richard B. "ΠΙΣΤΙΣ and Pauline Theology: What Is at Stake?" In *Pauline Theology: Looking Back, Pressing On*, edited by E. E. Johnson and D. M. Hay. Society of Biblical Literature, Symposium Series 4. Atlanta: Scholars, 1997.

———. *Echoes of Scripture in Paul's Letters*. New Haven: Yale University Press, 1989.

———. *The Faith of Jesus Christ: The Narrative Substructure of Galatians 3:1—4:11*. Grand Rapids: Eerdmans, 2002.

Hays, Richard B., and Joel B. Green. "The Use of the Old Testament by New Testament Writers." In *Hearing the New Testament*, edited by Joel B. Green, 222–38. Grand Rapids: Eerdmans, 1995.

Heitanen, Mika. *Paul's Argument in Galatians: A Pragmatic-Dialectical Analysis*, edited by Michael Labahn. London: T. & T. Clark, 2007.

Hengel, Martin. *Studies in the Gospel of Mark.* Translated by John Bowden. London: SCM, 1985.

Hens-Piazza, Gina. *1–2 Kings.* Abingdon Old Testament Commentaries. Nashville: Abingdon, 2006.

Henze, Matthias, ed. *Biblical Interpretation at Qumran.* Grand Rapids: Eerdmans, 2005.

————. *Jewish Apocalypticism in Late First Century Israel: Reading Second Baruch in Context.* Tübingen: Mohr Siebeck, 2011.

Hester, James D. *Paul's Concept of Inheritance: A Contribution to the Understanding of Heilsgeschichte.* London: Oliver and Boyd, 1968.

Hill, Andrew E., and John H. Walton. *A Survey of the Old Testament.* Grand Rapids: Zondervan, 1991.

Hodge, Caroline Johnson. *If Sons, Then Heirs: A Study of Kinship and Ethnicity in the Letters of Paul.* Oxford: Oxford University Press, 2007.

Hoehner, Harold. *Ephesians: An Exegetical Commentary.* Grand Rapids: Baker, 2004.

Hong, In-Gyu. *The Law in Galatians.* Journal for the Study of the New Testament. Supplement Series 81. Sheffield: Sheffield Press, 1993.

Paul. *1, 2 Kings.* New American Commentary 8. Nashville: Broadman & Holman, 1995.

————. *Old Testament Theology.* Downers Grove, IL: InterVarsity, 1998.

Howard, George. *Paul: Crisis in Galatia: A Study of Early Christian Theology.* Society for New Testament Studies 35. Cambridge: Cambridge University, 1990.

Hummel, Horace D. *Ezekiel 1–20.* Concordia Commentary: A Theological Exposition of Scripture. St. Louis: Concordia, 2005.

————. *Ezekiel 21–48.* Concordia Commentary: A Theological Exposition of Scripture. St. Louis: Concordia, 2007.

Jenni, Ernst, and Claus Westermann. *Theological Lexicon of the New Testament.* 3 vols. Translated and edited by Mark Biddle. Peabody, MA: Hendrickson, 1994.

Jeremias, Joachim. "Flesh and Blood Cannot Inherit the Kingdom of God." *New Testament Studies* 2 (1956) 151–59.

Jewett, Robert. *Romans.* Hermeneia—A Critical and Historical Commentary on the Bible. Minneapolis: Fortress, 2007.

Jobes, Karen H. "Jerusalem, Our Mother: Metalepsis and Intertextuality in Galatians 4:21–31." *Westminster Theological Journal* (1993) 299–320.

Johnson, S. Lewis, Jr. "Once in Custody Now in Christ: An Exposition of Galatians 3:23–29." *Emmaus Journal* 13 (2004) 212–20.

Kaiser, Walter C., Jr. "Leviticus." In *New Interpreters Bible,* 1:985–1191. Nashville: Abingdon, 1994.

————. "The Promise Theme and the Theology of Rest." *Bibliotheca Sacra* 130 (1973) 135–50.

————. "The Promised Land: A Biblical Historical View." *Bibliotheca Sacra* 138 (1981) 302–12.

Kappler, W. *Maccabaerorum Liber I.* Septuaginta: Vetus Testamentum Graecum 9.1. Göttingen: Vandenhoech & Ruprecht, 1967.

Keesmaat, Silvia. "Exodus and the Intertextual Transformation of Tradition in Romans 8.14–31." *Journal for the Study of the New Testament* 54 (1994) 29–56.

———. *Paul and His Story: (Re)Interpreting the Exodus Tradition*. Journal for the Study of the New Testament. Supplementary Series 181. Sheffield: Sheffield Academic, 1999.

———. "The Psalms in Romans and Galatians." In *The Psalms in the New Testament*, edited by Steve Moyise and Maarten J. J. Menken, 139–61. London: T. & T. Clark, 2004.

Kerr, A. J. "ΑΡΡΑΒΩΝ." *Journal of Theological Studies* 39 (1998) 92–97.

Kirkpatrick, A. F. *The Psalms Book*. Cambridge: Cambridge University Press, 1981.

Kittel, G., and G. Friedrich, eds. *Theological Dictionary of the New Testament*. Translated by Geoffrey W. Bromiley. 10 vols. Grand Rapids: Eerdmans, 1964–1976. Reprint, 2006.

Klein, Ralph. *1 Chronicles*. Hermeneia—A Critical and Historical Commentary on the Bible. Minneapolis: Fortress, 2006.

Klijn, A. F. J. "2 (Syriac Apocalypse of) Baruch: A New Translation and Introduction." In vol. 1 of *The Old Testament Pseudepigrapha*, edited by James H. Charlesworth, 615–52. Garden City, NY: Doubleday, 1983.

Knibb, Michael A. *Essays on the Book of Enoch and Other Early Jewish Texts and Traditions*. Leiden: Brill, 2009.

———. *The Ethiopic Book of Enoch: A New Edition in the Light of the Aramaic Dead Sea Fragments*. 2 vols. Oxford: Clarendon, 1978.

———. *The Qumran Community*. Cambridge: Cambridge University Press, 1987.

Koehler, Ludwig, and Walter Baumgartner. *Hebrew and Aramaic Lexicon of the Old Testament*. 2 vols. Translated and edited by M. E. J. Richardson. Leiden: Brill, 1995.

Kugel, James L. *A Walk through Jubilees: Studies in the Book of Jubilees and the World of Its Creation*. Leiden: Brill, 2012.

Kwon, Yon-Gyong. *Eschatology in Galatians*. Tübingen: Mohr Siebeck, 2004.

Laansma, Jon. *"I Will Give You Rest": The Rest Motif in the New Testament with Special Reference to Matt 11 and Heb 3–4*. Wissenschaftliche Untersuchungen zum Neuen Testament 2/98. Tübgingen: Mohr Siebeck, 1997.

Lea, Thomas D., and Hayne P. Griffin, Jr. *1, 2 Timothy and Titus*. New American Commentary. Nashville: Broadman, 1992.

Leithart, Peter J. *Deep Exegesis: The Mystery of Reading Scripture*. Waco, TX: Baylor, 2009.

Leonard, Jeremy M. "Identifying Inner-Biblical Illusions, Psalm 78 as a Test Case." *Journal of* Biblical *Literature* 127 (2008) 241–65.

Leupold, H. C. *Exposition of the Psalms*. Grand Rapids: Baker, 1959.

Liddell, Henry George, and Robert Scott. *A Greek-English Lexicon*. 9th ed. Oxford: Clarendon, 1996.

Lied, Liv Ingeborg. *The Other Lands of Israel: Imaginations of the Land in 2 Baruch*. Leiden: Brill, 2008.

Lim, Timothy H. *Holy Scripture in the Qumran Commentaries and Pauline Letters*. Oxford: Clarendon, 1997.

Lincoln, Andrew T. *Ephesians*. Word Biblical Commentary 42. Dallas: Word, 1990.

Lockwood, Gregory. *1 Corinthians*. Concordia Commentary: A Theological Exposition of Scripture. St. Louis: Concordia, 2000.

Lohse, Eduard. *Colossians and Philemon*. Hermeneia—A Critical and Historical Commentary on the Bible. Translated by William R. Poehlmann and Robert J. Karris. Philadelphia: Fortress, 1971.

Longenecker, Richard. *Galatians*. Word Biblical Commentary 41. Waco, TX: Word, 1990.

———. "The Pedagogical Nature of the Law in Galatians 3:15—4:7." *Journal of the Evangelical Theological Society* 25 (March 1982) 53–61.

MacDonald, Margaret. *Colossians and Ephesians*. Sacra Pagina. Collegeville, MN: Liturgical, 2000.

MacKenzie, R. A. F. *Sirach*. Old Testament Message. Wilmington, DE: Michael Glazier, 1983.

Marshall, I. Howard. *The Pastoral Epistles*. International Critical Commentary. London: T. & T. Clark, 1999.

Martens, Elmer A. "Land and Lifestyle." In *Old Testament Theology: Flowering and Future*, edited by Ben C. Ollenburger, 222–44. Winona Lake, IN: Eisenbrauns, 2004.

Martin, Oren R. *Bound for the Promised Land: The Land Promise in God's Redemptive Plan*. New Studies in Biblical Theology. Downers Grove, IL: InterVarsity, 2015.

Martin, Ralph. *Colossians: The Church's Lord and the Christian's Liberty*. Grand Rapids: Zondervan, 1972.

Matera, Frank. *Galatians*. Sacra Pagina. Collegeville, MN: Liturgical, 2007.

Mays, James Luther. *Psalms*. Interpretation. Louisville: John Knox, 1994.

McCarter, P. Kyle, Jr. *1 Samuel*. Anchor Bible. New York: Doubleday, 1980.

———. *2 Samuel*. Anchor Bible. New York: Doubleday, 1984.

McKinney, Richard W. A., ed. *Creation, Christ, and Culture, Studies in Honour of T. F. Torrance*. Edinburgh: T. & T. Clark, 1976.

Meek, Russell L. "Intertextuality, Inner-Biblical Exegesis, and Inner-Biblical Allusion: The Ethics of a Methodology." *Biblica* 95 (2014) 280–91.

Merrill, Eugene H. *Deuteronomy*. New American Commentary 4. Nashville: Broadman & Holman, 1994.

———. *Kingdom of Priests: A History of Old Testament Israel*. Grand Rapids: Baker, 2008.

Middendorf, Michael P. *Romans 1–8*. Concordia Commentary. St. Louis: Concordia, 2013.

Middleton, J. Richard. *A New Heavens and a New Earth: Reclaiming Biblical Eschatology*. Grand Rapids: Baker, 2014.

Miller, Patrick. "The Gift of God: The Deuteronomic Theology of the Land." *Interpretation* 23 (1969) 461–65.

Moo, Douglas J. *The Epistle to the Romans*. New International Commentary on the New Testament. Grand Rapids: Eerdmans, 1996.

Moore, Carey A. *Tobit: A New Translation and Commentary*. Anchor Bible. New York: Doubleday, 1996.

Morales, Rodrigo. "The Spirit and the Restoration of Israel: New Exodus and New Creation Motifs in Galatians." PhD diss., Duke Divinity School, 2007.

Motyer, J. Alec. *Isaiah: An Introduction and Commentary*. Tyndale Old Testament Commentaries. Downers Grove, IL: InterVarsity, 1999.

Moule, H. C. G. *Studies in Colossians and Philemon*. Grand Rapids: Kregel, 1977.

Moxnes, Halvor. *Theology in Conflict: Studies of Paul's Understanding of God in Romans*. Leiden: Brill, 1980.

Moyise, Steve. *Paul and Scripture: Studying the New Testament Use of the Old Testament*. Grand Rapids: Baker, 2010.

Murphy, Fredrick James. *The Structure and Meaning of Second Baruch*. Atlanta: Scholar's, 1985.

Nestle, Eberhard, Erwin Nestle, and Kurt Alan, eds. *Novum Testamentum Graece*. 28th ed. Stuttgart: Deutsche Bibelgesellschaft, 2012.

Nickelsburg, George. *1 Enoch 1: A Commentary on the Book of Enoch, Chapters 1–36; 8–108*. Hermeneia—A Critical and Historical Commentary on the Bible. Minneapolis: Fortress, 2001.

———. "The Bible Rewritten and Expanded." In *Jewish Writings of the Second Temple Period: Apocrypha, Pseudepigrapha, Qumran Sectarian Writings, Philo, Josephus*, edited by Michael E. Stone, 89–156. Philadelphia: Fortress, 1984.

———. *Jewish Literature between the Bible and the Mishnah: A Historical and Literary Introduction*. Philadelphia: Fortress, 1981.

———. "Stories of Biblical and Early Post-Biblical Times." In *Jewish Writings of the Second Temple Period: Apocrypha, Pseudepigrapha, Qumran Sectarian Writings, Philo, Josephus*, edited by Michael E. Stone, 33–88. Philadelphia: Fortress, 1984.

Nickelsburg, George, and James C. VanderKam. *1 Enoch 2: A Commentary on the Book of Enoch Chapters 37–82*. Hermeneia—A Critical and Historical Commentary on the Bible. Minneapolis: Fortress, 2012.

Nolland, John. *The Gospel of Matthew*. New International Greek Testament Commentary. Grand Rapids: Eerdmans, 2005.

Noth, Martin. *Exodus: A Commentary*. Old Testament Library. Philadelphia: Westminster, 1962.

Oropeza, B. J. "Echoes of Isaiah in the Rhetoric of Paul: New Exodus, Wisdom, and the Humility of the Cross in Utopian-Apocalyptic Expectations." In *The Intertexture of Apocalyptic Discourse in the New Testament*, edited by Duane F. Watson, 87–112. Leiden: Brill, 2002.

Oswalt, John. *The Book of Isaiah: Chapters 1–39*. New International Commentary on the Old Testament. Grand Rapids: Eerdmans, 1986.

———. *The Book of Isaiah: Chapter 40–66*. Grand Rapids: Zondervan, 1998.

Owens, Mark. *As It Was in the Beginning: An Intertextual Analysis of New Creation in Galatians, 2 Corinthians, and Ephesians*. Eugene, OR: Pickwick, 2015.

Pickering, P. E. "Did the Greek Ear Detect 'Careless' Verbal Repetitions?" *Classical Quarterly* 53 (2003) 490–99.

Pietersma, Albert, and Benjamin G. Wright. *A New English Translation of the Septuagint*. Oxford: Oxford University Press, 2007.

Piper, Otto. "Unchanging Promises: Exodus in the New Testament." *Interpretation* 11 (1957) 3–22.

Plato. *Laws*. Translated by R. G. Bury. Loeb Classical Library 11. Cambridge, MA: Harvard University Press, 1984.

Porter, Stanley E. *Verbal Aspect in the Greek of the New Testament, with Reference to Tense and Mood*. New York: Peter Lang, 1993.

Porter, Stanley E., and Christopher D. Stanley, eds. *As It Is Written: Studying Paul's Use of Scripture*. SBL Symposium Series 50. Atlanta: Society of Biblical Literature, 2008.

Puech, Émile. "Immortality and Life After Death." In *The Dead Sea Scrolls: Fifty Years After Their Discovery: 1947–1997*, edited by Lawrence H. Schiffman, Emanuel Tov, and James C. Vanderkam, 518–30. Jerusalem: Israel Exploration Society, 2000.

Rahlfs, Alfred, ed. *Psalmi cum Odis*. Septuaginta: Vetus Testamentum Graecum 10. Göttingen: Vendenhoeck and Ruprecht, 1979.

———, ed. *Septuaginta*. Id est Vetus Testamentum graece iuxta LXX interpretes. Stuttgart: Deutsche Bibelgesellschaft, 2006.

Robertson, A. T. *A Grammar of the Greek New Testament in Light of Historical Research*. New York: Hodder & Stoughton, 1923.

Ruiten, T. A. G. M. van. *Abraham in the Book of Jubilees: The Rewriting of Genesis 11:26—25:10 in the Book of Jubilees 11:14—23:8*. Leiden: Brill, 2012.

Runge, Steven. *Discourse Grammar of the Greek New Testament: A Practical Introduction for Teaching and Exegesis*. Peabody, MA: Hendrickson, 2010.

Ryrie, Charles. *Basic Theology*. Wheaton, IL: Victor, 1986.

Sailhamer, John H. *The Pentateuch as Narrative: A Biblical-Theological Commentary*. Grand Rapids: Zondervan, 1992.

Sanders, E. P. *Judaism: Practice and Belief, 63 BCE–66 CE*. London: SCM, 1993.

Sayler, Gwendolyn B. *Have the Promises Failed: A Literary Analysis of 2 Baruch*. Chico, CA: Scholars, 1984.

Schaefer, Konrad. *Psalms, Berit Olam: Studies in Hebrew Narrative and Poetry*, edited by David W. Cotter. Collegeville, MN: Liturgical, 2001.

Schlatter, Adolf. *Gottes Gerechtigkeit*. Stuttgart: Calwer Verlag, 1935.

Schnelle, Udo. *Apostle Paul: His Life and Theology*. Translated by M. Eugene Boring. Grand Rapids: Baker, 2003.

Schreiner, Tom. *Galatians*. Exegetical Commentary on the New Testament. Grand Rapids: Zondervan, 2010.

———. *Galatians*. Zondervan Exegetical Commentary on the New Testament. Grand Rapids: Baker, 2010.

———. *The King in His Beauty: A Biblical Theology of the Old and New Testaments*. Grand Rapids: Baker, 2013.

———. *New Testament Theology: Magnifying God in Christ*. Grand Rapids: Baker, 2008.

———. *Romans*. Baker Exegetical Commentary on the New Testament. Grand Rapids: Baker, 1998.

Schüpphaus, Joachim. *Die Psalmen Salomos: Ein Zeugnis Jerusalmer Theologie und Frömmigkeit in der Mitte des Vorchristlichen Jahrhunderts*. Leiden: Brill, 1977.

Schwartz, Daniel R. *2 Maccabees*. Commentaries on Early Jewish Literature. Edited by Loren T. Stuckenbruck. Berlin: Walter de Gruyter, 2008.

Schweitzer, Eduard. *The Letter to the Colossians: A Commentary*. Translated by Andrew Chester. London: SPCK, 1982.

Scott, James M. *Adoption as Sons of God: An Exegetical Investigation into the Background of ΥΙΟΘΕΣΙΑ in the Pauline Corpus*. Tübingen: Mohr Siebeck, 1992.

———, ed. *Exile: Old Testament, Jewish, and Christian Conceptions*. Leiden: Brill, 1997.

———, ed. *Restoration: Old Testament, Jewish, and Christian Perspectives*. Leiden: Brill, 2011.

Seifrid, Mark A. "The Gospel as the Revelation of Mystery: The Witness of the Scriptures to Christ in Romans." *Southern Baptist Journal of Theology* 11 (2007) 93–103.

———. "Paul's Use of Righteousness Language Against Its Hellenistic Background." In *Justification and Variegated Nomism: The Complexities of Second Temple Judaism*, edited by D. A. Carson, Peter T. O'Brien, and Mark A. Seifrid, 2:39–74. Grand Rapids: Baker, 2004.

———. "Righteousness Language in Hebrew Scriptures and Early Judaism." In *Justification and Variegated Nomism: The Complexities of Second Temple Judaism*, edited by D. A. Carson, Peter T. O'Brien, and Mark A. Seifrid, 1:415–42. Grand Rapids: Baker, 2001.

———. "Romans." In *Commentary on the New Testament Use of the Old Testament*, edited by G. K. Beale and D. A. Carson, 607–94. Grand Rapids: Baker, 2007.

Sherwood, Stephen K. *Leviticus, Numbers, Deuteronomy.* Berit Olam: Studies in Hebrew Narrative and Poetry. Collegeville, MN: Liturgical, 2002.

Silva, Moisés. *Explorations in Exegetical Method: Galatians as a Test Case.* Grand Rapids: Baker, 2001.

———. "Galatians." In *Commentary on the New Testament Use of the Old Testament*, edited by G. K. Beale and D. A. Carson, 785–812. Grand Rapids: Eerdmans, 2007.

Sizer, Stephen R. "Dispensational Approaches to the Land." In *The Land of Promise: Biblical, Theological and Contemporary Perspectives*, edited by Philip Johnston and Peter Walker, 142–71. Downers Grove, IL: InterVarsity, 2000.

Smith, Gary. *Isaiah 40–66.* New American Commentary. Nashville: Broadman and Holman, 2009.

Smyth, Herbert Weir. *Greek Grammar.* Revised by Gordon Messing. Cambridge: Harvard University Press, 1984.

Stahl, J. M. *Kritisch-historische Syntax des griechischen Verbums der klassischen Zeit.* Heidelberg: Carl Winter, 1907.

Stanley, Christopher D., ed. *Paul and Scripture: Extending the Conversation.* SBL Early Christianity and Its Literature 9. Atlanta: Society of Biblical Literature, 2012.

Stone, Michael Edward. *Features of the Eschatology of IV Ezra.* Atlanta: Scholars, 1989.

———. *Fourth Ezra: A Commentary on the Book of Fourth Ezra.* Hermeneia—A Critical and Historical Commentary on the Bible. Minneapolis: Fortress, 1990.

———, ed. *Jewish Writings of the Second Temple Period: Apocrypha, Pseudepigrapha, Qumran Sectarian Writings, Philo, Josephus.* Philadelphia: Fortress, 1984.

Stowers, Stanley K. *A Rereading of Romans: Justice, Jews, and Gentiles.* New Haven: Yale University Press, 1994.

Stuart, Douglas. *Exodus.* New American Commentary 2. Nashville: Broadman & Holman, 2006.

Stuckenbruck, Loren T. *1 Enoch 91–108.* Commentaries on Early Jewish Literature. Berlin: Walter de Gruyter, 2007.

Tate, Marvin. *Psalms 51–100.* Word Biblical Commentary 20. Dallas: Word, 1990.

Thielman, Frank. *Ephesians.* Baker Exegetical Commentary on the New Testament. Grand Rapids: Baker, 2010.

Thiselton, Anthony C. *The First Epistle to the Corinthians: A Commentary on the Greek Text.* New International Greek Testament Commentary. Grand Rapids: Eerdmans, 2000.

———. *New Horizons in Hermeneutics: The Theory and Practice of Transforming Biblical Reading*. Grand Rapids: Zondervan, 1992.

Thompson, J. A. *1, 2 Chronicles*. New American Commentary 9. Nashville: Broadman & Holman, 1994.

———. *The Book of Jeremiah*. New International Commentary on the Old Testament. Grand Rapids: Eerdmans, 1980.

Towner, Philip H. *The Letters to Timothy and Titus*. New International Commentary on the New Testament. Grand Rapids: Eerdmans, 2006.

Turner, David L. *Matthew*. Exegetical Commentary on the New Testament. Grand Rapids: Eerdmans, 2008.

VanderKam, James. "The Origins and Purposes of the Book of Jubilees." In *Studies in the Book of Jubilees*, edited by Matthis Albani, Jörg Frey, and Armin Lang, 3–24. Tübingen: Mohr Siebeck, 1997.

VanGemeren, Willem A., ed. *New International Dictionary of Old Testament Theology and Exegesis*. 5 vols. Grand Rapids: Zondervan, 1997.

———. "Psalms." In vol. 5 of *The Expositors Bible Commentary*, edited by Frank Gaebelein, 1–882. Grand Rapids: Zondervan, 1991.

von Rad, Gerhard. *Deuteronomy: A Commentary*. Old Testament Library. Philadelphia: Westminster, 1966.

———. *Essays on Old Testament Hermeneutics*. Translated by J. L. Mays, edited by Claus Westermann. Atlanta: John Knox, 1963.

———. *Old Testament Theology*. Vol. 2. Translated by D. M. G. Stalker. New York: Harper & Row, 1965.

———. *The Problem of the Hexateuch and Other Essays*. Norwich, UK: SCM, 2012.

Wallace, Dan. *Greek Grammar: Beyond the Basics*. Grand Rapids: Zondervan, 1996.

Waltke, Bruce. *Genesis: A Commentary*. Grand Rapids: Zondervan, 2001.

———. *An Old Testament Theology: An Exegetical, Canonical, and Thematic Approach*. Grand Rapids: Zondervan, 2007.

Waltke, Bruce, and M. O'Connor. *An Introduction to Biblical Hebrew Syntax*. Winona Lake, IN: Eisenbrauns, 1990.

Walvoord, John F. *The Millennial Kingdom*. Findlay, OH: Dunham, 1959.

Watson, Francis. *Paul and the Hermeneutics of Faith*. London: T. & T. Clark, 2004.

Watts, John D. *Isaiah 1–33*. Word Biblical Commentary 24. Nashville: Thomas Nelson, 2005.

Webb, Barry G. *The Book of Judges*. New International Commentary on the Old Testament. Grand Rapids: Eerdmans, 2012.

Wenham, Gordon J. *Genesis 1–15*. Word Biblical Commentary 1. Waco, TX: Word, 1987.

Wenthe, Dean O. "The Use of the Hebrew Scriptures in 1QM." *Dead Sea Discoveries* 5 (1998) 290–319.

Wevers, John William, ed. *Deuteronomium*. Septuaginta: Vetus Testamentum Graecum 5. Göttingen: Vandenhoech & Ruprecht, 1977.

———, ed. *Exodus*. Septuaginta: Vetus Testamentum Graecum 2. Göttingen: Vandenhoech & Ruprecht 1991.

———, ed. *Genesis*. Septuaginta: Vetus Testamentum Graecum 1. Göttingen: Vandenhoech & Ruprecht, 1974.

———, ed. *Leviticus*. Septuaginta: Vetus Testamentum Graecum 3. Göttingen: Vandenhoech & Ruprecht, 1986.

————, ed. *Numeri*. Septuaginta: Vetus Testamentum Graecum 4. Göttingen: Vandenhoech & Ruprecht, 1982.

Whybray, N. *Introduction to the Pentateuch*. Grand Rapids: Eerdmans, 1995.

Wilckens, Ulrich. *Der Brief an die Römer*. Evangelisch-Katholischer Kommentar zum Neuen Testament, vol. 1. Neukirchen/Vluyn: Neukirchener; Zürich: Benziger, 1978.

Wilcox, Max. "The Promise of the 'Seed' in the New Testament and the Targumim." *Journal for the Study of the New Testament* 5 (1975) 269–305.

Wilder, William N. *Echoes of the Exodus Narrative in the Context and Background of Galatians 5:18*. Studies in Biblical Literature 23. New York: Peter Lang, 2001.

Williams, Ronald. *Williams' Hebrew Syntax*. Revised by John C. Beckman. Toronto: University of Toronto Press, 2007.

Williams, Sam K. "Promise in Galatians: A Reading of Paul's Reading of Scripture." *Journal of Biblical Literature* 107 (1988) 709–20.

Williamson, Paul R. "Promise and Fulfillment: The Territorial Inheritance." In *The Land of Promise: Biblical, Theological, and Contemporary Perspectives*, edited by Philip Johnston and Peter Walker, 15–34. Downers Grove, IL: InterVarsity, 2000.

————. *Sealed with an Oath: Covenant in God's Unfolding Purpose*. Downers Grove, IL: InterVarsity, 2007.

Willits, Joel. "Isa 54, 1 and Gal 4, 24b–27: Reading Genesis in Light of Isaiah." *Zeitschrift für die Neutestamentliche Wissenschaft* 96 (2005)188–210.

Wilson, Gerald H. *Psalms*. The NIV Application Commentary 1. Grand Rapids: Zondervan, 2002.

Wilson, Todd. "Wilderness Apostasy and Paul's Portrayal of the Crisis in Galatia." *New Testament Studies* 50 (2004) 550–71.

Witherington, Ben. *Grace in Galatia: A Commentary on Paul's Letter to the Galatians*. Grand Rapids: Eerdmans, 1998.

Woudstra, Martin H. *The Book of Joshua*. New International Commentary on the Old Testament. Grand Rapids: Eerdmans, 1981.

Wright, N. T. *The Case for the Psalms: Why They Are Essential*. New York: HarperCollins, 2013.

————. *The Climax of the Covenant: Christ and the Law in Pauline Theology*. Edinburgh: T. & T. Clark, 1991.

————. *The Epistles of Paul to the Colossians and Philemon: An Introduction and Commentary*. Tyndale New Testament Commentaries. Downers Grove, IL: IVP Academic, 1986.

————. *Jesus and the Victory of God*. Minneapolis: Fortress, 1996.

————. *Justification: God's Plan & Paul's Vision*. Downers Grove, IL: InterVarsity, 2009.

————. "New Exodus, New Inheritance: The Narrative Structure of Romans 3–8." In *Romans and the People of God: Essays in Honor of Gordon Fee on the Occasion of His 65th Birthday*, edited by Sven K. Soderlund and N. T. Wright, 26–35. Grand Rapids: Eerdmans, 1999.

————. "Paul and Caesar: A New Reading of Romans." In *A Royal Priesthood? The Use of the Bible Ethically and Politically: A Dialogue with Oliver O. Donovan*, edited by Craig Bartholomew, Jonathan Chaplin, Robert Song, and Al Wolters, 173–93. Grand Rapids: Zondervan, 2002.

————. *Paul and the Faithfulness of God*. 2 vols. Minneapolis: Fortress, 2013.

————. *The Resurrection of the Son of God.* Minneapolis: Fortress, 2003.

————. *Romans.* New Interpreter's Bible 10. Nashville: Abingdon, 2002.

Zakovitch, Yair. "Inner-biblical Interpretation." In *A Companion to Biblical Interpretation in Early Judaism*, edited by Matthias Henze, 27–63. Grand Rapids: Eerdmans, 2012.

Ziegler, Joseph, ed. *Ieremias, Baruch, Threni, Epistula Ieremiae.* Septuaginta: Vetus Testamentum Graecum 15. Göttingen: Vandenhoech & Ruprecht, 1957.

————, ed. *Isaias.* Septuaginta: Vetus Testamentum Graecum 14. Göttingen: Dandenhoed & Ruprecht, 1939.

————, ed. *Sapientia Iesu Filii Sirach*, Septuaginta: Vetus Testamentum Graecum 12.2. Göttingen: Dandenhoed & Ruprecht, 1965.

————, ed. *Susanna, Daniel, Bel et Draco.* Septuaginta: Vetus Testamentum Graecum 16. Göttingen: Vandenhoech & Ruprecht, 1999.

Zimmerli, Walther. *Ezekiel 2: A Commentary on the Book of the Prophet Ezekiel Chapters 25–48.* Hermeneia—A Critical and Historical Commentary on the Bible. Philadelphia: Fortress, 1983.

CPSIA information can be obtained
at www.ICGtesting.com
Printed in the USA
LVHW081535030523
745968LV00001B/30